The Religious,
the Spiritual, and the Secular

SUNY Series in Religious Studies
Harold Coward, Editor

.

The Religious, the Spiritual, and the Secular

Auroville and Secular India

Robert N. Minor

State University of New York Press

Published by
State University of New York Press, Albany

© 1999 State University of New York

For information, address State University of New York
Press, State University Plaza, Albany, N.Y., 12246

Production by E. Moore
Marketing by Anne Valentine

Library of Congress Cataloging-in-Publication Data

Minor, Robert Neil, 1945–
    The religious, the spiritual, and the secular : Auroville and
secular India / Robert N. Minor.
        p.   cm.
    Includes bibliographical references and index.
    ISBN 0-7914-3991-7 (alk. paper). — ISBN 0-7914-3992-5 (pbk. :
alk. paper)
    1. Auroville (India)—Religion. 2. Sri Aurobindo Ashram—India-
-Auroville. 3. Secularism—India. I. Title.
BL1273.832.A876M56 1998
322'.1'095482—dc21   97-50628
                                                                CIP

10 9 8 7 6 5 4 3 2 1

Contents

List of Illustrations   *vii*

Foreword   *ix*

1. A Yogi, a City, and a Secular State   *1*

2. Sri Aurobindo and the "Religion"
   of the "Integral Yoga" Community   *18*

3. Auroville as the Mother's Vision   *36*

4. Auroville from the Mother's to the
   Government's Control   *55*

5. Auroville and the "Secular State" in Parliament   *77*

6. Auroville in Terms of India's and
   UNESCO's Mutual Goals   *96*

7. Auroville in the Court's Opinion   *112*

8. Auroville, the "Spiritual," and the "Secular"
   in the Post–Decision Debates   *130*

9. Clarity and Ambiguity in the
   Discussion of Auroville's Status   *150*

Notes   *169*

Bibliography   *197*

Index   *203*

Illustrations

Photos

1. The Main Building of the Sri Aurobindo Ashram in Pondicherry.   *47*

2. The "Samadhi," burial place of Sri Aurobindo and the Mother in the courtyard of the Ashram's main building in Pondicherry.   *47*

3. The Matrimandir, 1981.   *62*

4. The Matrimandir, 1993.   *62*

5. The marble urn in the amphitheater at the center of Auroville, where young people from 124 nations placed handfuls of soil from their countries at the Founding Ceremony on February 28, 1968.   *63*

6. The Banyan Tree at the center of Auroville where Aurovillians met for town meetings.   *63*

Photos by the author.

Map

1. A map of Auroville in 1982 from the *Auroville Review,* 1982.   *60*

Foreword

This study began in 1981 during a Senior Fellowship from the American Institute of Indian Studies. It has encompassed four trips to India since and numerous interviews with Aurovillians, Ashramites, and other devotees of Sri Aurobindo and the Mother in both India and the West. It involves issues that are heartfelt and held by sincere people, issues about Sri Aurobindo, the Mother, Auroville, and India. I thank these people for their sincerity and kindness for speaking with me and answering my questions. They had little idea what I would finally write.

Auroville continues to be a living idea, a growing community of people from all over the world. Those interested in Auroville's ongoing life might be interested in subscribing to the monthly periodical *Auroville Today*, published in Auroville, Kottakuppam, 605104, Tamil Nadu, India, or in accessing the following Web sites: http:// www.auroville-india.org and http://miraura.org/aa/av/av.html.

In the following work, I have tried to be clear, fair, and analytical without following the unsubstantiated. But I believe the process that brought Auroville under State control is an example of the down-to-earth workings of the "Indian Secular State" at this period in time and merits analysis in light of all of the theoretical discussions of the secular state, which are relatively clean and use normative definitions. As an old automotive tire advertisement put it: This is about where "the rubber meets the road." It also synthesizes much that I have written about before, as the notes will tell—Sri Aurobindo's thought, definitions, and ramifications of tolerance defined in terms of inclusivism and Radhakrishnan's influential definition of "Hinduism." Much of chapter 7 originally appeared as "Auroville and the Courts of India: Religion and Secular" in Robert D. Baird, ed. *Religion and Law in Independent India*, published in 1993 by Manohar Publishers in New Delhi.

I have included many quotations from the debate, particularly in Parliament, so the flavor of the discussion as well as its content will be readily available. For historical information I have often relied on my own copies of documents obtained from institutions and people involved. I have depended on the expertise of Inter-Library Services at the University of Kansas, as well as an international travel grant and a sabbatical leave from the University. Thanks to members of the Department of Religious Studies for encouragement and support, to Patrick Prohaska for reading the completed manuscript, to the editor of this series, Harold Coward, for his support, to Nancy Ellegate of the State University of New York Press for her encouragement, and to good friends and family for their indulgence and understanding. Thanks especially to Matt Minor and Paul Smith.

One

❦

A Yogi, a City,
and a Secular State

B y the time Sri Aurobindo passed from this world on December 5, 1950, he had become a world-renowned thinker as well as a source of inspiration for people who sought to explore and follow his "Integral Yoga." His major writings had been published in a variety of languages and were reviewed in such prestigious tomes as the *Times Literary Supplement*. When collected into his *Birth Centenary Library* in 1972, they constituted twenty-nine encyclopedic volumes. That he wrote the majority of his works in English enabled his readers to transcend the limits of regional languages, and the synthetic worldview he set forth appealed to those Westerners turning East for inspiration without the requirement that they enter the rigors of the study of traditional Eastern thought.

He left an international movement of devotees and inquirers who read his works, sought to apply his teachings to one degree or another, and organized centers and ashrams to delve into and practice his teachings. He established the authority of a second charismatic leader who would continue his direction. Known as "the Mother," she soon became the object of devotion and dedication by Eastern and Western devotees who reported seeing her in visions and dreams and who cherished memories of her physical presence when they had the opportunity to meet her.

It was the Mother who envisioned and established a "city" in Southeast India called "Auroville," which was to be a place where people from all corners of the world could settle to practice the active, world-changing elements of Sri Aurobindo's Integral Yoga. The city received international attention not only from devotees but, because of the moral and financial support of the government of India and its states, also from the United Nations Educational, Scientific, and Cultural Organization and its members. Just as Sri Aurobindo was a world figure, Auroville was a world city.

It was not long, however, before the nation of India, which defines itself as a "secular" state, had become the guardian and major promoter of this city of yoga. Three acts of Parliament with extended debates from 1980 through 1988 established the government's authority over Auroville and its mission, and a decision by the Supreme Court in 1982 ensured the legality and permanence of that authority. During the debates, questions naturally arose regarding the promotion of what appeared to be a religious enterprise by a so-called "secular state." In the midst of these events, the meaningfulness of the claim that India is a "secular state" was tested on a practical level. Though there had been, and continues to be, much theoretical discussion of the meaning of "secular" for India, these events provide an opportunity to observe how the concept might work in practice and whether in practice the term *secular* is a meaningful category.

"Secular State" as a Meaningful Designation

In November 1976, during a state of emergency that had lasted since June 1975, the two houses of the parliament of India passed the 42nd Constitution Amendment Act, which came into effect on December 18, 1976.[1] Among its extensive provisions[2] was the addition of the word "secular" to the description of India in the Preamble of the Constitution that had been ratified without the term twenty-seven years earlier. India would henceforth be constitutionally designated a "secular state."[3] As Robert Baird has pointed out, throughout the parliamentary discussion of the Amendment, "no one opposed the inclusion of the term 'secular' or objected in any way to India being designated as a 'secular state.' No one argued that the inclusion of the term 'secular' suggested a new departure."[4] It was accepted by all parties involved that India already was, and was meant to be, something called a "secular state."

The nature of this "secular state" had been discussed by the scholars long before the addition of the term *secular* in 1976, in a manner quite different from the discussions in the Constituent Assembly. In a 1958 dissertation, published in 1964 as *The Concept of the Secular State and India*, political scientist V.P. Luthera determined that, unlike the United States in particular and contrary to the intentions of the Parliament and Constituent Assembly, "India is not and cannot be a secular state."[5] He defined the term *secular* narrowly: "a secular state is one which is separated from, unconnected with and not devoted to religion."[6] He went on to add that in the context of the *"present* social circumstances" it is not even possible for India to be such a state. The continued use of the term *secular*, he concluded, creates confusion: "If a simpler term is to be used, it would perhaps be appropriate to describe it as a 'religiously impartial' or 'non-communal' (non-denominational) state."[7] To Luthera, these designations did not refer to a truly "secular state."

An American political scientist, however, was responsible for another study, entitled *India as a Secular State*, which has been cited more often than Luthera's work, both in India and abroad. Donald E. Smith read the typescript of Luthera's study and disagreed with both of his conclusions, saying that Luthera's definition of a secular state is too narrow and that he takes "too static a view of Hindu religion. . . ."[8] Smith's definition of a "secular state" included Luthera's definition as only one of its three components. For Smith, a secular state is "a state which guarantees individual and corporate freedom of religion, deals with the individual as a citizen irrespective of his religion, is not constitutionally connected to a particular religion nor does it seek either to promote or interfere with religion."[9] Smith concedes that by his own definition a *"completely* secular state" does not exist and, thus, India does not fit Smith's model either. Yet he answers a "qualified 'Yes'" to the question of whether India has succeeded as a secular state. Smith understands India to be "secular" in some "incomplete" or qualified sense then. It is not *fully* secular. What could this partially secular state be? The ideal, Smith says, is "clearly embodied in the Constitution," and, given the difficulties India is struggling to overcome, "it is being implemented in substantial measure."[10] Therefore, he is willing to designate India a "secular state" *relative to* its own history and to the current difficulties it is experiencing in the process of nation building, while admitting that India does not fully live up to his definition. In his response in the 1964 preface, Luthera remained unconvinced that this was essentially different from his own conclusion.

"Secular" as "Indian"

As a historian of religions, Robert Baird's interest is in the actual use of the term *secular* by the members of the Constituent Assembly and in subsequent parliamentary debates and judicial decisions. In a number of articles, Baird concluded that from its earliest discussions in the Constituent Assembly, no definitions of the *secular state* was made explicit. "Secular state" and "secular" were used freely without anyone questioning their value or defining their meaning. Assembly members were aware of some contrast between India as "secular" and their neighbor of partition, which was formed as an explicitly "Islamic" state. No one questioned the assumption that India should be a "secular state," but debates over a variety of proposals involving religion included the use of the term *secular* as a justification for arguments on all sides of the issues.[11] It was a term without an agreed-upon content, and that fact, Baird finds, allowed an important commonality in its use: "the designation 'secular state' functioned in a way that enabled political leaders with a variety of ultimate concerns to share in nation building without sacrificing their deepest convictions."[12]

Because the term remained undefined and yet was affirmed by all, religious conflicts could be held in check while the members were in the process of forming a constitutional nation. "It supported a common goal (nationhood), while its multivalent nature permitted ambiguity, which enabled religious people to retain their particular meaning for it."[13] As long as there was no attempt to agree upon the meaning of the term *secular*, there could appear to be agreement, and the creation of a nation on that appearance could take place. Had the members of the Constituent Assembly attempted to debate the meaning of the term, disagreements might have frustrated or torpedoed their overriding common concern of nationhood.

In a recent study, Gerald Larson agrees with Baird when he argues, then, that the terms *secular* and *secularism* are used as rough synonyms for the terms *nationalist* and *nationalism*.[14] The ambiguous designation of the nation in such a way that began officially with the Constituent Assembly continues to be the common element of their use.

A recent collection of essays entitled *Secularism in India: Dilemmas and Challenges* brings together writers from a broad political and theoretical spectrum to clarify the "true" meaning of Indian secularism as opposed to other things the writers designate "pseudo-secularism," or "Western," that is non-Indian, secularism, or even "Nehruism." The essays contain the common thread that identifies "secularism" with something that the writers think India is, or something that India is supposed to be. Being "secular" is clearly the true ideal for India, they write, though the content of that term, as it becomes more explicit, divides many of the writers considerably.

For example, in response to previous critics of "secularism," University of Delhi Professor of Law Upendra Baxi defines the "real" meaning of the Indian secular state by attempting to determine what it means for the "Indian people" as defined in the Constitution itself and by Indian courts. "Politicians, in their deep ambivalence towards judiciary, find it congenial to overlook all that courts have said and done, more so when it suits the here-and-now expedient interests."[15] Baxi's own concern is for "the Indian people's struggle" to win social justice, and he thus approves of judicial decisions that provide political and social guidance and reform of what he views as religious activities that offend "public morality." Therefore, he argues, the legislators and the judiciary have moved toward true secularism. To the critics, he warns, "in attacking 'secularism' theoretically and politically, in desymbolizing its potential, in calling for its total redefinition—rubbishing 'secularism,' in short—neither the future of human rights nor social justice in India is enhanced."[16]

Two other contributors to the volume who are "General Secretaries" of the conservative, right-wing religious movement called the Rashtriya Swayam Sevak Sangh ("National Assembly of Volunteers") criticize current "misunderstandings" of "secularism," such as that of Baxi, because, they say, such interpretations actually mean, "you support and justify the Muslim communalism, you are secular; you oppose it, you are communal, anti-secular, fundamentalist and whatnot."[17] One of them concludes: "It is high time that we disabuse our minds of the politicalised and perverted concept of secularism" and replace it with "Dharma Rajya" or "Ramarajya" which is not "anti-Hindu" and, we may conclude, a nonpoliticized and nonperverted "secularism."[18] The other, K.S. Sudarshan, argues as well that the problem is not true "secularism" but that, "Today in the Indian context the words 'Secular' and 'Secularism' have lost their original meaning and purpose."[19] True "secularism" is found in the traditional "Hindu" state. "Hindu state has always remained secular as far as its treatment to different religious sects is concerned." For all of these writers, the term *secular* is appropriate to describe a goal of India, but they believe the term is misunderstood, consciously or unconsciously, by those who disagree with each writer's definition of the term.

In a similar manner, the term *religion* was left undefined by the Indian constitution, yet it is accepted by the constitutional model and contemporary discussion that there are two recognizable categories of activities, beliefs, and entities in reality. One is "religion" and the other is an opposing realm which is other than religious.[20] Again, as Baird has shown, the category "religion" and the category "secular" have become axiomatic "so that neither side of a litigation is able to deny the categories themselves." The very acceptance of the idea that reality is divided into two realms of existence, one "religious" and one "secular," he points out, is religious change, for the idea that there are two such realms "run[s] counter to much traditional religious thinking in India which sees life as homogeneous."[21]

Thus with both categories and the ability to distinguish them accepted as an integral part of the constitutional model of reality, it is up to the legislature and ultimately the courts of India to define both categories. Baird concluded that "subsequent legislative history" will produce whatever official definition the term *secular* will gain, and also traced the judgments of the Supreme Court in the attempt to define both.[22] Admitting in the beginning that there are difficulties in defining "religion," the Supreme Court of India also knew it must set itself to define it. The "secular," then, would be that which is not "religion." Baird traced the difficulties in the process of definition, noting that though the Court never clearly defines the terms, it continues to use the terms as agreed-upon categories to handle conflict between religious groups and the State.

Clearly, the assumption that there are two realms designated "religion" and "secular" is firmly established. These are taken for granted by the Constitution and the Supreme Court, not argued for nor definitively defined. It is clear that this assumption is accepted even by those who have argued that the State is interfering with religion. That traditional religious views of reality have not distinguished these categories but treated all life as one is also clear. From the perspective of this constitutional model of "religion," the traditional claim that there are not two categories of reality called the "religious" and the "secular" is merely a false one, an encroachment of "religion" on the "secular."

The Supreme Court of India has continued to accept the responsibility of determining what falls within these two categories, but with the earlier precedents, it no longer speaks of the determination as difficult, even if observers see inconsistencies in the means by which the judges arrive at their opinions. From its earliest case, the Court has noted that the Constitution allows the State to regulate and even administer economic, financial, and political activities carried on by religions. Therefore, when the State steps in to administer properties of a religion, that is clearly acceptable. The Court, in declaring an activity, institution, or idea as a "secular" matter, acts thereby as the authority that promotes religious change. If the "secular" is a new category, its progressive definition is an expansion of the power of the State to make what from a traditional view are religious pronouncements.

In its attempt to define "religion," the Court has introduced further categories, as Baird has shown.[23] The Court advanced "essentiality" as a category and said it was important to decide whether an activity was "essential to a religion." At first it stated that what was essential would be determined in terms of the religion itself, but when a religious institution explicitly claimed that how income from a temple should be spent was a religious matter, the Court refused that claim. The religious community's explicit statement of "essentiality" was not taken as a basis for accepting whether an activity was religious or essential to the religion. The Court declared it a "secular" activity that happens to be practiced by "religion."

Likewise, other claims made by religious individuals and communities have been rejected, and the realm of the "secular" has appeared to expand. The Supreme Court declared that the scale of expenses and the provision of proper materials for rituals are "secular" matters, that the actual determination of which priestly duties are "religious" is a "secular" task, and that the appointment of a priest is "secular." It appears to have had little trouble doing this without clear definitions of the categories, but in the process it has, from a traditional standpoint, expanded the realm of the "secular" at the expense of more traditional views. Historically, the Court by doing so has enforced religious change.

Propagating an Ambiguous "Indian Secularism"

Larson's study also has underscored an important set of assumptions that stand behind the use of the phrase "the *Indian secular state*" when the phrase is used in discussions of the nature of that "secular state," especially as such a state relates to "religion" and the "religions." After noting that "secular" means "national," as pointed out earlier, he shows that the content of "secular" as "national" is for many a religious position he identifies as "Neo-Hindu." Larson goes on to argue that this "Neo-Hindu" position is, in fact, a "Gandhian-Nehruvian Indic civil religion."[24]

Though Gandhi envisioned a state that affirmed "religion" as he defined it and the "religions" as he understood them, Gandhi himself functioned not as a systematic and an effective theoretician but more as an activist symbol of this "Neo-Hindu" position, just as he became a symbol of Indian nationalism, "Indianism," and the Indian Independence movement. He was popular foremost as an activist, not a theorizer, nor was he the major proponent of the basic theory of the Indian secular state. Nehru soon diverged from him, and others affirmed Gandhi without accepting his basic premises or by reading their own ideas into Gandhi's thought and action. Nehru, for one, understood the significance of Gandhi's symbolic and activist role, as he chose from Gandhi what was useful while admitting he was bothered by Gandhi's religious emphasis. "But I was powerless to intervene, and I consoled myself with the thought that Gandhiji used the words because they were well known and understood by the masses. He had an amazing knack of reaching the heart of the people."[25]

There were, in fact, two important approaches to the "Civil Religion" Larson identifies as "Gandhian-Nehruvian," which operated side by side from the Constituent Assembly on. Each assumed a different definition of "secularism." The most visible and widely known thinker who defined and promoted the first definition of this "Neo-Hindu" position and identified it with the term *secular* was philosopher/statesman and second president of India Sarvepalli Radhakrishnan. His speeches and writings functioned as introductions to Indian philosophy and religious thought for many, both inside and outside of India, including many who called themselves "Hindus."

Radhakrishnan was well known for his defense of "Hinduism" or "Neo-Hinduism," more specifically as a "Neo-Advaita." He was inspired by the previous work and defense of India and "Hinduism" of Swami Vivekananda, the fiery preacher of the Ramakrishna Mission, and by the tradition of the eighth-century Indian thinker Shankara, the most renowned thinker of the Indian school of thought known as Advaita Vedanta. Radhakrishnan's version of

"Neo-Advaita" was most known for its "tolerance," an inclusivism that subordinated other positions to its own.[26] He also served as vice president of India from 1952 to 1962, and as India's second president from 1962 to 1967, succeeding Rajendra Prasad as president with India's first prime minister, Jawaharlal Nehru. Nehru had opposed Prasad's initial nomination, and their relationship remained uneasy. Nehru was concerned with Prasad's stand on a variety of issues and his activities as president, which Nehru felt were less than modern, scientific, and "secular." In 1956, Nehru supported a change of president and favored Radhakrishnan for the position, but it was not until 1962 that Radhakrishnan succeeded Prasad.

To Nehru, Radhakrishnan was an accomplished, world-renowned philosopher and writer, one who understood "Hinduism" and who would not compromise the "secular state" as Nehru understood it. Nor, he assumed, would Radhakrishnan interfere in politics. To Radhakrishnan, the office of the presidency was in public detached from the affairs of government and politics and, instead, symbolized the nation itself. Thus Radhakrishnan never joined the Congress Party nor even voted in an election. The ideal president he sought to portray publicly was that of an advisor, a "*rajaguru*" (the king's teacher) to Nehru and all of India, or, in even more traditional terms, he was to be a brahmin, not a kshatriya—a teacher, philosopher, scholar, and grand theorizer, not a politician, bureaucrat, or warrior.[27] Nehru apparently hoped that Radhakrishnan would embody a quiet, advisory aloofness, for in spite of Radhakrishnan's active life already he was known best as a philosopher and an academician more than a this-worldly politician.

Publicly, Radhakrishnan appeared to fill this role. Part of that advisory role to the State and the nation was to admonish Indian leaders and citizens about the true nature of "Hinduism" and Indian "secularism." By the time of India's independence, Radhakrishnan's writings on the former were already well known and well regarded by India's English speakers, including members of the Constituent Assembly.[28] One hears Radhakrishnan's words and ideas quoted, both with and without credit given to him, in the Constituent Assembly and later in the Parliament and the Supreme Court when issues involving "religion" and the definition of "Hinduism" arise.

Radhakrishnan himself was a member of the Constituent Assembly from its first session on December 9, 1946, until his resignation on August 24, 1947, to become India's ambassador to the Soviet Union. His speeches included his familiar words proclaiming India's essential historical and cultural tolerance, its cultural and "spiritual" unity that embraced all religions, and, underneath it all, his "Neo-Hindu" (as "Neo-Advaita") understanding of reality and religion. Often these assumptions were there if only subtly: "Swarajya," he told one session, "is the development of that kind of tolerant attitude which sees in brother man the face Divine."[29] In the Assembly he referred to the ideal leader as one who affirms what he called "Raja Dharma," though he meant that leaders should act in a spirit of detachment.[30]

Here he first stood to teach what he understood to be the essentially Indian model of a "secular state." Later, as vice president and president, his speeches and writings provided regular opportunities to correct others regarding the "true" meaning of "the Indian secular state." The definition he proclaimed was also an integral part of, and, therefore, consistent with, his own religious position, which he at this point in life designated "the religion of the spirit."[31] "Secularism," as he defined it, does not mean the state is antireligion or indifferent to religion, but that it is only "nonsectarian." The secular state can promote religion (in the singular) but not one of the religions (in the plural), and that religion it promotes is Radhakrishnan's inclusivistic "religion of the spirit," which he believed is the essence of all religions. "Religion of the spirit," a position he earlier dubbed "Vedanta" and, then, "Hinduism,"[32] he believed, is not one of the sectarian religions but "religion" (the term used in the singular for the essential nature of all religions) itself. The state, therefore, can actually promote "religion" without promoting religions. For example, in 1955, while vice president, he wrote: "Secularism lays stress on the universality of spiritual values which may be attained by a variety of ways." He went on to define these values in Neo-Advaitin terms in the tradition of such earlier Neo-Advaitins as Swami Vivekananda and consistent with Radhakrishnan's own writings.[33] Consistently, then, out of his Neo-Advaitin assumptions about "religion," which included his belief that experience of the Absolute within is the essence of "religion," he, as president, could declare that the principles of "religion" are the basis for the Indian Constitution: "Today the Constitution proceeds on that principle, the principle saying that religion is to be regarded as experience of the Supreme."[34] His evangelistic spirit, which encouraged the transformation of other views into his own, also was clear when he spoke of correcting other religions so they would transform into this "religion of the spirit," his "Neo-Advaita." For example,

> We can so transform the religion to which we belong as to make it approximate to the religion of the spirit. I am persuaded that every religion has possibilities of such a transformation. We must look upon Hinduism or Christianity as part of an evolving revelation that might in time be taken over into the larger religion of the spirit.[35]

In his life as a teacher in and an administrator of a number of Indian universities, and as Chairman of the University Education Commission in 1948–49, which was to recommend improvements to higher education in India, Radhakrishnan expressed his conviction that universities should be the institutions that promote this "religion of the spirit."[36]

This, then, is the theory for the promotion of a "secular state," with the definition of the term *secular* based upon the "Neo-Hindu" or "Neo-Advaitin" perspective of Radhakrishnan. By this definition, the "secular state" would mean a state that will promote, and even enforce, through its institutions, a "Neo-Advaita." It would be a state that would attempt to promote a "Neo-Advaitin" understanding not only of the variety of religions but other non-Neo-Advaitin positions (officially religious "denominations") that other self-identified "Hindu" believers have thought of as essential "religion" and often called "Hindu" as well.

These inclusivist "Neo-Advaitin" assumptions, however, are to be found not only behind the position of those who would promote this "secular state" in the manner Radhakrishnan recommends. The understanding of "Hinduism" as "tolerant" in this inclusivistic manner is also behind the more conservative understandings of the nature of a "truly Indian secular state" by such groups as the right-wing Rashtriya Swayam Sevak Sangh (RSS). The RSS leader K.S. Sudarshan describes "true secularism" as practiced in "the Hindu state" as a concept based upon "Hinduism's" inclusiveness: "Equal respect was given for all religions (sarva mata samabhava) because they were the different aspects of the same reality."[37] He can openly speak of the "Indian secular state" as a "Hindu state" without understanding why there are objections. While those outside of this understanding believe this inclusivistic language sounds particularly "Hindu" rather than the essence of their own religious positions, and even that it threatens their positions, RSS leader H.V. Seshadri can speak of "Dharma Rajya," "the true Hindu secularism" the RSS promotes, in inclusivistic terms that are quite similar in theory and definition to the words of Radhakrishnan. "It encompassed at once a strictly non-sectarian approach and yet inclusive of the highest moral and spiritual purpose of man as elaborated by the enlightened souls all over the world." Seshadri finds this in line with the thought of the same great cultural heros of modern India that Radhakrishnan would cite: Swami Vivekananda, Sri Aurobindo, Bipin Chandra Pal, and Lokmanya Tilak.[38] In words similar to Vivekananda and Radhakrishnan, Sudarshan goes beyond this to make the generalized claim that this understanding is historically the definition of Indian "secularism" that the people of the country accepted: ". . . all [religions] coexisted catering to the different temperaments, tastes and needs of the people. *'Ekam sat viprah bahudha vadanti'* (Truth is one, the learned describe it in different ways) was the guiding principle. It was ingrained in the psyche of the people of this country that all paths lead to the same ultimate reality."[39] Even the coalition of parties called the Janata (People's) Party proposed in response to the 42nd Constitution Amendment Bill a similar definition of "secular," which they suggested should actually be added to the Constitution: "Equal respect to all religions."[40]

Thus the concept of "inclusivism" behind this "Neo-Hindu/Neo-Advaitin" definition of "secular" as nonsectarian has led to what those outside of this position believe is actually the threat, sometimes subtle and sometimes not, of the destruction of their own positions. It has been argued that this is inherent in inclusivism in one degree or another, because inclusivism of this "Neo-advaitin" sort

> does not consider the viewpoint of the believer as objector as significant. Though the believer may say otherwise, it eliminates the viewpoint . . . as a significant other. This is quite unlike the person who considers the alternative viewpoint of another seriously, believes that that other does understand his or her own position though it may be wrong, and then agrees to tolerate that person in a civil and humane manner. Radhakrishnan's position does not consider that other a significant viewpoint and does not consider that the other understands his or her position accurately. In fact it destroys the sense that there can be a significant other. The other is dissolved into the inclusivistic viewpoint, understood only in terms of the inclusivist's view. As a result of not viewing other viewpoints as significant others, such an inclusivistic view is never challenged by the other, for there is no other to

challenge it. It cannot in itself understand why there is even the claim of a challenge by what are only apparently other positions. It considers none wrong because there are ultimately no other options.[41]

The key is that this position, if held consistently, insulates one from objections and objectors. Objectors are looked upon as "not understanding" or, as Kaylor puts it, this inclusivism "often seems to be that of a superior who tolerates the weakness of an inferior: truth is one, and those who have realised it can look benignly upon those whose inferior ideas and practices show that they still have ways to go."[42]

> Radhakrishnan's position, if held consistently, admits no serious confrontation, no other to consider, no challenge to cause one to analyze one's own position. It allows only for a sense that others plainly do not understand not only Radhakrishnan's position, but their own position, or that of religion in general. As such there is no real and essential pluralism for Radhakrishnan; plurality is unreal at the essential level and unimportant where it seems real.[43]

Though there are other factors that result in the difference between the application of the "secular state" as interpreted through the "inclusivism" of Radhakrishnan by the "Neo-Hindu right" and by other "Neo-Hindus," they all may claim the same inclusivism in theory. To identify the "secular state" as a "truly Hindu state" can, therefore, be an application of what appears to "non-Neo-Hindus" as a religious imperialism that flows from an inclusivism that affirms that "The sun never (really) sets on such an (religious) Empire."

The definition represented by Radhakrishnan is one of the positions and one of the definitions of the "secular" that is promoted as a "Civil Religion," to use the phrase Larson brings to the discussion from studies of American Civil Religion. There is, however, a second definition of "secular" that also is promoted as true "secularism," that of Nehru, which includes an agnosticism regarding the category "religion." Larson calls this second definition "a kind of 'demythologization'" of the Neo-Hindu vision of Gandhi, and, thus, of the position for which Radhakrishnan was responsible.[44] This Nehruvian position has existed among members of the government and the judiciary alongside the "Neo-Advaitin" position, which the Nehruvian definition in some ways ignored as being nonthreatening to its own definition of "secular." It is this second definition that the more conservative groups have criticized as "pseudosecularism," "non-Indian secularism" and "Nehruism," though they may have included representatives of the first in their criticism.

Much has been said about Nehru's definition of the Indian "secular state" and its treatment of "religion."[45] Nehru was troubled by what he called the "religious element" injected into political discussion by Indian leaders: "Their history and sociology and economics appeared to me all wrong, and the religious twist that was given to everything prevented all clear thinking."[46] Since he supported Gandhi as one who could mobilize the masses with his message, he said he had to stifle any criticism of their disagreements. Yet his writings show that what he frequently had to remain silent about was his criticism of Gandhi's injection of "religion" into what Nehru believed were "secular" matters. For example, Gandhi's use of fasting, Nehru asserted, is "sheer revivalism, and clear thinking had not a ghost of a chance against it."[47] In Nehru's eyes, "religion" was acceptable if it did not interfere with India, but it should be rejected as a basis for achieving national unity, or for nation-building.[48] The attempt to relate religion and the state, he wrote, is an outmoded idea, which "was given up by the world some centuries ago and has no place in the mind of the modern man."[49] And, as Baird has pointed out, Nehru's conception of the "secular state" was based upon Nehru's affirmation and valuing of the "rational and scientific," the "Indian," and the "modern." "When a debate over his position actually arises, it is not an appeal to a sacred tradition, but these values which are offered to clinch the validity of his approach."[50]

These two approaches have existed side by side, as illustrated by the service of the First Prime Minister and the Second President of India together. The one, however, had no need to justify the present by the past in "religious" terms, for it considers "religion" irrelevant to a modern nation–state, while the other sought to use what it defines as the "essential" and truly "Hindu" elements of the past in the present. To cite one example, unlike Nehru, who had no desire to affirm or rehabilitate the caste system, calling "the caste system and much that goes with it . . . wholly incompatible, reactionary, restrictive, and barriers to progress. . . ,"[51] Radhakrishnan defended its theoretical basis and proclaimed it as a universally applicable solution to modern societal problems.[52]

For Nehru, the two positions could exist together in their ambiguity because Radhakrishnan's position as Nehru understood it was theoretical and did not actively interfere with the goals of Nehru's vision of "secularism." Likewise, Radhakrishnan could accept Nehru's position in the inclusivistic manner in which he accepted all positions that "apparently" disagreed. After all, Radhakrishnan had done this throughout his historical interpretations of Indian philosophy. All of it, even the most extreme anti-Advaitin positions, he wrote, "tended toward monism."[53] Radhakrishnan, at least publicly, spoke and wrote of Nehru as he had of Rabindranath Tagore, Gandhi, and other cultural heros. Nehru was essentially, if not explicitly, a follower of "the religion of the spirit."[54] He saw no significant other viewpoint represented by Nehru on these matters.

Finally, the two positions could exist as if they were the same because many did not see, or would not consider looking for, a difference between the two. As cultural heros referenced by later leaders, particularly members of the Congress Party, which dominated national politics for decades, nationhood and party loyalty would not incline one to ferret out differences at all, particularly in their use of the politically important term *secular*. The two perspectives continued as part of the ambiguity of the term *secular* on the Indian scene.

The courts, and the Supreme Court in particular, however, were required to reduce, if not eliminate, the ambiguity for the very practical reason that they were confronted with cases to decide. The judges took on the challenge, and in the process promoted a definition of "secularism" that came closest to that of Nehru while using the "Neo-Advaitin" theories and definition of "Hinduism" from Radhakrishnan to justify and promote their positions. In Marc Galanter's terms, the Court delivered "reformist decisions" while using "religious justifications" to enhance the effect of the decisions.[55] It promulgated religious reforms particularly, but not exclusively, regarding "Hindu usage." These reforms conformed to the "Hinduism" that is the "Neo-Advaitin" interpretation of "Hinduism" defined by Radhakrishnan. His definition of what was essential to "Hinduism" provided religious justification in matters called "Hindu," if not also a "Neo-Advaitin" inclusivistic view of other religions.

Analyses of judicial decisions, particularly at the level of the Supreme Court, indicate the counterplay of these two definitions with the favor going in some notable cases to Nehru's agnosticism toward "religion." Baird's analysis of the influential Supreme Court Chief Justice (1963–1965) and Chairman of the Law Commission

(1971–1978) P.B. Gajendragadkar, who "strides across Indian jurisprudence in the sixties,"[56] lays bare an example of an influential nation builder who accepted an ideal notion of what "religion" that is guaranteed freedom by the Constitution means and, through judicial decision and opinion, sought to enforce a reconception of the religions in light of this ideal and to propagate that reconception to the masses. His ultimate purpose was to further the "secular" goals of the Indian nation.[57] The task of "secularism," he said, "is to separate the secular from the essentially religious," so the state can govern the truly "secular."[58] Therefore, "religion as it is practiced by ignorant men" or "as preached by [an] ignorant and bigoted priestly caste belonging to different religions" is not acceptable.[59] Instead, accepting the definition of an essential, "tolerant" "Hinduism" proclaimed by Radhakrishnan as true, the chief justice asserted that "Hindus" should adjust their current religion to one of tolerance. The relevant legacy of "Hindu" thought, he wrote, and "the cornerstone of secularism" is "the spirit of tolerance, born out of a firm conviction that all religions are entitled to freedom and each one of them has an element of truth, while none has the monopoly on truth. . . ."[60] Yet, like Nehru, Gajendragadkar has no desire to identify "secularism" with any religious position, even a reconceived one: "Indeed, the state as such has no religion."[61] The function of reconstructing religion is not to provide a definition of "secularism," which would be undergirded by "religion," for "secular matters are out of bounds for religions of all kinds."[62] Instead, "religion" needs to be reshaped to end all religious interference in the state and, thus, to enable India to proceed unhindered in the building of a "modern" society with the accompanying social, political, and other "secular" reforms. In the creation of a "secular India," "religion" will have to take its proper place. "Religion will, in this process, have to renounce its claim to intervene in the material life of the community and will have to confine itself to its legitimate sphere of facing the eternal riddle of the universe."[63]

A similar case, though with yet more commitment to "socialist, reformist" jurisprudence, was another influential Supreme Court judge, Justice V.R. Krishna Iyer, who also had been a member of the Law Commission, a judge of the Kerala High Court, and a minister in the Communist government in the state of Kerala (1957–1959). He sought a more active program of socialist reform with a definition of "secularism" thoroughly that of Nehru. "We need more activist judges accepting the humanist ideology of the Constitution," he pleaded.[64]

Thus the debate over the nature of the "true Indian secular state" on the level of the national leaders who engaged in the debate as more than an academic discussion continued in ambiguity. In practice it illustrates how the concerns, ultimate or penultimate, of various parties work against each other in the midst of building a "sovereign socialist democratic republic." While the definitions of "religion" and "secular" are still unresolved, much less even made explicit by the various parties in the disputes, the intentions and goals of the numerous parties involved in various issues vie for a hearing and search for words and power to attain their goals.

One such case follows. In the midst of the discussion of "secular" and "religious" by writers and theoreticians, what happens in the actual debates and discussions to navigate through the problems created by the distinction between "religion" and the "secular" while promoting perceived interests of the nation, groups, and individuals? What are the various interests of the parties involved in such disputes, and how are these categories used to promote the various interests of the parties? The case of the disposition of the township of Auroville provides one example. Founded by the inspiration of two gurus and culture heros, the government of India is now committed to promote (could we say propagate?) the goals for which it was founded in some form, and the Parliament, the courts, and even an international organization, the United Nations Educational, Scientific and Cultural Organization (UNESCO), were involved in what appears to be government interest in promoting the teachings of an Indian guru and his followers. This is a study of the competing interests of groups involved, the necessary decisions that the organs of the state made, and the ambiguity of the discussion in terms of the meaning of the categories: the "religious," the "spiritual," and the "secular."

Two

⊸◈⊷

Sri Aurobindo and the "Religion" of the "Integral Yoga" Community

O n February 6, 1893, Aurobindo Akroyd Ghose (1872–1950), a man who would become an Indian cultural hero, a renowned activist in the Indian independence struggle, and the first guru of a modern "religious" movement, returned to India after fourteen years of study in England. Taken to England by his father, Dr. Kristo Dhone Ghose, to prepare him for a career in the Indian Civil Service, Aurobindo instead returned with other plans.

Upon his arrival in Bombay, Aurobindo took up service under the Maharaja of Baroda, Sayajirao Gaekwar, and eventually rose to the status of vice president of Baroda College. He brought with him a classical British education, which had culminated with a year and a half of study at King's College, Cambridge. He had excelled in Greek and Latin as well as in English composition, French, English literature and history, and Italian. His Indian Civil Service course included law, economics, Sanskrit, Bengali, and Indian history and geography. During his last year at Cambridge, he also was introduced to Indian religious thought and, in English, first read the ancient Sanskrit scriptures most often cited by "Neo-Advaitins," the *Upanisads.*[1]

In England, Aurobindo's desire to play a part in the overthrow of British imperialism began and grew in intensity. He joined other Indian students to form "The Lotus and Dagger," a group that required each member to vow to work for the liberation of India.

His failure to complete the horseback riding requirement for the Civil Service probably stems from this turn in his political leanings. In addition, during this period he was first introduced to Indian thought, and the idea that began to capture his mind was the unifying concept of a universal Self (*ātman*) behind the universe.

At Baroda, Aurobindo studied Indian religion and culture in a manner that set the stage for the system of thought he developed years later at the French colony of Pondicherry in southeast India.[2] Central to his system of thought at Baroda were (1) the importance and centrality of the intuitive, revelatory, yogic experiences of the seers who wrote the ancient texts called the *Upanisads*; (2) a definition of the Highest Reality in terms of an Absolute Unity, traditionally designated Brahman; and (3) the setting forth of the goal of life as the realization of a harmony with this Highest Reality, which emphasizes the Unity behind the diversity of this world.

Aurobindo also attended sessions of the Indian National Congress, an organization of elite, English-educated Indians, most of whom believed that British rule was a necessary, even providential, stage in the progress of India toward modern nationhood. In its leaders' eyes, the purpose of the Congress was to petition the British government with its grievances. As early as 1893, Aurobindo criticized the Congress for what he considered selfish elitism: "Whatever theatrical attitude it may suit our vanity to adopt, we are not, as we pretend to be, the embodiment of the country's power, intelligence and worth: neither are we disinterested patriots striving in all purity and unselfishness towards an issue irreproachable before God."[3] Aurobindo came to identify with a growing group of Congress "Nationalists" who favored immediate independence from British rule and even revolution to achieve that end. At the 1902 Congress, he met the most famous Nationalist leader of this more extreme faction, B.G. (Lokamanya) Tilak.

Indian Nationalism and the Rejection of a "Secular" Realm

In August 1905, the British declared that the state of Bengal would be partitioned, a decision perceived by many Nationalists as a British colonialist attempt to divide and conquer. Between that time and February 1910, Aurobindo, now in Calcutta, became one of the major exponents of the Nationalist position, publishing his political–religious essays in three journals: first, *Bande Mataram*, and later, *Karmayogin* and *Dharma*. With this move toward a leadership role in the Nationalist cause, there was little change in his *Weltanschauung*, but a fiery spirit moved the independence of India to the center of his concern.

In these Nationalist articles, Aurobindo defined the cause of Indian independence in a manner that rejected any real distinction between Nationalist activities that were "religious" and those that were "secular." He conceived of India as "the Mother," identifying the nation with the Goddess, the *śakti*, or the "power" of the Absolute at work in the universe. The ultimate goal of Indian independence, he wrote, was to present India to the world as the world's spiritual teacher. As "the *guru* of the nations," India has been set apart by the Divine "as the eternal fountain-head of holy spirituality."[4] "It is she who must send forth from herself the future religion of the entire world, the Eternal Religion which is to harmonise all religion, science and philosophies and make mankind one soul."[5] Identifying his nationalism with the teachings of the *Upanisads*, Aurobindo defined the goal as "the final fulfilment of the Vedantic ideal in politics, this is the true Swaraj for India."[6]

The cause of India in which Nationalists worked was not really a "secular," political one in Aurobindo's mind. Work for India involved a recognition that the Divine itself was at work in everything, and, thus, that the work of the true Nationalist was, in actuality, a yoga, a spiritual discipline.

> Do you hold your political creed from a higher source? Is it God that is born in you? Have you realised that you are merely the instruments of God, that your bodies are not your own? You are merely instruments of God for the work of the Almighty. Have you realised that? If you have realised that, then you are truly Nationalists; then alone will you be able to restore this great nation.[7]

To work for Indian national liberation was to obey the will of the Divine and, thus, the true Nationalists were those who realized they were Divine instruments. Aurobindo did not hesitate to call it "religion" or use other religious language.

Under Aurobindo's editorship, *Bande Mataram* came to be identified as the organ of the "Extremists." Though it originated in Bengal, it was known throughout much of India. In 1907, the government began to prosecute the Nationalist press, and on August 14 a warrant for the arrest of Aurobindo as editor of *Bande*

Mataram was issued. In September, Aurobindo was found inno-
cent, because no documents were submitted that supported the
contention that Aurobindo was actually the editor, but the trial
served to bring national attention to Aurobindo.

On May 5, 1908, Aurobindo was again arrested, this time as a
suspect in a bombing case centering around his brother Barinda.
During the year of the trial, Aurobindo was incarcerated in the Alipore jail, and when he was acquitted he was the most well-known
Nationalist extremist still free in India.

Upon his release, he began the two new journals: the English
language *Karmayogin*, which appeared first on June 19, 1909, and
its Bengali counterpart, *Dharma*, which began publishing on
August 23. In these he further, and even more self-consciously,
incorporated politics and religion. He credited his spiritual experiences during the year of his incarceration for what he said was a
new approach to Indian nationalism. He experienced, he said, a
more meaningful realization of the Truth that he had previously
understood only intellectually, and, thus, he emerged from prison
"a new being, a new character, intellect, life, mind, embarking on a
new course of action. . . ."[8]

On May 30, 1909, twenty-four days after his release, in his
famous Uttarpara Speech, he spoke of these experiences as the realization in his total being of "the utter truth of the Hindu religion."[9]
There was no hesitation to speak of his experiences as "religious,"
but they were more than that. The experiences, he was convinced,
were experiences of the truth of the "Sanatan(a) Dharma," which
he translated into English as the "eternal religion" behind all religions. By using this designation, he joined those Indian thinkers
and modern "Neo-Hindu" apologists such as Swami Vivekananda
and, later, Radhakrishnan, who taught that there was a position
behind the variety of religious positions that transcended or under-
girds them all. Even though this position was usually identified
with one of the historical positions in the history of religions in
India, usually a form of Advaita Vedanta, Aurobindo, like the other
advocates of this position, did not see it as merely one of them. He
saw it as the essential truth of all religions, or, at least, as the one
position behind all so-called "Hindu positions." Thus, to treat it as
one of the historical options, he and they believed, was to misunderstand their own view.

This *sanātana dharma*, Aurobindo believed, encompassed all
that people call religion, politics and society, both the "religious"
and the "secular." It provided a vision of politics and society that

would raise these to a higher level. It also eliminated any and all distinctions between religion, politics, social action, and national uplift.

Though these Alipore jail experiences added no radically new content to Aurobindo's *Weltanschauung*, he believed they had changed his emphasis.

> I spoke once before with this force in me and I said then that this movement is not a political movement and that nationalism is not politics but a religion, a creed, a faith. I say it again today, but I put it in another way. I say no longer that nationalism is a creed, a religion, a faith; I say that it is the Sanatan Dharma which for us is nationalism.[10]

He would not hesitate to designate the cause of Indian nationhood "a creed, a religion, a faith," but there was to be a change of order in his Nationalist work. The nation of India was no longer the priority; the *sanātana dharma* had become more important. No longer would he promote India to raise the *sanātana dharma*. Instead, he would promote the *sanātana dharma* because that is in fact the promotion of India, and in this work all distinctions between religious and secular were eliminated. "The Sanatan Dharma," he concluded, "that is nationalism."

The difference in emphasis from his writings in the *Bande Mataram* might have seemed subtle to the casual reader of his two new journals. Political comment continued to occupy a large place in the *Karmayogin*, and Aurobindo continued to act as a public spokesperson for those nationalists called "Extremists." In the February 5, 1910, *Karmayogin*, though, Aurobindo reflected on the "disproportionate space" he had given to politics in the light of the intended goals of the new journal. Because of the current political situation, he vowed to spend more time pursuing these original goals,[11] but he found himself torn between his position as an Extremist spokesperson and the pursuit of the development of his personal yogic discipline with its larger goals.

In the meantime, the political situation in India continued to intensify. Revolutionaries stepped up their activity, and the Bengal authorities decided to act decisively against the Extremists. In February 1910, Aurobindo learned of his impending arrest and chose not to remain and fight. On February 14, he left British India for Chandernagore, a town in French India, twenty miles up the Ganges River from Calcutta. On April 4, he arrived in Pondicherry, a French territory in southeast India, where Tamil Nationalists received him. Later, he wrote that he had left Calcutta and the Nationalist fight in India as a result of spiritual guidance. "While considering what should be his attitude, he received a sudden command from above to go to Chandernagore in French India. He obeyed the command at once, for it was now his rule to move only as he was moved by the divine guidance and never to resist and depart from it. . . ."[12]

The initial reaction from other Nationalists was disappointment. Aurobindo would never leave Pondicherry to act directly in the Nationalist movement again, though he remained in touch with Nationalist activities and received requests to return to the fray. For example, on August 30, 1920, he responded in the negative to a request to take the presidency of the Indian National Congress. In his answer, he indicated his new priorities.

> The central reason however is this that I am no longer first and foremost a politician, but have definitely commenced another kind of work with a spiritual basis, a work of spiritual, social, cultural and economic reconstruction of an almost revolutionary kind, and am even making or at least supervising a sort of practical or laboratory experiment in that sense which needs all the attention and energy that I can have to spare. It is impossible for me to combine political work of the current kind and this at the beginning.[13]

His new approach was to withdraw physically to develop a yoga that would affect the political situation in what he believed was the most basic manner. And since, he believed, the yoga he continued to develop and practice was the yoga of the *sanātana dharma*, it could not be separated from politics, or social, cultural, or economic reconstruction.

His withdrawal should be seen in light of that *Weltanschauung*. It was not an ascetic withdrawal of worldly denial, but a withdrawal that he believed would more deeply affect politics and society over the long term. It was, he said, the recognition that there is nothing "secular," that all relates to the "spiritual" activity he espoused. "I have always laid a dominant stress and I now lay an entire stress on the spiritual life, but my idea of spirituality has nothing to do with ascetic withdrawal or contempt or disgust of secular things. There is to me nothing secular, all human activity is for me a thing to be included in a complete spiritual life, and the importance of politics at the present time is very great."[14] Like traditional religious positions, his own did not distinguish between the categories "religious," "spiritual," and "secular." All was to be included in this *sanātana dharma* that he would fully develop and define in his writings from Pondicherry, until his death on December 5, 1950.

If Aurobindo had done no more, he would have been honored by future Indians as a great leader of the freedom movement as a patriot and an activist. The disappointment of Nationalists in 1910 gave way to pride and exaltation of Sri Aurobindo. The Indian nation builders came to see him as almost larger than life, as do their counterparts in other nations for such cultural heroes. His yogic period and subsequent writings would bring him international renown and would only further Indian pride in their hero. The Indian nation would own him as it did Lokamanya Tilak and Mahatma Gandhi, though it would often ignore the fact that he promoted a particular *Weltanschauung* or religious position that ultimately eliminated the basis for a distinction between the two realms designated the "religious" and the "secular."

Sanatana Dharma as Integral Yoga

Sri Aurobindo lived in Pondicherry until his death. He wrote voluminously in English, corresponded with the growing number of *sadhaks*, seekers or disciples, who gathered around him, and gained a worldwide following. Most important to him, however, was the development of his own personal discipline, his yoga. As the years passed, he became less and less accessible, except to a handful of followers.

His ultimate concern was the perfection of the individual, society, and the entire phenomenal reality.[15] These three were integral parts of his goal. Perfection began with the individual but could not end there.

> It is, then, this spiritual fulfillment of the urge to individual perfection and an inner completeness of being that we mean first when we speak of a divine life. It is the first essential condition of a perfected life on earth, and we are therefore right in making the utmost possible individual perfection our first supreme business. The perfection of the spiritual and pragmatic relation of the individual with all around him is our

second preoccupation; the solution of this second desideratum
lies in a complete universality and oneness with all life upon
earth which is the other concomitant result of an evolution
into the gnostic consciousness and nature. But there still
remains the third desideratum, a new world, a change in the
total life of humanity or, at the least, a new perfected collective life in the earth–nature.[16]

The individual, society, and the larger environment of the Universe
were to be united in perfection, a perfection envisioned in terms of
his definition of reality, his view of the Absolute, and his particular
notion of the evolution of the environment toward that perfection.

Aurobindo denied that the position he was affirming was to be
accepted on the basis of philosophical arguments. The key to truth
was in realization, what he sometimes called "true intuition." The
emphasis was to be on experiential knowledge, but experience for
Aurobindo was not limited to the sensual. The practice of yoga
could provide experiences of consciousness far beyond the limits of
the mind and physical senses.[17] These experiences would not negate
those in the physical world, he taught, but fulfill, complete, and
integrate them.

Aurobindo believed that through these ongoing personal yogic
experiences he had discovered a key to the universe that was best
manifested in a system of thought and practice he called "Integral
Yoga." He, therefore, wrote as a yogi who saw realization as a
process and saw himself in the midst of that process of realization.
He spoke authoritatively, but not with finality, for at times he
would speculate on certain issues and questions on the basis of
what he believed had already been revealed in his yoga. He believed
he had discovered, or, identifying with the Upanisadic sages, redis-
covered, levels of consciousness that transcended those open to the
methods of the ordinary mind.

The knowledge he believed he had realized in these experiences was "integral." Though it came from higher, more intuitive
levels of consciousness that were beyond reason, it was capable of
integration with lower levels of consciousness, such as that of
Mind. "These truths present themselves to our conceptual cogni-
tion as the fundamental aspects in which we see and experience the
omnipresent Reality."[18]

Aurobindo's system explains his claims for the centrality of
these integral, supramental experiences. Crucial is the affirmation
of the integral nature of the Absolute. Using traditional Upanisadic

terms, it is *saccidānanda* (*sat*, "being, existence"; *cit*, "consciousness–force"; *ānanda*, "bliss, freedom"). This Absolute transcends the limitations inherent in the distinctions of the intellectual process, the level of consciousness he called "Mind." The Absolute is both eternal, static Being and eternal, dynamic Becoming. As the former, it is the Brahman of the Advaitin thinkers, which is One and All, unchanging and *nirguṇa*, without characteristics. It is *neti . . . neti*, "not this, not that." As Becoming, it includes the universe of phenomena and the totality of spiritual forces behind it in a cyclical involution to lower levels of consciousness and in evolution from lower to higher levels of consciousness.

The evolutionary process of the Absolute assumes its prior involution down into the level of the least conscious, the physical, Matter. It then proceeds from Matter through Life, Psyche, Mind, Higher Mind, Illumined Mind, Intuitive Mind, Overmind, Supermind, Saccidananda ("Being, Consciousness–Force, Bliss") in Manifestation and, finally, to the highest consciousness, the Supreme Saccidananda Unmanifest. The evolution takes place through the activity of the level of consciousness known as "Supermind," an eternal reality of the Divine which is a consciousness that sees and acts upon both the Unity and the multiplicity.[19]

The world of phenomena is therefore real. It is not an illusion, but the Absolute in real Becoming; and this level of Becoming is as real, as ultimate, as the Absolute as Being. ". . . It is a progressive self-expression, a manifestation, an evolving self-development of That in Time which our consciousness cannot yet see in its total or its essential significance."[20]

Even though static Being and ever-changing Becoming are logical opposites to Mind consciousness, on the basis of his yogic experiences, Aurobindo believed that the Absolute transcends distinctions such as these contradictions of that lower-level consciousness.

> But the Absolute, obviously, finds no difficulty in world–manifestation and no difficulty either in a simultaneous transcendence of world–manifestation; the difficulty exists only for our mental limitations which prevent us from grasping the supramental rationality of the co-existence of the infinite and the finite or seizing the nodus of the unconditioned with the conditioned. For our intellectual rationality these are opposites; for the absolute reason they are interrelated and not essentially conflicting expressions of one and the same reality.[21]

It was the reconciliation of the affirmation of the One and the Many as equally real that Aurobindo said occupied "decades of [his] spiritual effort." In fact, he actually only accepted his yogic experiences as fully authoritative when they had confirmed that both the One and the Many were ultimate realities.[22] In any case, the result was the affirmation of the world and its plural entities as real and ultimately significant.

Though the essential human being is identical with Supermind, outwardly its consciousness is on the level of evolutionary consciousness that Aurobindo labels "Mind." This level is that of "Nature become partially conscious of her own laws." Mind consciousness is able to participate consciously in the evolutionary process itself to either promote or hinder it. The means for such promotion of the perfection of the world is Integral Yoga. It is, in essence, a personal acceleration of the evolutionary process itself, beginning with the individual whose achievements both directly and indirectly affect the earth consciousness. "The aim of the yoga is to open the consciousness to the Divine and to live in the inner consciousness more and more while acting from it on the external life, to bring the inmost psychic into the front and by the power of the psychic to purify and change the being so that it may become ready for transformation and be in union with the Divine Knowledge, Will, and Love."[23]

The very nature of these assertions that higher levels of consciousness transcend the limitations of rational categories requires those who wish to begin Integral Yoga to accept the guidance of another, not guidance by what the Mind consciousness allows to be true. If the limitations of reason are not ultimate clues to the nature of Reality and if in particular the law of contradiction is not ultimately valid, one must surrender to this view of truth and to its purveyor and be willing to admit the ultimate errors of reason's skepticism. Aurobindo's system and claims require the acceptance of his authority. The disciple, or sadhak, must accept that Aurobindo knows in a manner that the disciple does not.

This yoga, that is, the theory he spoke of in his voluminous writings and the method he practiced daily, was called "integral" for a number of reasons,[24] one of which was that it did not reject or subordinate the world and its plurality but affirmed it as a Divine diversity essential to human beings, "integrated" the Many into the system. This meant human beings also were diverse, and the Supermind was working in and through them in diverse ways. There was, therefore, no fixed system of yogic practice for all who sought to follow his yoga, but a variety of methods that share certain basic requirements, the most crucial being surrender to the guru.[25]

Those who eventually attain supramental consciousness, the "gnostic beings," would join with others to provide an atmosphere on earth that would further their evolution and prepare the social, political, and biological environment (the "earth consciousness") itself to rise to higher consciousness.[26] The collective spiritual influence of these communities would affect the world, in the same way that it was traditionally believed that the *tejas*, or splendor, of a realized yogi would exude out to the world about him and bring observable change. This change would encompass all that others might designate "religious" and "secular." As integral, it must integrate everything and, therefore, could not be relegated merely to one portion of what Aurobindo saw as real.

This is the closest Aurobindo came in his writings to a discussion of what might be conceived of as the basic conception of a township such as Auroville, though it could just as easily be merely a retreat, or ashram, such as the one that began to grow up around him in Pondicherry. "At a certain stage it might be necessary to follow the age-long device of the separate community, but with a double purpose, first to provide a secure atmosphere, a place apart, in which the consciousness of the individual might concentrate on its evolution in surroundings where all was turned and centered towards the one endeavour and, next, when things were ready, to formulate and develop the new life in those surroundings and in this prepared spiritual atmosphere."[27] His conception of this community, in any case, was one fully rooted in, and inseparable from, his *Weltanschauung*, his religious/philosophical position, not just in any position whatsoever, and it was a system that sought to influence all elements of life on earth.

Religion and the Religions

Mind, however, is a limited and only indirectly illuminated consciousness that is ignorant, because it views reality only in its dividedness. On the basis of what he believed were his intuitive experiences of higher levels of consciousness, he criticized unenlightened reason as "out of its province and condemned to tread either diffidently or else with a stumbling presumptuousness in the realm of a power and a light higher than its own."[28] Intellectual systems and religions are located on this level of partial consciousness.

On the basis of the authority he believed his experiences had, he felt free to evaluate the other positions, the religions. Essentially, he said, as did other "Neo-Hindu" thinkers, religion and the religions are based upon experience, not doctrines, creeds, or practices. The knowledge one gains in religious experience is intuitive rather than intellectual, and must, therefore, bring its insights to bear on the intellectual level. Other positions have not done this, but have tried to make the Mind consciousness limit the higher insights.[29]

When speaking of the variety of religious positions, he treated them monolithically as reified entities, as "isms" (e.g., Christianity, Buddhism, Islam, Judaism). One exception was the manner in which he treated the traditions with which he had become most familiar, which he included under the category "Hinduism." In this category, he recognized the existence of a variety of positions, but, again, as other modern "Neo-Hindu" religious figures such as Swami Vivekananda and Sarvepalli Radhakrishnan did, the reified "Hinduism" was defined as a unity based in a common religious experience.[30] And also as with these other thinkers, this experience was defined as the essence of all religions, though many who profess these religions foolishly do not recognize this fact.

This essential religious experience—which the members of all of the religions should recognize as the essence of every religion and, thus, religion itself—is the experience of the Absolute as both Being and Becoming as he experienced it. This essential religious experience affirms the ultimate reality of both the one, inner Self and also the plurality of the ever-changing world. He criticized the religions in traditional form because they value the present life less than other realms and portray themselves merely as the means to another life beyond the grave. "The orthodox religions looked with eyes of pious sorrow and gloom on the earthly life of man and were very ready to bid him bear peacefully and contentedly, even to welcome its crudities, cruelties, oppressions, tribulations as a means for learning to appreciate and for earning the better life which will be given us hereafter."[31] The affirmation of the evolution of the Supermind instead provides the basis of the significance and ultimacy of this world.

Aurobindo's view of the Absolute as Becoming not only affirms the world but provides him with a basis for the actual transformation of the world. The true devotee is to perform activity in this ultimately significant world that is actually an acting out of the evolution of the Divine consciousness's eternal becoming and thereby promotes the earth's perfection. The sadhak is to raise the world–consciousness by bringing down the higher levels of consciousness the sadhak has experienced to transform the lower levels. Aurobindo's writings are one example of the transformation, for he believed they integrated his intuitive insights into Mind and, thus, transformed that level of consciousness.

In contrast to his confidence that his own position will achieve the perfection of the world, he criticized the religions for their failure to transform it. His criticism is universal and absolute, asserting not only that *all* religions have failed but that all non-religious attempts are failures as well.

> Altruism, philanthropy and service, Christian love or Buddhist compassion have not made the world a whit happier, they only give infinitesimal bits of momentary relief here and there, throw drops on the fire of the world's suffering. All aims are in the end transitory and futile, all achievements unsatisfying or evanescent; all works are so much labour of effort and success and failure which consummate nothing definitive: whatever changes are made in human life are of the form only and these forms pursue each other in a futile circle; for the essence of life, its general character remains the same for ever.[32]

Only his Integral Yoga can solve the world's problems. The religions have more often worked against the natural improvement inherent in the world's progress through the evolutionary movement of the Spirit: ". . . historically and as a matter of fact the accredited religions and their hierarchs and exponents have too often been a force for retardation, have too often thrown their weight on the side of darkness, oppression and ignorance. . . ."[33] Unlike Integral Yoga, which Aurobindo believed accomplishes the preliminary step necessary for societal change, that is, it changes the inner being, the religions "at best modify only the surface of the nature. Moreover, they degenerate very soon into a routine of ceremonial habitual worship and fixed dogmas."[34] They are, therefore, incapable of success unless they return to their essence, which is expressed in Aurobindo's position.

Since the Becoming is essential to Aurobindo's critique and since this Becoming is understood in terms of the evolutionary scheme Aurobindo believed his experiences of higher levels of consciousness had made authoritative, he interpreted the cause of the inadequacies of the other religious positions in terms of his evolutionary scheme.[35] Higher and truer knowledge is that of higher levels of evolution, those above the level on which humanity currently finds itself—Mind. True religion, therefore, sees that reason is incapable of knowing Reality any more than partially. Though reason is useful on the level of Mind to sharpen and order one's expression of Truth, it must actually find the Truth in higher levels. Reason is not in error but in ignorance. It is a limited knowing. To truly understand, religions must, therefore, recognize the limited nature of reason and its products: creeds, dogmas, and forms.

Aurobindo credited the problems he saw with other Indian religious positions to their lack of extensive intuitive vision of the levels of supramental consciousness he affirmed as being authoritative. Instead they placed emphasis on Mind, giving it an exclusive status instead of recognizing, as he did, that rational limits are not ultimate when speaking of the Being and Becoming that is Saccidananda. For example, Gandhi's central commitment to *satyāgraha* (nonviolent resistance), Aurobindo taught, was a commitment to limited mental theories. In fact, he says, so inferior are viewpoints such as Gandhi's, which are limited to the level of Mind, that they are hardly worth attention.

> Gandhi's theories are like other mental theories built on a basis of one-sided reasoning and claiming for a limited truth (that of nonviolence and passive resistance) a universality which it cannot have. Such theories will always exist so long as the mind is the main instrument of human truth-seeking. To spend energy trying to destroy such theories is of little use; if destroyed they are replaced by others equally limited and partial.[36]

Likewise, Aurobindo rejected Theosophical teachings because, he taught, they arose out of Mind or even "raw imagination" rather than the higher supramental consciousness.[37] In his letters, Aurobindo criticizes Vivekananda too for making *seva*, or service itself, into a universal requirement. No matter how essential *seva* was to Vivekananda, Aurobindo saw this as being a case of making one relative side of truth absolute. "His ideal of *seva* was a need of his nature and must have helped him—it does not follow that it must be accepted as a universal spiritual necessity or ideal."[38]

The authority Aurobindo placed upon his experiences, therefore, resulted in the judgment of those whose experiences, descriptions of their experiences, or systems that they espoused, were not like Aurobindo's. They had not actually experienced the highest levels of truth but were most often working out of the level of Mind. It is not that the other positions and the religions affirm what is completely unworthy of belief and practice in a particular space and time, but that they do not recognize that those beliefs and practices are only relative and partial. As a consequence they take these partial truths and nonessential elements as universal. Still identifying his own position as "religion," in *The Human Cycle* he calls the emphasis upon these partial truths by others "religionism," and not the "true religion," which is the essence identical with his own affirmation.

> There are two aspects of religion, true religion and religionism. True religion is spiritual religion, that which seeks to live in the spirit, in what is beyond the intellect, beyond the aesthetic and ethical and practical being of man, and to inform and govern these members of our being by the higher light and law of the spirit. Religionism, on the contrary, entrenches itself in some narrow pietistic exaltation of the lower members or lays exclusive stress on intellectual dogmas, forms and ceremonies, on some fixed and rigid moral code, on some religio-political or religio-social system."[39]

By universalizing and absolutizing relative and partial truths, the religions set themselves up in opposition to the very nature of Reality and the evolution of the Universe as Aurobindo envisioned them. This evaluation of the religions as being guilty of egoistically universalizing and promoting partial views is more than a declaration of their relative place in the evolutionary scheme. It is, as argued elsewhere, "an application of Aurobindo's belief that evil is the result of the egoistic tendency of principles that arise in the evolutionary process to extend themselves beyond their partial and temporary place in the Supermind's scheme."[40] Evil, for Aurobindo, is anything that retards the evolutionary process. "To the extent, then, that religions hinder or retard the evolutionary process, to that extent they are evil; as evil as anything can be in Aurobindo's view of reality."[41] Though built upon a positive foundation—the experience that is essentially integral—the religions are egoistic hindrances to the Divine plan.

Aurobindo entitled chapter 34 of *The Ideal of Human Unity*

"The Religion of Humanity." He wrote of his own position in terms of a "spiritual religion" that alone, he said, is the hope of the future. Though he spoke of this "religion" as one based upon a realization and not a "universal religious system, one in mental creed and vital form," he defined it in terms that are propositional and, one might say, creedal, affirming his own ontological stance with its emphasis upon evolution and the oneness of the Divine and the universe.

> A religion of humanity means the growing realisation that there is a secret Spirit, a divine Reality, in which we are all one, that humanity is its highest present vehicle on earth, that the human race and the human being are the means by which it will progressively reveal itself here. It implies a growing attempt to live out this knowledge and bring about a kingdom of this divine Spirit upon earth. By its growth within us oneness with our fellow men will become the leading principle of all our life, not merely a principle of cooperation but a deeper brotherhood, a real and an inner sense of unity and equality and a common life. There must be a realisation by the individual that only in the life of his fellow men is his own life complete. There must be the realisation by the race that only on the free and full life of the individual can its own perfection and permanent happiness be founded. There must be too a discipline and a way of salvation in accordance with this religion, that is to say, a means by which it can be developed by each man within himself, so that it may be developed in the life of the race.[42]

As the truth about the universe, he believed, and as based upon true realization, there would be no need for forceful promotion, yet its "creed and ideal" would be upheld "as a light and inspiration" to all.[43] Until sufficient members of the human race realize this truth, "the attempt to bring it about by mechanical means must proceed."[44] While the "religion of humanity" that is Integral Yoga makes itself "more explicit, insistent and categorically imperative,"[45] other religions should outwardly be treated as stages in the evolution that have become problematic by egoistically overemphasizing nonessential elements beyond their limited place in the evolutionary scheme. One must allow the existence of a variety of paths to the goal, as India has done.[46] Yet the process of upholding integral truth is understood as the integration of the essentials of these other positions that are partial yogas into Integral Yoga, affirming thereby their true insights. Beyond this, one need not worry about the ultimate fate of these views as separate positions. With confidence in the evolutionary process as set forth in Aurobindo's position comes confidence that this process in itself will result in the eventual elimination of the other positions as absolutes and the integration of spiritual seekers into that highest truth seen in Integral Yoga. Religion has evolved through stages in the past and will continue to evolve in the future. Aurobindo is convinced that someday humanity will recognize this Higher Vision.[47]

The theoretical foundation Aurobindo expounded included a specific view of Reality, a *Weltanschauung*, which, he believed, understood the Truth of the Universe. Its relationship to other viewpoints was to see these as misunderstandings of Reality. What they said may not have been wrong unless they claimed absolute truth for those viewpoints. Only Aurobindo's viewpoint had that status because he believed it was "integral," it had greater vision, sweep, and insight, and it was revealed by essential religious experiences. He believed he had "seen" from higher levels of consciousness and that those who did not also "see" were speaking only from their limited vision. They could not but absolutize what Aurobindo's own viewpoint saw was only relatively true. It is on the basis of this higher vision, this "Integral Yoga," that communities like Auroville can be successful. Success would be assured there because they are in touch with Reality.

Throughout Aurobindo's life, his viewpoint called for the rejection of the distinction between "religion" and the "secular." There is one realm, not two, and thus he ultimately rejected the very category of "secular." Politics, economics, social issues, and religion are all part of the same realm. At times, then, Aurobindo called his position "religion," but distinguished it from "the religions" or "religionism." "The religions" and "religionism" are of course based upon the essential position he himself affirmed and sometimes called "true religion," "the religion of humanity," or "a spiritual religion." Yet the religions err by affirming what is not in fact ultimately true. They absolutize and universalize what is truly relative and particular.

If a community of people then is to fulfill this vision of things, it can only be based upon this particular worldview, for its goal is not merely to help people work together in harmony in some general and vague sense, but to change individuals, relationships, and the environment, to correspond to the view of their destiny expounded and attempted in Integral Yoga. And Aurobindo did not hesitate to call that view "religion," though it was not one of "the religions" that understand reality only partially. He rejected the idea that anything fell outside of this "religion," that there was anything "secular," because an essential, superior characteristic of his *Weltanschauung* was that it was all-encompassing, leaving nothing out of its scope. This, then, is like traditional religious models, which rejected the division of the world into distinct religious and secular realms. However, in Aurobindo's language, it meant that everything is the arena of the thought, experience, and activity of what he called "the religion of humanity," "true religion," "spiritual religion," or "Integral Yoga." That would mean then that everything was the work of a community that practiced such "Integral Yoga," and it would be a misunderstanding to call it "secular."

Three

◁◈▷

Auroville as the Mother's Vision

Sri Aurobindo envisioned and wrote about communities that would practice this "religion of humanity," this active life of yogic experimentation that in its integral view would not accept the idea that anything was outside of its purview. In his terms, they would accept nothing as "secular." As Integral Yoga communities, these would be centers where followers would collectively practice not only a meditative, consciousness-raising yoga, but also a *karma-yoga*, an active, world-changing life that would bring the supramental consciousness he saw down into the "earth-consciousness" to enable, encourage, and promote its evolution toward Divine manifestation. Here was the basis for community action.

Aurobindo would not be the founder or "hands-on" leader of such enlightened communal activity. That task would be the work of the second leader, or guru, of the movement that began to grow around him. This second leader's authority was assured because Aurobindo passed on the mantle of leadership, what sociologist Max Weber would call its accompanying "charisma," to this successor before he personally left the "earth-consciousness."

November 24, 1926, has come to be known as Aurobindo's "Day of Siddhi," or "Day of Perfection," in the movement that followed him and in the Sri Aurobindo Ashram that was built around him. Aurobindo believed it was a day of particularly significant supramental experience along the path of yogic experimentation on which he had set his feet. As a result, the day also marked a change in his relationship to the twenty or so disciples that had gathered around him and extended a period of literary silence that had begun six years earlier. On this day, he is said to have experienced the descent of a level of consciousness he labeled "Overmind," a consciousness that stood between the level of Mind and the higher consciousness that is the key to the universe, Supermind.[1] In some ways this revelation was a surprise, for it began the process of revelation of intermediary levels of consciousness he had not previously detected. As a result of this process, during the period 1939–1940, he would revise some of his earlier writings to include these newly revealed levels in his evolutionary schema, levels he came to call Higher Mind, Illumined Mind, Intuitive Mind, and Overmind.[2]

One response to this breakthrough was that Aurobindo curtailed his public activities and ceased to meet regularly with his disciples. In February 1927, he moved to an adjoining house to remain in solitude for the remainder of his life. Henceforth, he appeared for his disciples only three times a year, giving them "darshan" (the blessing of his sight) and corresponding with them. But even this extensive correspondence ended after five years.

It is on this date as well that the Sri Aurobindo Ashram was officially founded.[3] Sri Aurobindo placed the Ashram in the charge of Mirra Alfassa (1878–1973), who is known by the name Aurobindo came to call her, "the Mother." She would effectively become the movement's second leader. As Aurobindo slipped further into the background, he would provide the inspiration in increasingly more distant terms. The existential experience of the followers came to center more and more on "the Mother."

The Person, Place, and Authority of the Mother

Mirra Alfassa was born in Paris on February 21, 1878, to an Egyptian father and a Turkish mother. In later recollections she portrays herself as a spiritualist, a practitioner of yoga at the age of four, one who developed an early interest in "occultism," and the subject of numerous paranormal or spiritual experiences throughout her early life.[4] She studied drawing and painting at the Ecole des Beaux Arts and at the age of nineteen married Henri Morisset. On August 23, 1898, she gave birth to a son, Andre.

Between 1905 and 1906, Mirra Alfassa studied in Tlemcen,

Algeria, with Max Theon, a Polish or Russian Jew, and his wife. He was known for his accomplishments in religious experience, had worked with the Theosophical Society leader and founder, Helena Petrovna Blavatsky (1831–1891), had traveled to India for "initiation" into a religious order, and had founded a group for "spiritualist experiences" in Egypt, before settling in Algeria. Mirra Alfassa's accounts of his teachings show the strong influence of theosophical theories and methods of study. Upon her return to Paris, she conducted a number of study groups whose goals were the examination of mystical and spiritual experiences. In 1912, she lead a twelve-member group known as "Cosmique" and introduced Indian texts such as the *Bhagavad-gita*, the *Yoga Sutras*, and the *Upanisads*.

Mirra ended her marriage to Morisset after a few years, entrusted her son to his sisters, and married a lawyer, philanthropist, and former Christian pastor in Lille, France, Paul Richard. Having studied modern philosophy during his seminary training, Richard's growing interest in Indian thought, along with his own political ambitions, took him to Pondicherry in 1910. He sought out Aurobindo and met with him several times. When he returned to France, he told his wife about Aurobindo and they began a correspondence.[5] On March 5, 1914, the Richards both left Paris for Pondicherry. On the afternoon of their arrival in Pondicherry, on March 29, they met Aurobindo at his residence in Rue Francois Martin. Thereafter they met with him daily, often talking from the afternoon into the late evening. Paul Richard proposed the publication of a philosophical magazine that could spread Aurobindo's message to the world, and on Aurobindo's forty-second birthday, August 15, 1914, the Richards published the first edition of the *Arya*. The monthly journal contained numerous articles by Aurobindo that would be revised and reprinted as some of his major works: *The Life Divine, The Synthesis of Yoga,* and *The Human Cycle,* for example.

Six months later, Paul Richard was called back to France for service in the French Reserve Army to fight in what developed into World War I. Aurobindo and the Mother carried on a continuing correspondence. After one year of military service, Paul Richard's service ended and he and Mirra moved to Japan, where he had found work. They remained there for four years. In April 1920 they returned to Pondicherry, where the Mother would stay. Her relationship with Paul Richard had basically ended. She had turned her attention completely to Aurobindo. Paul left Pondicherry, traveled in northern India, and then returned to Europe.

In November 1920, the Mother joined Aurobindo at Rue Francois Martin, and in 1922 they both moved to a new house on Rue de la Marine, keeping the former house for disciples and visitors. She began to make the arrangements for the household of disciples, though she remained in the background until November 24, 1926. Collective meditations with Aurobindo, the members of the group, visitors, and herself took place. At some point in 1926, Aurobindo began to call Mirra "Mirra Devi" (Goddess Mirra) and "Mother," and on November 24 of that year, Aurobindo's "Day of Siddhi" occurred.

Immediately the Mother became the authority over the new Sri Aurobindo Ashram. Aurobindo withdrew and told his disciples that she would be responsible for their further development. She not only organized Ashram activities and supervised its programs but became for many the representative presence of the Divine. She developed a regular balcony darshan that she held for most of the remainder of her life. Three special darshan days involving both Aurobindo and the Mother were celebrated—Aurobindo's birthday, his Day of Siddhi, and the Mother's birthday. The number of disciples grew to about 150 by 1930.

The leadership transition from Aurobindo to the Mother was not without question by followers. All of the evidence that remains of these questions is found in Aurobindo's responses to his followers' correspondence.[6] He continually affirmed, in spite of their concerns and objections, that there was no disagreement between the Mother and himself.

> The opposition between the Mother's consciousness and my consciousness was an invention of the old days (due mainly to X,Y and others of that time) and emerged in a time when the Mother was not fully recognised or accepted by some of those who were here at the beginning. Even after they had recognised her they persisted in this meaningless opposition and did great harm to them and others.[7]

So united were the two of them, he claimed, that, "If one is open to Sri Aurobindo and not to the Mother it means that one is not really open to Sri Aurobindo."[8] In fact, the yoga of Aurobindo, he said, "is the joint creation of Sri Aurobindo and the Mother. . . ."[9] Regarding questions about her authority and methods in running the Ashram, he responded, "The work here is the Mother's and she has the right to give her orders in whatever way she pleases and they must be obeyed."[10] As late as 1945, Aurobindo continued to defend the Mother's activities against the complaints and "revolt" of some followers.

> I do not find that Mother is a rigid disciplinarian. On the contrary, I have seen with what a constant leniency, tolerant patience and kindness she has met the huge mass of indiscipline, disobedience, self-assertion, revolt that has surrounded her, even revolt to her very face and violent letters overwhelming her with the worst kind of vituperation. A rigid disciplinarian would not have treated these things like that.[11]

The *mantras* he prescribed for the focus of the disciples' minds were either a combination of Aurobindo and the Mother's names or the Mother's name, Mirra, alone. "Usually the Mother's name has the full power in it; but in certain states of consciousness the double Name may have a special effect."[12]

Not only was Aurobindo direct in his support of the Mother taking the position of leadership in the Ashram and able personally to reinforce the transfer of leadership from his own hands, but his theory of the Mother's being and presence as she fit into his total *Weltanschauung* provided an explanation for the exalted position he gave her. She was not merely a human being, but the Mother, the *śakti*, the "energy" behind the evolution of the Universe and, thus, the incarnation, the *avatāra* or "descent," of Supermind consciousness into the "earth-consciousness." Though he never claimed to have had the experience of Supermind consciousness himself, only of the lower Overmind consciousness, the Mother, he says, "comes in order to bring down the Supramental."[13] "Her embodiment is a chance for the earth-consciousness to receive the Supramental into it and to undergo first the transformation necessary for that to be possible."[14] Though Aurobindo said he himself had only ascended to the level of Overmind, or, alternatively, that he had experienced the descent of the Overmind consciousness into his own, Mirra, the Mother, was the actual descent of the even higher Supermind.

Such references by Aurobindo to the concept of the Mother, the Mother as goddess, and the Mother as the "energy" or *śakti* behind the activity of the Universe are nothing new. In his Nationalist days, Aurobindo not only regularly referred to this Divine Energy, but identified India with the Energy. He not only considered India the present instrument of the Energy but its very *avatāra*, or incarnation. India was not just the Motherland but the Mother. "It is not a piece of earth, nor a figure of speech, nor a fiction of the mind. It is a mighty Shakti, composed of the Shaktis of all the millions of units that make up the nation."[15] Such language of the *śakti*, taken from devotional and Tantric traditions and applied to the nation, affirmed that there was an overriding energy pushing the universe forward. When this energy was identified with the level of consciousness called Supermind, the Mother was that very consciousness-force.

In the language of Aurobindo's later thought at Pondicherry, he called the Spirit (or level of consciousness) that was responsible for the Becoming of this evolving world Supermind and identified this with the traditional Indian idea that the energy or *śakti* of the Universe was a goddess. Therefore, he called this energy, this Spirit, the Mother.

In the person of Mirra Alfassa Richard, Aurobindo thus saw the descent of the Supermind. He believed she was its *avatāra* or descent into the earth plane. As the incarnate Supermind she was changing the consciousness on which the earth found itself, and as such her work was infallible. His letters are therefore filled with answers to followers' questions that identify the Mother, Mirra Alfassa Richard, and Supermind. She does not merely embody the Divine, he instructed one follower, but is in reality the Divine appearing to be human.

> The Divine puts on an appearance of humanity, assumes the outward human nature in order to tread the path and show it to human beings, but does not cease to be the Divine. It is a manifestation that takes place, a manifestation of a growing divine consciousness, not human turning into divine. The Mother was inwardly above the human even in childhood, so the view held by "many" [that she was actually human but now embodies the Divine Mother] is erroneous.[16]

This identification provided the justification for the Mother's authority over the Ashram and for his, and later her, admonitions to recognize not only her authoritative and effective place in the Universal evolution itself but also in the disciples' personal yogic paths. Her mission on earth, he said, is to prepare the lower consciousness by transforming it so it will be able to receive the supramental. She is, thus, actually always at work in material nature, in the disciples' souls, minds, and bodies, and in all of reality.[17]

Through Aurobindo's personal intervention regarding the questioning of the Mother's authority and through his theory of the Mother, the mantle of authoritative leadership, the "guruship," was successfully passed on. By the time of Aurobindo's death on December 5, 1950, the Mother's authority had been firmly established.

The Mother's Agenda and Religion

The Mother added little to Aurobindo's thought, and she did not intend to do so. The members of the movement, however, turned their attention increasingly toward her, for she was the more available leader who was directly involved with the activities of the Ashram. Her personal interests, her personality, and even her hobbies, such as tennis, gardening, and stamp collecting, were viewed by her followers as profound statements about the nature of the universe. They began to speak of her appearances to them in visions and dreams and cherished her words, her touch, and her methods. They viewed her approach and emphases as similarly profound. Though the focus of members of the movement was on her own activities, this focus also included her influence on their interpretation of those activities, on their interpretation of Aurobindo and his thought and writings, and her influence upon which elements within the vast range of Aurobindo's Integral Yoga and its application would be emphasized within the movement.

The Mother was more uncomfortable than Aurobindo with the term *religion*. She, therefore, did not consider Integral Yoga as a "religion" and sought to further distance it from "religion" and the religions. She, in fact, spoke often of Aurobindo's theories, experiences, and practices in contrast to "religions." However, in one response to the question of whether religion is "a necessity in the life of the ordinary man," she used the term *religion* in a broad sense that might include even Aurobindo's path as a "religion," though she was pointing to "ordinary life," not the life of the Integral Yogin.

Something might be a "religion," she said, even when its followers do not consider it so or might claim to be irreligious. Here she defines religion as an ideal that seems to the ordinary believer to be "the most precious thing in life," or "something which may seem to be worth consecrating one's life to."

In ordinary life, an individual, whether he knows it or not, always has a religion but the object of his religion is sometimes of a very inferior kind. . . . The god he worships may be the god of success or the god of money or the god of power, or simply a family god: the god of children, the god of the family, the god of the ancestors. There is always a religion. The quality of the religion is very different according to the individual, but it is difficult for a human being to live and to go on living, to survive in life without having something like a rudiment of an ideal which serves as the *centre* for his existence. Most of the time he doesn't know it and if he were asked what his ideal is, he would be unable to formulate it; but he has one, vaguely, something that seems to him the most precious thing in life.[18]

She goes so far as to say, "Every political or social ideal is a sort of lower expression of an ideal which is a rudimentary religion."[19] In this instance, in agreement with Aurobindo's writings, there is no distinction between "religion" and "secular."

In most cases, however, the Mother makes a clear distinction between Integral Yoga and "religion" and, as Aurobindo did, between Integral Yoga and the religions. She equates "religion" with ideas on the level of Mind, with teachings and dogmas, whereas Aurobindo's system, first, is based upon experience and, second, is not a single viewpoint but a synthesis of the various viewpoints. By her definition, then, Aurobindo's position is above mental notions. For example, when asked if Aurobindo's teaching constitutes a new religion, she responded

People who say that are fools who don't even know what they are talking about. You only have to read all that Sri Aurobindo has written to know that it is impossible to base a religion on his works, because he presents each problem, each question in all its aspects, showing the truth contained in each way of seeing things, and he explains that in order to attain the Truth you must realise a synthesis which goes beyond all mental notions and emerge into a transcendence beyond thought.[20]

Even though his system constitutes a stance, a position, a viewpoint, toward the Universe, "something worth consecrating one's life to," in the manner of many religions, she saw it not as the affirmation of one position but as a synthesis of notions that transcends other stances. As such, it is considered above the "religions," a True position that is validated in experience, not conceptualization, and, thus, not one of the "religions." As a transcendent position, she says, it is an "action of the Supreme; no religion can be founded on that."[21] To the Mother, Aurobindo's system is not mental doctrine but Yoga, "free from all mental dogma." By her usual definition, religion is organized, containing fixed laws and ceremonies, and, most importantly, it is exclusivistic. In contrast, yoga, she says, is an effort of personal discovery based upon the sense that there is something to be discovered, which is like the Divine that is there, but yoga is personal, fluidly experimental, and characterized by an effort to discover what this Divine is.[22]

When the Mother rejected the notion that Aurobindo's teaching is a "religion" then, she meant by the term *religion* an organized system of beliefs and practices characterized by the requirement that its followers adhere to fixed ideas handed down to them by others in an organization. Since she understood Aurobindo's view as a position based on his experiments, open to experimental verification by any who would wish to follow his position, she did not define it as "religion." Her assumption was that all who so experimentally seek the Divine will find it as Aurobindo did, since his view is the Truth about Reality.

Regarding the "religions," each "religion" expresses "one aspect of the single and eternal Truth,"[23] which Aurobindo's position understands in its fullest. In this, she, like Aurobindo, was not unlike the hierarchically inclusivistic Neo-Advaitins of nineteenth- and twentieth-century India who treated their own position as the synthetic, inclusivistic, and experientially verifiable stance that encompasses all religions, believing that, unlike her own view, these "religions" view Reality in a partial and historically conditioned manner.

Not only are the "religions" merely in touch with a partial, nonintegral view of Reality and Divinity, each religion expresses its one partial aspect exclusively as if it were the highest stance or the only true aspect of the Divine.[24] Like these other religious thinkers and Aurobindo, she too did not ask whether her own position is only one of the available alternatives from which humanity may choose. In contrast, she was clear that the synthetic position of Aurobindo is ultimately the only fully True position, the one which sees the single Truth in its fullest.

From this transcendent stance she recommended to her followers that they practice "an enlightened indifference towards all religions."[25] They should recognize that "the time of religions is over."[26] Religions may have been helpful in a past state of human evolution, but no longer. Religion is being replaced today by Aurobindo's stance toward Reality. The very evolution of the universe is making these "religions" irrelevant and will ultimately result in their death.[27] To promote the evolutionary process, one might assume, would be to quicken the end of the "religions."

The Mother thus distinguished Truth from "religion." Truth is expressed by Aurobindo's vision and system. She also used another ambiguous term, *spiritual*, to distinguish "spiritual" teaching from "religious" teaching, but defined both terms on the basis of their acceptance or rejection of Aurobindo's *Weltanschauung*, particularly its experiential and evolutionary claims.

> You must not confuse a religious teaching with a spiritual one.
>
> Religious teaching belongs to the past and halts progress.
>
> Spiritual teaching is the teaching of the future—it illumines the consciousness and prepares it for future realisation.
>
> Spiritual teaching is above religions and strives towards a global Truth.
>
> It teaches us to enter into direct relation with the Divine.[28]

By this definition, Aurobindo's teaching is "spiritual," and "religions" are merely "religious," that is, exclusivistic and partial in understanding. In fact, the test here set forth about whether a teaching is "spiritual" or "religious" is whether or not it furthers the evolution of the Divine as defined by Aurobindo and the Mother. This means "spiritual" teachings are those that agree with the teaching and evolutionary goals of Aurobindo and the Mother, or, alternatively, accept the relativity and transitory nature of their own teachings as part of the evolutionary scheme Aurobindo and the Mother affirmed. If they do not do so, they are defined as "religious," not "spiritual." The "spiritual" agrees with the Mother's teachings about Aurobindo's experience and the resulting evolutionary truth; the "religions" do not.

Many of the religions would make some of these same claims for their positions as well, but the Mother was convinced of the truth of this position, just as the teachers of many of the religions are convinced of the truth of theirs. As such, she was unable to ask of her own position the questions she asked of other religions. But she warned followers not to formulate Aurobindo's system "in a way that is elegant and imposing and has a force," for that would make it a religion.[29]

Envisioning the "City of Dawn"

The Sri Aurobindo Ashram continued to grow in membership and facilities as the Mother created numerous organizations such as the Sri Aurobindo International Centre of Education in 1952[30] and procured buildings throughout Pondicherry. In the late 1950s, the Mother began to conceive of the development of another collective community that would express Aurobindo's more active ideals. Some of the members of the movement speak of a dream she had in 1956 as the major catalyst for the new community, but in any case in the Mother's mind this new community clearly would be a part of the working out of Sri Aurobindo's vision and aspirations.

The Mother expressed this aspiration as early as August 1954 in the Ashram *Bulletin,* beginning with the words

> There should be somewhere on earth a place which no nation could claim as its own, where all human beings of goodwill who have a sincere aspiration could live freely as citizens of the world and obey one single authority, that of the supreme Truth; a place of peace, concord and harmony where all the fighting instincts of man would be used exclusively to conquer the causes of his sufferings and miseries, to surmount his weaknesses and ignorance, to triumph over his limitations and incapacities; a place where the needs of the spirit and the concern for progress would take precedence over the satisfaction of desires and passions, the search for pleasure and material enjoyment.[31]

Though this was intended to be a description of the original Sri Aurobindo Ashram of disciples in Pondicherry, the Ashram did not completely fulfill her vision. So with the assumptions about Reality found in Aurobindo's *Weltanschauung* as the basis of the project, she sought to develop an experimental community, a living laboratory that would have no specific agenda but would allow the working out of the evolution inherent in the Becoming of the Spirit. The resulting vision was to be called Auroville, "the city of Dawn," a community that would be a collective yoga, a living acceleration of the evolution of the Universe.

Photo 1
The Main Building of the Sri Aurobindo Ashram in Pondicherry. (Photo by author.)

Photo 2
The "Samadhi," burial place of Sri Aurobindo and the Mother in the court-yard of the Ashram's main building in Pondicherry. (Photo by author.)

Though some of the disciples record references by the Mother from the early sixties to the land on which Auroville would be built, or to an "ideal city,"[32] and though the "dream" of such a city was apparently in the Mother's mind throughout that period, the Mother took up the active planning of Auroville in 1965. Specifically in June 1965 she said

> For a long time, I had a plan of the "ideal town," but that was during Sri Aurobindo's lifetime, with Sri Aurobindo living at the center. Afterwards I was no longer interested. Then the idea of Auroville—I gave the name Auroville—was taken up again, but from the other end: instead of the formation having to find the place, it was the place—near the lake—which gave birth to the formation, and until now I took only a very minor interest in it, for I had received nothing directly.[33]

In this early talk the Mother spoke of visions of such a place during her days with Max Theon. Upon receiving a recent letter from a devotee who had set up her house on that place "near the lake," the early memories returned and, she said, "All at once I had my plan for Auroville." Auroville would be separate from the Ashram in purpose and government. Put succinctly in June 1968, "The Ashram will retain its true role of pioneer, inspirer and guide. Auroville is the attempt towards collective realisation."[34] Since Aurobindo had died, of course, he could no longer physically be its center, and the Mother would not move there either. She worked through liaisons.

The Mother was convinced that the evolutionary, divine force that was inevitably behind the progress of the universe was behind both the idea and manifestation of Auroville, and that, as a result, the city would undoubtedly one day be a reality. Though other forces might slow down its completion, all events were under the Supermind's control and, thus, would be used to bring about the realization of her vision.

> . . . no thought preceded the birth of Auroville; it was simply, as always, a Force, a kind of absolute manifesting, and it was so strong that I was able to say to people, "Even if you don't believe it, even if all the circumstances seem quite unfavourable, I KNOW THAT AUROVILLE WILL BE. It may take a hundred years, it may take a thousand years, I don't know, but Auroville will be because it is decreed."[35]

You say that Auroville is a dream. Yes, it is a "dream" of the Lord and generally these "dreams" turn out to be *true*— much more true than the human so-called realities![36]

The Mother also was convinced that Aurobindo himself was behind Auroville. She reports that she continued to speak with him about it regularly.[37] Often she spoke of its crucial role in human history.

A new world will be born; if men are willing to make an effort for transformation, to seek for sincerity, it is possible. From animal to man, thousands of years were needed; today, with this mind, man can will and hasten a transformation towards a man who shall be God."[38]

Though there was clearly a specific theory of Reality behind these intentions, a *Weltanschauung* that molded the very definition of the experiment, in June 1967 the Mother set down only two "psychological" convictions that she said were necessary for those who sought to become members of the Auroville community.

(1) To be convinced of the essential unity of mankind and to have the will to collaborate for the material realisation of that unity;

(2) To have the will to collaborate in all that furthers future realisations.

The material conditions will be worked out as the realisation proceeds.[39]

On February 7, 1968, the Mother decided to prepare a "Charter" for Auroville. There were two suggested examples, one by a future Aurovillian and another, called a "Dedication," written by the director of education. The first read:

1. Auroville is the first crucible of planetary man.
2. Auroville offers itself for the discovery of the profound sources of the unity of man and the universe, of knowledge in joy and love.
3. Everything in Auroville belongs to the whole earth and the members of Auroville are beings of the whole earth.
4. This day Auroville is solemnly consecrated to serve forever and ever the union of heaven, earth and life.

The "Dedication" by the Director of Education read:

1. We do solemnly found this city as the first seat of a planetary society, the society of tomorrow.
2. We do solemnly consecrate this city as the constantly renewed synthesis of the latest conquests of science and the most ancient wisdom.
3. We do solemnly establish as the chief function of this city the preparation of each child towards his highest spiritual and planetary destiny so that the city may become the cradle of a new humanity.

The Mother considered both close to her intentions, but unsatisfactory.[40] Instead she wrote another which, Satprem records, she believed she was "OBLIGED to write" and had come "from somewhere up there."[41]

The final "Charter," as she conceived it, put the goals of Auroville in terms that are accurately understood in the context of Aurobindo's and the Mother's ontology.

1. Auroville belongs to nobody in particular. Auroville belongs to humanity as a whole.
   But to live in Auroville one must be the willing servitor of the Divine Consciousness.
2. Auroville will be the place of an unending education, of constant progress, and a youth that never ages.
3. Auroville wants to be the bridge between the past and the future.
   Taking advantage of all discoveries from without and from within, Auroville will boldly spring toward future realisations.
4. Auroville will be a site of material and spiritual researches for a living embodiment of an actual human unity.[42]

First, the Charter's goals assume the truth of Aurobindo's vision and definition of an eternally becoming, immanent Divine Consciousness that is the force of the Universe and its evolution. Aurobindo had retired from direct control of his followers to continue to develop his yoga, based, he was convinced, on his own experiences of supramental consciousness and revealing the *Weltanschauung*, which saw Reality as characterized equally as an Eternal Static Being and an Ever-changing Becoming. Reality, seen from these supramental standpoints, transcended the contradiction in these two concepts and relegated the contradiction to the lower level of consciousness known as Mind, a level out of which the world will continue to evolve.

The evolution as understood here, and the spiritual as well as the physical nature of it, were assumed as being true by Aurobindo, the Mother, and the members of the movement. The Charter also assumes them. They are not seen as a "religious" view, in the sense that they are a set of beliefs of one of "the religions," but as the Truth of things, as brute facts. Hence, the Charter refers to this "Divine Consciousness" and assumes that "progress," or evolution, so defined, is a fact of reality.

The term *Divine* in the phrase "Divine consciousness" turned out to be the most controversial word in the Charter. Some suggested that it reminded them too much of the term *God*, but the Mother responded that, "It doesn't remind ME of God!"[43] She rejected the substitution of the phrase "universal consciousness," saying it "belittled" the idea, but unenthusiastically accepted approximations such as "perfect consciousness" in the Russian translation and "highest consciousness" in the German so "Divine" would not be confused by others with the idea of a god. But "Divine" remained her preference.[44] Aurobindo used the term regularly, and she understood its meaning in terms of his *Weltanschauung*.

Second, the Charter assumes the truth not only of Aurobindo's *Weltanschauung* but of the "spiritual researches" that Aurobindo believed he was carrying out through his own yogic practices. It assumes he was a yogi in the process of realization and, thus, that his experiences were revelatory.

Third, on the basis of the aforementioned assumptions, the Charter calls Aurovillians to continue research such as that of Aurobindo in their own lives and to work to seek to rise to higher levels of consciousness that Aurobindo and the Mother believed existed and believed they embodied. It calls members of Auroville to take the role of a willing servant toward this Divine Consciousness. The "Integral Yoga" Aurobindo espoused was viewed as the assumption of this role, because Integral Yoga was the compression of years or decades of evolution into a short period.

The Mother regularly spoke of Auroville in terms of these underlying assumptions. For example, on September 20, 1969, she defined Auroville as "a place where human beings, freed from all slavery to the past, can devote themselves wholly to the discovery and practice of the Divine Consciousness that is seeking to manifest."[45] On December 12, 1972, she said, "Auroville has been created not for the satisfaction of the egos and their greeds, but for the creation of a new world, the supramental, expressing the divine perfection."[46] On March 27, 1973, she reminded her disciples that Auroville was a place to realize the ideal as Aurobindo defined it through "karma yoga," the path of action "done for the Divine."[47] Throughout her life she understood Auroville to be the result of supramental leading: "The conception of Auroville is purely divine and has preceded its execution by many years."[48] Likewise, it was not to realize just any ideal but that envisioned by Aurobindo through the revelations of his experiences.

> Auroville is created to realise the ideal of Sri Aurobindo who taught us the Karma Yoga. Auroville is for those who want to do the Yoga of work.
> To live in Auroville means to do the Yoga of work. So all Aurovillians must take up a work and do it as Yoga.[49]

In other words, Auroville would be a place for spiritual experimentation, a city where individuals becoming progressively enlightened could promote the evolutionary progress of the Universe, envisioned as the Becoming of the Absolute. Each individual would seek and attain individual perfection, understood in terms of Aurobindo's *Weltanschauung*, which would lead the world to become a manifestation of the Absolute. Such perfection was not to be limited to the inner spirit, for Aurobindo's yoga included the perfection of the material and the psyche as well. In fact, one record includes the Mother's declaration of the uselessness of "meditation" or "spiritual discipline" to Auroville, because such practices might not include physical activity, which she saw as central to Auroville as a laboratory on earth.[50]

For the Charter, "human unity," therefore, is more than agreement or passive and peaceful coexistence. It is a manifestation in the physical world of the real and essential ontological unity affirmed by Aurobindo and the Mother.

Auroville and "Religion"

Granted the Mother's definition of "religion" as an entity contrary to the basic principles of Sri Aurobindo's and her thought, and her definition of their own position as being not a "religion" nor "religion" itself, Auroville was conceived as a place that was nonreligious, a place of "peace, in sincerity and Truth." "Religion" as she defined it, is exclusivistic, transitory, partial in its understanding, egoistically a hinderance to the evolutionary progress, and non-"spiritual." "Auroville," she said, "should be at the service of Truth, beyond all social, political and religious convictions."[51]

Consistent with her belief that "religion" is becoming outmoded on the evolutionary scheme that she and Aurobindo affirmed, when a disciple asked her in 1965 whether one can retain one's religion in Auroville, she answered in terms of "religion" as an outmoded need, "if one has not gone beyond that."[52] She went further, though, on May 2, 1970, and asserted that Auroville is built on "Truth" and, thus, it includes the rejection of all religions. "Auroville is for those who want to live a life essentially divine but who renounce all religions whether they be ancient, modern, new or future."[53] Its emphasis will be on "experience of the Divine," which will include the "objective" study of religions, but the program she proposed for life in the township is "A life divine but NO RELIGIONS."[54] The Mother's rhetoric by then had become much stronger: Auroville and "religion" were incompatible. As early as April 20, 1968, a close disciple reports she refused to recommend the inclusion of Aurobindo's photograph in an exhibition because it would seem that the goal was to start a new religion. Instead, she said, "I don't want any religions, finished with religions!"[55] In 1969, in discussing the central architectural feature of Auroville, he reports that she declared: "NO RELIGION, no religion, no religious forms. . . . we DON'T WANT religion."[56]

Though Aurobindo, the Mother, and the Aurovillians denied that their own stance toward the Universe and the accompanying practices were "religion" or a "religion" as they defined the terms, the conception of Auroville was clearly one of the many ontological-ethical options available to humanity, and its goal was to promote that option out of the confidence that it is "integral," that is, that it embraces the other options. It is, as the Mother said, not "religion" but the "Truth." By other definitions, what she espoused might be called "religion," and, as we have seen, Aurobindo had at times used the term to designate his own position while relativizing "religions."

In light of the Mother's understanding and definition of "religion" as well as the acceptance of Aurobindo's evolutionary theory, vision, and *Weltanschauung* as the obvious truth of Reality, "religion" and "the religions" could confidently be ignored and even renounced. They would die out of themselves and would do so more quickly if people would not cling to them. The Mother moved a step further in her discussion of "religion" then. Unlike Aurobindo, she would not use the term to describe their beliefs, not even as "religion" itself in an essentialist manner or the "religion of humanity." "Religion" and the "religions" were opposed to the Truth and vision in which she believed. Furthermore, as she developed further the notion that "religion" was a prior, exclusivistic stage on the evolutionary path of humanity, she declared it a hindrance to that evolution of the Spirit. It, therefore, must be rejected.

Therefore, Auroville was no place for it. For the Mother, to affirm Auroville was not merely to be nonsectarian but to reject "religion." Yet she also was clear that Auroville was built on Aurobindo's particular vision and ideals, not that of just any theory but a *Weltanschauung*, which to her was, in her own words, "something which may seem to be worth consecrating one's life to," even "the most precious thing in life."

Four

Auroville from the Mother's to the Government's Control

On February 28, 1968, Auroville was officially founded five miles northeast of Pondicherry, about three miles inland from the Bay of Bengal. Young people from 124 nations placed handfuls of soil from their native lands into a marble urn situated at what would be the center of the township. It then consisted of about 2,000 acres of deforested and eroded land used by 30,000 local Tamil villagers.

There was no need in the Mother's mind for an overarching authority to legislate Auroville's development, thus there was no need to set down rules for its operation or control. Consistent with the overall *Weltanschauung* she and Aurobindo affirmed, the Mother was convinced that the Divine, the Spirit, the Supermind within, was the Force at work providing individuals with direction and internal motivation. It was leading each individual to self-perfection, but not in an egotistic sense, which would result in an individualism that competed with the interests of others. That would be inconsistent with the fact of unity. It has worked, she believed, and would continue to do so, in terms of unity and diversity. Hence all would be coordinated without external compulsion.

"Nothing is compulsory" in Auroville, she stated.[1] When asked how people with different values can live and work together in harmony, her answer was that they could do so through a deeper harmony than that which could be envisioned by organizations that define unity superficially. "The solution is to go deep within oneself and find the place where all the differences combine to constitute the essential and eternal Unity."[2] Any organization that would appear in Auroville would only be temporary, "flexible and progressive." But the political organization most suited to Auroville, she said, was

> a divine anarchy. But the world will not understand. Men must become conscious of their psychic being and organise themselves spontaneously, without fixed rules and laws—that is the ideal.
>
> For this, one must be in contact with one's psychic being, one must be guided by it and the ego's authority and influence must disappear.[3]

The Mother, therefore, wanted no rules for Auroville.

The Mother as Authority in Auroville

In actuality, her own charismatic presence back in Pondicherry functioned as the authority not only in the Ashram but in Auroville. Thus, for example, from March through August 1970, a number of Aurovillians from one of the earliest communal settlements, Aspiration, met with the Mother in her room in Pondicherry for advice.[4] In addition, the Mother made it clear that she alone spoke for Auroville as its sole authority. "Nothing on any Auroville project can be published without my approval," she reminded a disciple as early as March 22, 1966, for example.[5]

She was the arbiter of its disputes and its legislator. Both her writings in her *Collected Works* and the remembrances of her conversations in *Mother's Agenda* record her constant concern that the absence of laws had become an excuse for some to live out their egoistic desires. "Satisfaction of desires" became a designation for what could go wrong in Auroville. In 1968, her messages included the following reminders: "Auroville is meant not for the satisfaction of desires but for the growth of the true consciousness."[6] "It is not for comfort and satisfaction of desires that one comes to Auroville. . . ."[7] In a 1969 message, she wrote, "To unite with the Divine one must have conquered in oneself the very possibility of desire."[8] Freeing oneself from "all desires, all preferences and all repulsions," she said, was the duty of every good Aurovillian.[9] On June 13, 1970, she made this the second point of a six-point list of what it means to be "a True Aurovillian."

2. One lives in Auroville in order to be free from moral and social conventions; but this freedom must not be a new slavery to the ego, to its desires and ambitions.

The fulfilment of one's desires bars the way to the inner discovery which can only be achieved in the peace and transparency of perfect disinterestedness.[10]

This was to be a continuing concern.[11] Thus, in her last public talk, on March 30, 1972, she dealt with this issue in the context of the maternity clinic she had established. Her concern was that it was being used as a place for "illegitimate children" and, thus, as an aid for the "satisfaction of desires" in Auroville.

Since we have set aside all conventions, immediately everybody thinks: "Ah! nice place to satisfy our desires." And they nearly all come with that intention. . . .

I am not concerned about legality, I am not concerned about laws or conventions. But what I do want is a more divine life and not an animal life.

And they turn freedom into license, they use it to satisfy their desires. And all the things that we have truly worked all our lives to master, they indulge in—a dissipation. I am absolutely disgusted.[12]

Auroville was intended to be a place to "give up desires and turn towards the Divine."

There were recurring specific issues for which she would have to set down rules. An April 6, 1968, talk included, "I didn't want to make rules for Auroville, but I'm going to be forced to begin formulating certain things because . . . it so happens there are difficulties."[13] On June 15, 1968, she declared that there will be no marriages in Auroville. "If a man and a woman love each other and want to live together they may do so without any ceremony. If they want to separate they can also do so freely."[14] Though she knew of earlier drug use, in February 1971 she made clear a ban on the use of drugs while discouraging alcohol and tobacco.

Drugs are prohibited in Auroville.

If there are any who take them, they do it deceitfully.

The ideal Aurovillian, eager to become conscious of the Divine Consciousness, takes neither tobacco, nor alcohol, nor drugs.[15]

Very early she had forbidden begging as well.[16]

Though she was questioned about how consistent these pro-
hibitions were in light of her rejection of rules for Auroville, she did
not appeal to the Divine within each individual but to her own
superior consciousness of Reality. "Perhaps Aurovillians have not
attained the level of consciousness that is expected of them."[17]
Apparently, they were not following the inner light at this point
and, thus, needed external guidance.

Money was an issue the Mother pondered early in her planning for the township. She envisioned no use of money within
Auroville. Conflicts arising from money, she said, are actually conflicts of ownership.

> This idea of possessing money has warped everything. Money
> should not be a "possession": like power it is a means of
> action which is given to you, but you must use it according
> to . . . what we can call the "will of the Giver," that is, in an
> impersonal and enlightened way.[18]

Her recommendation was that money should be used as "a collective possession," and in the charge only of those "who have an integral, comprehensive and universal vision." She also added that
their vision must be "*true* as well; a vision which can tell the difference between a use which is in accord with the universal
progress, and a use which could be termed fanciful."[19] She offered
no more specifics. The Auroville experiment would have to work
the details out as part of its growth to the full manifestation of the
Divine. Should there be mistakes and waste in the process, she said,
even that would help the general progress as "lessons learned the
hard way."[20] Difficulties should be expected, she told the Aurovillians. "We have to bear in mind that we are starting from the present state of humanity. So you must face all the difficulties; you
must find the solution."[21] During her lifetime, then, she would be
the one with true, integral, comprehensive, and universal vision,
and therefore she provided the authority "external" to her followers for Auroville and the movement.

As early as 1960 the Mother had founded the Sri Aurobindo
Society in Pondicherry, and she was its honorary president until her
death in 1973. Sri Navajata (Keshavdev Poddar) became its General
Secretary. The Society's stated purpose was to coordinate and
administer the institutions of the Aurobindo movement worldwide
and to collect funds for the Ashram.[22] It gained legal status through
its registration in Calcutta under the West Bengal Societies Regis-

tration Act of 1961, and its management was vested in its Executive Committee. Hence it became the organization responsible for the practical and legal beginnings for Auroville. The Society gave Auroville legal status, since Auroville had none of its own, and through this connection Auroville received its government tax exemption under the "Income Tax Act, 1961," for scientific and social research.

In 1966, the Sri Aurobindo Society approached the government of India to propose the support of Auroville to the United Nations Educational, Scientific, and Cultural Organization (UNESCO) in commemoration of UNESCO's twentieth anniversary. The Indian government began its active part in the promotion of the project and UNESCO commended Auroville to its member states, passing resolutions of support in 1966, 1968, and 1970.

In 1968, the Mother designated the Sri Aurobindo Society the official overseer of the finances and administration of Auroville. It was the official channel for gifts to Auroville, including those from the Indian government and UNESCO.

The Sri Aurobindo Society accepted the growing financial support for Auroville from organizations in India and abroad. Indian state governments contributed Rs. 6,650,000 and the Central government Rs. 2,614,000. UNESCO contributed less than Rs. 40,000. Even before Auroville's foundation, the Mother knew that there were government leaders who were unhappy with Auroville. In October 1967, her analysis was that there was mixed support in the Tamil Nadu state government, among others.

> . . . there is a whole section of the government which is quite keen on it [Auroville], and then three or four people here, in Madras State, who are totally against it and who have a frightful energy: they are blocking everything. Some ministers (as usual) who come, we see them, they make promises, they tell you, "I am with you, you will get everything you want"; they leave the room and they send a telegram to their "executor" saying, "Don't sign the paper." This kind of falsehood you see everywhere.[23]

She was not enthusiastic about such support. Yet government monies did arrive for environmental and other projects.

By 1970, Auroville, the city, whose goal was 50,000 inhabitants, consisted of fifty residents scattered throughout its barren, fifteen-square-mile landscape. Its dirt roads connected the indige-

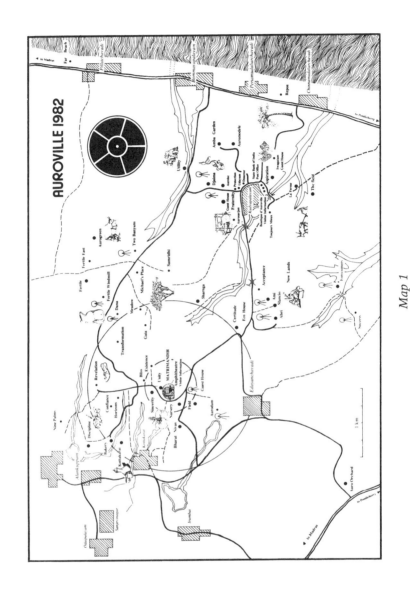

Map 1

A map of Auroville dated 1982, from the Auroville Review, 1982.

nous Tamil villages with the small isolated autonomous groups of foreign "pioneers" and their small industries, craft centers, schools, and projects. One of the earliest existing settlements was "Aspiration," where fewer than forty residents, most from a group that had arrived from France in October 1969, and most in their twenties, had settled. Adapting to rural south India, living in huts through the seasons of dry heat and relentless monsoon, they struggled with community living. For six months representatives met regularly with the Mother for guidance.[24] They began a school for their own and Tamil children in December 1970, which would become "Last School" with a modern, abstract concrete building designed by Roger Anger, a Parisian architect who was offered the initial position of "Chief Architect" of Auroville by the Mother. Because the landscape was heavily eroded and deforested, the first projects attempted were soil conservation, reforestation, and refertilization projects. They were in full swing by 1972 and consumed the largest percentage of Auroville's resources.

The Mother's vision of Auroville as an experimental, anarchical city focused attention on its geographical and spiritual center called "Peace." Symbolic of the actual spiritual center was to be the 100-foot-high, spherical Matrimandir ("House of the Mother"), a banyan tree, and an amphitheater with the urn containing soils from the nations attending the founding of Auroville. Radiating out from the center as if spun off from a rotating star were to be four zones for cooperative activities serving cultural, industrial, residential, and international needs. The outermost sphere would have fluid boundaries. Here agricultural activity would meld into the native Tamil villagers' farming culture.

The Mother spent much time and energy reflecting on this center as the focus of the total project.[25] Likewise, the construction of the Matrimandir continually took priority in the minds of many of the Aurovillians as symbolic of the total city and the reason for struggling in the middle of the unforgiving land. The literature from Auroville gave considerable attention to this project and continues to do so. A "Matrimandir Newsletter" began publication in February 1978 to report the progress of its construction. It was hoped that the structure's completion could coincide with the Mother's birth centenary, February 21, 1978, for it was seen as a symbol of her aspirations as well as her very presence. It, however, was still incomplete as of 1998.

Criticisms about the effort and expense put into the Matrimandir in light of surrounding needs were met by answers that

Photo 3
The Matrimandir, 1981. (Photo by author.)

Photo 4
The Matrimandir, 1993. (Photo by author.)

Photo 5
The marble urn in the amphitheater at the center of Auroville, where young people from 124 nations placed handfuls of soil from their countries at the Founding Ceremony on February 28, 1968. (Photo by author.)

Photo 6
The Banyan Tree at the center of Auroville where Aurovillians met for town meetings. (Photo by author.)

reflect the symbolic and spiritual importance Aurovillians saw in the structure and process of its construction. Typical is one view written after the Mother's death and during the ensuing legal conflict over whether Auroville is a religious project. In a 1982 issue of the *Auroville Review*, in addition to denying that the project involves "religion, a temple, or a monument," an Aurovillian says, "This extraordinary work of building a soul for a city will make possible what we call Auroville."[26] A later, but still representative, interpretation understands the Matrimandir itself as the "body of the Mother": of the Mother who envisioned it, of the Supermind that is the Divine unfolding in the world's evolution, and of Mother earth.

> We are now talking about bridging the gap between *unmateri-alised* matter and *materialised* matter. Matrimandir—Materia-mandir—is only one first cell of the body of Mother Earth which offers itself for the transformation, but ultimately every spot, every corner, every cell, each and every atom of Earth will be in for it.[27]

It is more than a concrete and steel sphere. It has been viewed by numerous Aurovillians as the central project, the sacred center, symbolizing the movement of the Ultimate toward ultimate manifestation. Though not identified as "religious," it is seen as a place for meditation and the symbol of the ultimate transformation of the earth and all of its inhabitants, physically and spiritually.

This is all in keeping with the Mother's own understanding of the Matrimandir, "the soul of Auroville." She called it ". . . the symbol of the Divine's answer to man's aspiration for perfection. . . . , the symbol of the Universal Mother according to Sri Aurobindo's teaching. . . . , the living symbol of Auroville's aspiration for the Divine. . . . , the symbol of a progressive Unity. . . ." Its four pillars were symbols of four *sakti*, goddesses of Indian tradition, while the Matrimandir itself "is directly under the influence of the Divine. . . ."[28]

And even more so, after the Mother's death in 1973, it became for many a symbol of "the Mother," not only as the force at work in all but as the legacy of the presence and inspiration of the Mother who led Auroville while in the body on earth. It was often referred to in conversations as "the Mother's project." It is being lovingly constructed for her. She took a special interest in the Matrimandir, and it was even seen by some as a replacement for her physical presence. In reply to the criticism that both Aurobindo and the Mother died without accomplishing the work of universal transformation, Ruud Lohman, a central figure in its construction, wrote about the Matrimandir taking the place of their physical and, possibly, spiritual presence.

> All right, I replied—and I myself was surprised at the strength of the inner conviction with which I said it and how firmly I believe it—all right, let's say that you're right, that he [Aurobindo] didn't make it and that she [the Mother] also left. Let's agree that the first anchor on Earth was lifted and the second one too. But . . . there is a *third* anchor: Matrimandir. That, precisely, is the point, a big, concrete-and-golden point in *matter, on the Earth*, where it has a hold, where the flow-through, the transformation, takes place. We don't really know what it is, we don't understand fully what it is we're building, but for myself I call it the 'transformer.' It's the third step.[29]

For this key member of Auroville, the Matrimandir is the representative presence of Aurobindo and the Mother and continues to lead the world's transformation. This is its importance, though it clearly cannot guide the movement by the methods a "human" guru could.

The Struggle for Authority in Auroville

The Mother died on November 17, 1973. A committee of trustees took over the management of the Ashram.[30] But with her death, the absence of officials or institutions allowed the Auroville township to move closer to anarchy. She left no individual whom the followers could agree was an authoritative leader of the movement, nor did she clearly pass her leadership to other Ashram members or invest it in an organizational structure.

On the contrary, the Mother believed it was unnecessary to do so. She was convinced that with her own incarnation, the Supermind was here working within each individual. The Supermind within would therefore provide all with guidance, would lead the individuals forward, though there would in that process be temporary setbacks. Instead she left a number of organizations, particularly the Sri Aurobindo Ashram and the Sri Aurobindo Society (SAS). The latter was most directly concerned with the community she had established and guided.

The issue of succession became more important to the move-ment.[31] One of the members of the Ashram and a resident from the period 1956–1973, B.V. Reddy, brought his fourteen-year-old niece, Kamala Reddy, to the Ashram in 1974 as the Mother, or the Mother's Spirit, reincarnate. Known as Mother Meera, they pro-claimed that she was to continue the work of Sri Aurobindo and the Mother. She had, Reddy said, received visions of both Sri Aurobindo and the Mother in which they told her that she was entrusted with the work of completing the transformation of the world they had begun. The language of Aurobindo and the Mother are regularly a part of her descriptions of these visions, but often, she said, Aurobindo and the Mother actually appeared to her and in their conversations commissioned her to continue the work. In one vision, for example, Aurobindo gave her his soul in the form of a golden rose. Then, she said, "I merged in Sweet Mother and Sweet Mother merged in me. I was told by Sweet Mother that I must look after the affairs of the whole world, that I must bear very heavy responsibilities and work unceasingly for the Divine."[32] She returned to Reddy's home the following year, and they both returned to the Ashram again in February 1978. Though some were interested in her claims,[33] the majority of the Ashram ultimately rejected the claim that she was to speak for the Mother. After a visit to Canada in 1979, a Mother Meera Society was founded there. So she and a handful of followers left the Ashram in 1981 for Canada and, finally, for Thalheim, Germany, where Reddy died. She remained in Thalheim and has a small, but devoted, following.[34]

The symptoms of the actual "anarchy" that resulted from the absence of the Mother's authority were clearly visible to outside observers in the summer of 1975. During a two-month visit to Auroville at that time, Professor Larry Shinn observed the site to have 400 inhabitants living in "more than twenty nearly autonomous communities spread across an area more than five miles in diameter and linked by mud roads often impassable during monsoon season." He noted, for example, that with the increased autonomy for each Aurovillian and since all therefore could choose their occupation regardless of community needs, there were five "Auroville photographers" in a community of less than 300 adults.

When inter-community bickering arose in competition for scarce material and monetary resources in the absence of the Mother's dictums, no one person or group was accepted as the official proclaimer of Divine will and adjudication. Likewise, when an Auroville marriage based upon inner spirit instead of social contract failed, who could say which party was responsible for or could claim a right to the child who technically belonged to the whole Auroville community?[35]

Even before Shinn's visit, questions of authority and leadership arose within the movement. Without its honorary president and the guiding hand of the Mother, leaders of the Sri Aurobindo Society moved to clarify and consolidate the Society's leadership role in relationship to Auroville. On November 27, 1973, Navajata, its general secretary and founder, proposed a resolution making him president and leader of the Society's Executive Committee. Leaders of the Ashram objected, for the presidency had been an honorary position and the Mother its "Permanent President." Instead, he was named "Chairman" of the Executive Committee and Shyamsundar Jhunjhunwala, a lawyer, its General Secretary and Treasurer.[36]

As Auroville's legal representative and its sole organizational body, the Society assumed that Auroville was a subordinate agency. It thus exercised financial authority, believing the Mother had meant it to be the permanent authority over the township. Its leaders saw the Society as the heir in institutional form of the authority of the Mother. It continued to be the receptor of funds to Auroville, and it began to consolidate Auroville's activities. It managed the "General Fund" on which Auroville's economy was based. Aurovillians were expected to place their personal possessions into the "Fund" and from it the Society would support Auroville. It also was the depository for other outside financial gifts from public and private donors. The Aurovillians themselves were not personally represented in the Society as it made decisions regarding Auroville's economic future. Without the consent of the Aurovillians, the Society began to lease the harvest of Auroville's fruit and nut trees to outsiders. In September 1973, it declared that it was no longer able to provide the funds for food for Auroville's community kitchens.

Outside institutions understood the Society to be the authoritative representative of Auroville, for even before the Mother's death, it was the representatives of the Society, particularly its General Secretary, who spoke to the public for the township. Governments had dealt with the Society, not directly with Auroville's residents, and UNESCO dealt only with these governmental representatives. Navajata himself would become an advisor with the Indian UNESCO delegation. Thus, in January 1975, at the "All India Conference on the Relevance of Sri Aurobindo Today," sponsored by the Sri Aurobindo Samiti in Calcutta, whose members included the Governor, Chief Minister, and Chief Justice of the state of West Bengal, the Chief Minister of the state of Orissa, and ministers in the Government of India, as well as the "President" of the Sri Aurobindo Society, Navajata, it was Navajata who spoke for Auroville.

In his conference speech entitled "Auroville—A Model of Human Unity," Navajata spoke of the goals, the progress, and the "spiritual aspiration" of Auroville. The project's purpose, he said, is to realize "human unity," and its goal is "accelerated evolution from man to the next species."[37] There have been "problems," he told the conference, but the only problem he listed concerned the Aurovillians.

> We had the problem of laziness, some of the Aurovillians just would not work. When the matter was referred to the Mother, She remarked, "Do not disturb them. They will get fed up with their laziness." Today they are amongst some of our best workers.[38]

Regarding the issue of "religion" in Auroville, his use of the term was similar to that of the Mother. "Faith and spiritual aspiration are common to all Aurovillians, where religions in their dogmatic sense do not exist."[39] For Navajata, terms like *faith* and *spiritual* are appropriate descriptions, but not "religion" in its "dogmatic sense." Thus, he said, Auroville's essential structure is "based on a synthesis of spiritual and material life. . . ."[40] Navajata and the Sri Aurobindo Society then were taken as the voices of Auroville, particularly by governmental agencies.

Most Aurovillians, however, felt that attempts by the Society to assert its control were high-handed and contrary to the Mother's intentions. They did not recognize any authority in the Society as an institution or in its leaders. The only authority was the Divine within or the Mother herself. So any decisions regarding Auroville should be made, they believed, in the midst of the experiment itself. In a 1974 booklet, an Aurovillian spokesperson rejected the Society's authority and assumed any relationship it did have to Auroville was only temporary.

> The Society, however, is not a policy-making organ for Auroville or those who inhabit it. . . . Its role is that of a sponsoring body and will continue to function in this respect pro-

portional to Auroville's transitional capacities, receding in accordance with an emergent internal initiative. Decisions evolve from within Auroville as does the organisation of individual and collective disciplines, rather than as arbitrary imposition from without. This is a basic element in the theme and fabric of Auroville's experiment.[41]

To most of the foreign "pioneers" who populated Auroville, the Society's activities betrayed the Charter's claim that Auroville belonged to "nobody in particular." They developed among themselves a town meeting form of democracy and began to seek outside funding for themselves. Savitra, an Auroville resident, negotiated Auroville's first American grant independent of the Society in 1973 from the Point Foundation.[42]

The government of India continued to be interested in Auroville as an "important undertaking." On October 26, 1974, at UNESCO's eighteenth General Conference in Paris, it introduced a resolution calling for UNESCO to invite member states and non-governmental organizations to establish national pavilions in Auroville to commemorate Auroville's tenth anniversary. The draft resolution was amended in a Programme Committee but not passed.[43] The Indian pavilion, Bharat Nivas, was already under construction in one of the four principal zones, the International Zone, in which the nations of the world were to have pavilions displaying their culture, arts, and technology.

Tensions between the Society and the Aurovillians continued to build, however, and as the year 1975 wore on, the struggle heightened. The Society revived the Comite Administratif d'Auroville for the purpose of "Consideration and finalization of [an] objective programme for Auroville."[44] Its members had diverse agendae. Navajata and the General Secretary and Treasurer of the Society, Shyamsundar, who built a second residence in Auroville, engaged in an open debate over issues of control. One account quotes a letter from Shyamsundar to Navajata that reflected these debates.

> Both by its composition and its acts it (the CAA) is now an imposition on Auroville by yourself, Roger [Anger] and some others none of whom is a resident of Auroville. . . . You repeatedly refer to the resolution dated 2 December '73 perhaps because you forget that you are not the President of the Society and the resolution (Delegation of Powers) is applicable to a president and not to you. . . .[45]

Though the Comite failed, the controversy grew. On November 11, 1975, Shyamsundar was removed from his position by a resolution from the Society's Executive Committee.

To ensure financial independence from the Sri Aurobindo Society, a group from Auroville on November 4, 1975, registered "Auroville" with the government of India in Cuddalore, the seat of local district government, as a legally incorporated, independent society. Ashram trustees objected, and on November 15, Navajata, as chairman of the Sri Aurobindo Society, filed suit in the Second Additional Munsiff's Court in Pondicherry for a permanent injunction against the new Auroville Society. The Chairman of the Sri Aurobindo Society, the suit declared, was the sole proprietor and manager of the funds and assets of Auroville.

The case was repeatedly delayed. Forty-five Aurovillians signed a petition presented to the court reading

> Every Aurovillian has a right to live in Auroville. We declare our solidarity and readiness to protect any Aurovillian threatened by expulsion, unless it is a case of clear offense against the Charter of Auroville or the Law of the country.[46]

The Society responded on December 2 with a Rejoinder Affidavit which declared that Auroville "is a project which is part and parcel of the Sri Aurobindo Society" and that Auroville is the property of the Society and under the management of the Executive Committee of the Society. In addition, the Society appealed to the term *spiritual* when describing the Auroville Charter, and thereby attempted to argue that the application of the Charter to Auroville was not a legal matter enforceable by law. "The Charter of Auroville is a spiritual declaration. It is inappropriate to quote from the Charter in a legal document."[47]

On December 24, the Court issued an interim injunction against the Sri Aurobindo Society, which the Society immediately appealed. The interim injunction was removed on February 5, 1976, but the stay order against the Auroville Society requested by the Sri Aurobindo Society also was refused.

By the end of 1975, the Sri Aurobindo Society was withholding money from the General Fund that had been donated specifically for the development of Auroville, and on December 30, Navajata created "Aurotrust" as an agency whose purpose was "to assist in the establishment, development, and maintenance of the SAS and its projects, including Auroville."[48] It thereby declared that

Auroville was one of the projects of the Sri Aurobindo Society, with Aurotrust as its business agency.

In response to the end of funding to Auroville from the Society in late 1975, the Aurovillians looked to their central food purchase and distribution system, Pour Tous, as a deposit for monies they generated. In January 1976, the "Pour Tous Fund" ("For All Fund") increased its functions to embrace the total economy of Auroville, but in April the Society's Executive Committee, which legally held control of the fund, froze the account's assets of Rs. 15,000.

There were growing indications of financial irregularities in audits done for the Society. A letter from a chartered accountant to the Society dated May 26, 1976, warned of serious deficits related to Auroville (over one million rupees by March 31, 1976), "heavy bank overdrafts," and the diversion of government moneys received for Auroville to "other purposes." The accountant's recommendation concluded

> Therefore, in the above circumstances it is absolutely necessary that earliest steps be taken to correct the situation, before serious audit objections are raised by the Government Auditors. We are afraid to say that we ourselves would be constrained to make a qualified report of audit, if the state of affairs does not get corrected immediately.[49]

The Society charged that Auroville was being used for foreign interference in Indian affairs by the United States Central Intelligence Agency and that gross licentiousness and the widespread use of drugs were being practiced by the foreigners under the guise of freedom.[50] It refused to continue to guarantee the visas for foreign residents unless they supported the Society's policies. Beginning in February, 1976, leaders of the Aurovillian opposition received notices from the government of India that they would no longer be permitted to remain in India.[51] One group of Aurovillians declared themselves "neutral" in the dispute and thereby colluded with the Society.[52]

Meetings between the two parties failed. The Aurovillians appealed to the central government in New Delhi. On May 29, 1976, eight Aurovillians were arrested in the village of Aspiration. They were charged with trespassing, housebreaking, theft, and unlawful assembly by the Society. On May 9, Aurovillians had removed belongings from an unoccupied house in Aspiration that had been briefly occupied by Navajata but had been vacant for months. Their stated intention was to make it available to a family of three. After discussions with the police, the police placed the Aurovillians in custody for a week.[53]

Followers of Aurobindo and the Mother outside of India were alerted to the problems. Some groups supported the Society, some the Aurovillians, and others maintained neutrality.[54] In June, one combined group of centers from Belgium, France, Great Britain, Italy, the Netherlands, Spain, Sweden, Switzerland, and West Germany approached the Indian government with a declaration that was certain to alert the central government to problems. The government had promoted Auroville in international terms to UNESCO, so international reactions were even more important to it. The declaration read

> We, as representatives of the undersigned European Centers, at a meeting in Paris on June 11th, 1976, herewith openly declare that we no longer have any confidence in the Trustees of the Ashram, the Sri Aurobindo Society and the Aurotrust.
>
> The Way in which of late they have been handling affairs is, we are convinced, in important respects inconsistent with the teachings of Sri Aurobindo and the Mother and with the Charter of Auroville.
>
> We therefore withdraw our support, financial and otherwise, from the above-mentioned bodies under their present administration, and will advise all people concerned to do likewise.
>
> We will continue in every lawful and practical way to encourage the implementation of the vision of Sri Aurobindo and the Mother, the diffusion in our countries of their ideals, and to support the progressive growth of Auroville.[55]

The Aurovillians themselves were now joined by international interests in pleading for intervention by the Indian government. On July 24, 1976, the Union Minister for Home Affairs visited Auroville. An inquiry was conducted by the Chief Secretary of Pondicherry, who noted irregularities and suspected mismanagement, and recommended a further probe into the financial matters of the Society.

On December 21, 1976, the Ministry of Home Affairs responded by setting up a three-member committee to inquire into the matter. It was chaired by the Lieutenant Governor of

Pondicherry, B.T. Kulkarni, and included the Chief Secretary of the state of Tamil Nadu, V. Kartikeyan, and the Additional Secretary of the Ministry of Home Affairs, S.S. Siddhu. It was charged "to consider the problems of Auroville in depth and in their entirety and help in their solution with a view to promoting the objectives set forth by the Mother in the Auroville Charter." It was also to "evolve an appropriate procedure for the clearance for entry into and stay in Auroville of foreigners."[56]

The Committee visited Auroville and met with the parties involved. Its report confirmed instances of serious irregularities in the management of the Society and misuse of its funds and their diversion to other purposes. Professional services were paid for but not rendered; funds from state governments for state pavilions were diverted to fund other facilities; Rs. 100,000 received for the "Project of World University" were reported to have been utilized while "There is no such World University in Auroville"; and so on. In addition, the system of verification and record keeping was inadequate, so the auditors could not verify many of the other expenses.[57] Government reports indicated that clarifications that had been requested from the Society were evasive, but as a result of the Committee's recommendations a bank account was opened to channel collected funds directly to Auroville. The Society claimed that it had not been given a sufficient opportunity to present its own case.

The elections in the spring of 1977 following the lifting of the Emergency by the Congress-I Government resulted in a change of government. The Janata Party coalition took office and Indira Gandhi's Congress Party was out. The new government took no action regarding the Committee's recommendations. The Society set up an office in the abandoned Indian cultural pavilion in Auroville, Bharat Nivas.

During October and November 1979, the new Ministries of Education and Home Affairs decided that there were no legal grounds for government intervention in Auroville, since the Society had given assurance that the irregularities noted by the audit report would be corrected and proper management would be guaranteed in the future.[58]

But this also had been a period of actual physical confrontation within Auroville itself. Reports of fighting came to government attention and the government of Tamil Nadu attempted to restore order. The month of August 1977 was one of confrontations in Auroville that involved the local authorities. On Sunday, August 7, a group of Aurovillians met near the Matrimandir under the banyan tree in response to a report that the Society was to have regular Sunday meetings there. When the Society's bus arrived, the Aurovillians locked arms to prevent their entrance to the area. The next day, police arrived with local officials who ordered the Aurovillians to disperse. A violent confrontation was averted when the Aurovillians yielded and the police escorted the group from the Society to the Matrimandir.

On August 11, a group of Aurovillians occupied the hut of Jagadish, a leader of the "neutral" faction in the Auroville village of Fidelity unsupportive of the majority of Aurovillian leaders. Jagadish had been a major figure in the confrontation of August 7 and 8, supporting the Society. The Aurovillians' report to the government indicates that this action was taken after an open meeting of Aurovillians on August 10 under the banyan tree at the Centre decided that "Jagadish, a non-Aurovillian lodged in 'Fidelity'" should be evicted from Auroville. A delegation left the meeting to inform Jagadish on the eleventh. Not finding him home, they remained in the hut. The police were called but the Aurovillians remained. Members of the Sri Aurobindo Society arrived on August 13. The Aurovillians decided "to prevent the SAS from further intrusion into the [Indian Pavilion under construction,] Bharat Nivas."[59] On August 21, a large contingent of riot police arrived. Though the Aurovillian contingent, now totaling about ninety, presented a statement explaining their actions as a protest against the misuse of the Bharat Nivas by the Society, the police ordered them to disperse. A number of Aurovillians were charged with "unlawful assembly."

On August 23, the former sub-inspector from Kottakuppam called a meeting of Aurovillians at the Centre of Auroville with police and government officials and read a list of twenty-two Aurovillians who were under arrest. With the help of officials from the Society, they identified those on the list. The police forcibly arrested them, as well as others attempting to prevent their arrest. Forty Aurovillians were taken into custody in Killianur and Tindivanam and eventually seventy were charged. On August 27, all were released on bail.

Aurovillians appealed to the government of Prime Minister Morarji Desai as did the Sri Aurobindo Society, with little resulting action. Reports of possible expulsion from India of the leaders of the Aurovillian dispute continued. In 1978 deportation orders were served on forty-five foreign nationals but not implemented.

The Aurovillians continued to petition the government. On

April 17, 1978, a further confrontation at Bharat Nivas in Auroville ultimately involving police intervention pitted agents and employees of the Society against Aurovillian leaders. One Aurovillian was hospitalized, apparently beaten by employees of the Society.

Outside support for the Aurovillians came from high quarters, as it did for the Society. To provide a legal basis to challenge the Society, "Auromitra," or the "Friends of Auroville Research Foundation," was established by a number of outside supporters, including the Indian industrialist, J.R.D. Tata, and a minister of Parliament, Bijoy Singh Nahar, along with Satprem, the author of works on Aurobindo, collector of the *Mother's Agenda*, and a leader of the Aurovillian faction. It was registered in New Delhi on February 21, 1978.

In February and March 1980, further confrontations between Aurovillians and representatives of the Society took place over the right to harvest cashews and fruit.[60] In the same year, Indira Gandhi's Congress Party was returned to office and the new government ordered an examination of the Sri Aurobindo Society's books by the Central Bureau of Investigation. Over the protests of the Society and its supporters,[61] the president of India responded with "The Auroville (Emergency Provisions) Ordinance" on November 10. On December 2, 1980, the Lok Sabha, and, on December 9, the Rajya Sabha, passed "The Auroville (Emergency Provisions) Act "to take over, for a limited period, the management" of Auroville. It became effective with the president's assent on December 17, 1980. Auroville was put officially under government control.

In the meantime, on August 18, 1980, the Sri Aurobindo Society filed a civil suit in the Calcutta High Court contending that the government of India was interfering with a "religious" institution and, thus, that its action was unconstitutional. The Court issued an anticipatory injunction against the ordinance that was soon vacated, but this and other petitions were transferred to the Supreme Court of India. The Court was to make its decision in January 1981, but its decision was postponed a number of times.

In May 1981, the Court issued several orders regarding the case and on November 8, 1982, it upheld the Act as constitutional, stating that neither the Sri Aurobindo Society nor Auroville is a religious denomination and that the teachings of Sri Aurobindo do not constitute a religion.

The force of the Act was continued through "Amendment Acts" in 1985 and 1987, justified on the basis of the delay in implementation of the original Act while awaiting the Supreme Court's decision. Then, what appears to be a final resolution was passed in September 1988. The "Auroville Foundation Act, 1988" made the central government the owner of all property and assets related to Auroville and set up a permanent foundation with a "Governing Board" appointed by the government as the main authority within the foundation. By doing so, the government of India became the authority that would encourage, continue, and consolidate the activities of Auroville. Some members of the movement even believed that the Mother herself had directly intervened in history to solve Auroville's problems by creating the Auroville Act.[62]

Five

⊲◈⊳

Auroville and the "Secular State" in Parliament

G iven the alternatives of indifference, promotion, or civil and criminal investigation and prosecution of suspects, why would the state of India choose the alternative that would find the "secular" state apparently promoting the *Weltanschauung* and yoga of Sri Aurobindo? Other alternatives were suggested, such as that expressed by a Minister of Parliament from Tamil Nadu, who told his Rajya Sabha colleagues in 1980 during the debate over "The Auroville (Emergency Provisions) Act" that the world would be better if the project, or at least the Sri Aurobindo Society, were dissolved.

> . . . I would be very happy if this society was dissolved and we, at least the residents of Pondicherry town and Pondicherry State, and the whole of Tamil Nadu, not only Pondicherry, but the people of the whole of Tamil Nadu, would be happy, if the Government dissolved the society, because they are the people who are witnesses to what is happening there. The people sitting here [in Parliament] are just taken by the grandiose words of aims and objectives. They do not know what is happening there. But the entire people of Tamil Nadu . . . are sick of the institution. The sooner that institution is finished, the better for the country and better for the world.[1]

The ambiguity of the terms *religious* and *secular*, as seen in the debates of India's Constituent Assembly, the decisions of the

Supreme Court, and the minds of leaders of India's government, functioned well in the official debates regarding Auroville and the nation of India's relationship to, and responsibility for, its success. The existence of a variety of nonexplicit definitions was crucial to the Parliamentary debates as well.

Also important, however, was the nature of the government's actual interest in the success of Auroville. The government and members of Parliament came to have their own stake in Auroville's success, an interest based upon Indian pride and prestige in the international arena. India's commitment to Auroville as presented to UNESCO in particular involved the issue of national pride. To the world, India was committed to the promotion of human unity and international cooperation. Auroville's success came to represent India's success at such a commitment. Auroville's failure would reflect badly on India's image. In the midst of the debates over Auroville, it was clear that government interest was different from that of the Mother or the Aurovillians. Though the language and intentions of the national leaders often included the invocation of the term *spiritual*, a major concern of the state was in both the appearance and reality of its own commitment to international unity and cooperation in the international arena. Auroville's success then was a matter of national pride.

Sri Aurobindo as a Cultural Hero

Long before Auroville was presented to the state for support, leaders of the Indian state were interested in Sri Aurobindo. Both his role as a freedom fighter in the Indian independence movement and his international prestige as a modern Indian thinker were important to the nationalist understanding of Aurobindo's image as a cultural hero. The representatives of both strands of the official ambiguity in the definition and application of the phrase "secular state" to India, Nehru, and Radhakrishnan heralded Aurobindo as a living example of what it is to be "Indian."

Nehru spoke of Aurobindo as an inspiring freedom fighter in *Toward Freedom*,[2] and quoted Aurobindo's words in *The Discovery of India*, both to inspire fellow Indians to see the importance of seizing the opportunities of the present moment for action and to criticize those who, through ignorance of India's dynamic past, would counsel stagnation and prevent or discourage India from modern change.

Aurobindo Ghose has written: "If an ancient Indian of the time of the Upanishad, of the Buddha, or the later classical age were to be set down in modern India . . . he would see his race clinging to forms and shells and rags of the past and missing nine-tenths of its nobler meaning . . . he would be amazed by the extent of the mental poverty, the immobility, the static repetition, the cessation of science, the long sterility of art, the comparative feebleness of the creative intuition."[3]

For Nehru, Aurobindo functioned as one of the inspiring "leaders of thought and action" in modern India. However, Nehru's reference to Aurobindo as a nationalist thinker is a reference to a national icon to support Nehruvian ideals for India, such as the application of modern psychology to yoga,[4] or the importance of religious tolerance: ". . . as Aurobindo Ghose has pointed out, every truth, however true in itself, yet, taken apart from others which at once limit and complete it, becomes a snare to bind the intellect and a misleading dogma; for in reality each is one thread of a complex weft, and no thread must be taken apart from the weft."[5] For Nehru, Aurobindo was a cultural hero useful as the embodiment of what he understood to be India's independent spirit, its welcome embrace of "modern" ideals, and its affirmation of a nondogmatic attitude toward religions.

Radhakrishnan also was committed to the exaltation of Aurobindo as a representative of India's ideals as he conceived them. As president and vice president, Radhakrishnan spoke of Aurobindo as a "freedom fighter" and one of the "great leaders who moulded our thought in the last century" as well.[6] He did not, however, hesitate to point out that Aurobindo, like many of "the [Indian] leaders of politics are men of religion. . . ." In a 1963 speech entitled "Solidarity Among Indians," Aurobindo and the other cultural heros were examples of what he considered an essential Indian ideal. They put "spiritual values" above "material things."[7]

Aurobindo was evoked and quoted regularly by numerous politicians and national leaders to support Indian nationalism. To celebrate the centenary of Aurobindo's birth on August 15, 1972, "in a befitting manner in all the States," a "National Committee for Sri Aurobindo Centenary" was formed under the Chair of Prime Minister Indira Gandhi. As part of the celebrations, the Indian Posts and Telegraphs Department issued a gold and blue commemorative stamp designed by a member of the Sri Aurobindo Ashram, depicting the symbol of Aurobindo (a six-pointed star made of two triangles, one pointing upward and one downward, in the center of which is a lotus), surrounded by a sun which, it said, "represents the supermind." The accompanying brochure describes the life of "this honoured son of India," particularly his activism in the independence movement (". . . he gave expression to his ideas of patriotism, love of freedom and sacrifice in the cause of the motherland."), and his later "spiritual work" ("Fate had cut out Sri Aurobindo for a very different type of leadership.").

Aurobindo was thus praised at a variety of levels of government. In his home state, the government of West Bengal established the "Sri Aurobindo Bhavan" and the "Sri Aurobindo Samiti" by a special Act, the "West Bengal Act XXIV of 1972." Aurobindo's birthplace and boyhood home at 8 Shakespeare Sarani in Calcutta was renovated, and a memorial shrine, library, and reading room were constructed within its premises as "the Sri Aurobindo Bhavan."

The Sri Aurobindo Samiti was an organization established by the state government "for propagating the teachings of Sri Aurobindo among the masses so as to help them raise their mental and moral outlook and to solve their social, economic, cultural and spiritual problems in the light of such teachings."[8] Not only was the state of West Bengal thereby to be involved in the "propagation" of Aurobindo's teachings to "the masses," but the membership of the Samiti designated the Governor of West Bengal as its "Chairman" and the chief minister of West Bengal as an ex-officio member. Other members of the committee at the time of the birth centenary celebrations included the chief justice of West Bengal, the Honorable Sri Sankar Prasad Mitra, another minister of West Bengal, two union ministers of the government of India, Dr. Karan Singh and Dr. Debiprasad Chattopadhyaya, the chief minister of the state of Orissa, and the chairman of the Sri Aurobindo Society, Navajata.

The "All India Conference on the Relevance of Sri Aurobindo Today" was held at the Sri Aurobindo Bhavan on December 30, 1974, and on January 3–5, 1975, as part of this plan of propagation. It was inaugurated with a speech by Fakhruddin Ali Ahmed, president of India, who spoke of Aurobindo as a "citizen of the world." The themes of human unity and India's unique role in its promotion, themes the Indian government also used in its promotion of Auroville, were central to President Ahmed's address.

> Sri Aurobindo believed that out of this turmoil a new spirit of oneness will take hold of the human race. In the new world

order he envisioned, India had a great role. He believed that the spiritual gift of India to humanity would bring about the new age of world unification. He considered India as the repository of the spiritual consciousness, the Guardian of Truth.[9]

The term *religion* was not used, but the term *spiritual* seemed appropriate to most officials, designating something other than the "material," but still ambiguous.

The union minister of commerce, however, went further in both his nationalist depiction of Aurobindo and the identification of Aurobindo's specific line of thought. D.P. Chattopadhyaya spoke of Aurobindo as one who expressed in his personality and writings "whatever best that is in the heritage of Indian culture." He identified Aurobindo's "very comprehensive philosophy of life" as a specific position, "*Purnadvaitavad* or integral monism," and as a "spiritual" philosophy but not, he said, in a "narrow" sense. He proclaimed that Aurobindo "acted according to his vision" and affirmed that Aurobindo had "spiritual realization." The union minister also spoke of the unity of humanity, but noted that such an internationalism is best facilitated by the specifics of Aurobindo's thought, which he interpreted in "Neo-Advaitin" terms.

> When man realises himself, he perceives God within and therewith all other men as integral parts of a spiritual whole. Similarly, when we look into the soul of a nation to discover its true identity, the difference between nation and nation appears to be more and more external and inessential. . . . Man, society and humanity are three graded aspects of one and the same dynamic spiritual reality.[10]

Finally, he spoke of Aurobindo not only as "a religious teacher or mystic yogi," but a "great social reformer" who shows the world the path of progress ahead.[11] To the union minister, it mattered little whether Aurobindo was a "religious" teacher. He identified Aurobindo's thought as the best of India and the basis for future progress. His stake in Aurobindo was high.

Governmental representatives of the state of West Bengal who spoke at the Conference emphasized the need to spread Aurobindo's thought. They apparently saw no problem with doing so in and by a "secular" state. The governor of West Bengal, A. L. Dias, emphasized the need to propagate Aurobindo's thought in the present age, which is characterized by "an erosion of the moral and

ethical values which give meaning and stability to life." He
expressed the hope that the Conference would produce "a practical
programme to bring Sri Aurobindo's message to the masses."[12] Likewise, Siddhartha Shankar Ray, the chief minister of West Bengal,
who warned that Sri Aurobindo must not be turned into "an object
of worship," spoke of the dissemination of Sri Aurobindo's thought
"among the masses and the younger generation in particular."[13]
Here then were federal and state government officials encouraging
the propagation of Aurobindo's beliefs to the citizens of the "secular" state of India. Their commitment to Aurobindo and his legacy
was already high, even before the government was called in to consider the status of Auroville.

When Navajata rose to speak to interpret Auroville to the Conference, the chairman of the Sri Aurobindo Society emphasized
human unity, "the greatest need of the hour," and Auroville as the
solution to human disunity. Quoting India's own Malcolm Adiseshiah when he was deputy director general of UNESCO, Navajata
hailed the project as being internationally important, as if the world
looked to the success of India's Auroville to fulfil this "greatest
need." It was no less than an internationally recognized figure who
said, "We have tried UNESCO . . . we have tried every way, and we
have failed. And so now we turn to Auroville, and to its foundations,
the firm foundations on which its human unity, its universal harmony is to be built. That foundation is MAN. . . ."[14] Nothing less
than the entire world itself, he said, has placed its trust in Auroville,
and Auroville, thereby, has "a special responsibility on it."[15] Navajata quoted Prime Minister Indira Gandhi as one who was committed to Auroville's success. Her description of Auroville was: ". . . an
exciting project for bringing about harmony among different cultures and for understanding the environmental needs for man's spiritual growth."[16] By the time Auroville's problems drew the attention
of Indian leaders, the project was of interest not only because of the
funds India's central and state governments had invested in it, not
only because of a distant hope of human unity, but because India's
international prestige was at stake. Something would have to be
done to protect all three concerns.

Guaranteeing Auroville's Success

When the president of India responded to Auroville's problems
with "The Auroville (Emergency Provisions) Ordinance" on

November 10, 1980, this was the beginning of an extended and open debate over the nature of Auroville, and what was the appropriate interest of the Indian "secular" state in the promotion of such a project as a matter "in the public interest." On November 25, "Bill No, 188 of 1980" was introduced in the Lok Sabha, "A Bill to provide for the taking over, in the public interest, of the management of Auroville for a limited period and for matters connected therewith or incidental thereto."[17] The bill would move through both houses of Parliament, but, in spite of the debates, it would emerge as "The Auroville (Emergency Provisions) Act, 1980," with little change from the initial form introduced by the government.

The Act's preamble listed seven reasons for its existence. The first noted Auroville's initial purpose as the promotion of human unity. In doing so, it recognized the Sri Aurobindo Society's place as a channel for funds "for the setting up of a cultural township known as Auroville, where people of different countries are expected to live together in harmony in one community and are expected to engage in cultural, educational, scientific and other pursuits aiming at human unity."[18]

The second, third, and fourth, purposes of the Act emphasized the government's interest in Auroville because of the international attention given to the project by UNESCO. The second stated purpose spoke in terms of UNESCO's first resolution in which UNESCO, "being of the opinion that the project aforesaid would contribute to international understanding and promotion of peace, by a resolution passed in 1966, commended Auroville to those interested in UNESCO's ideals." The third also reflected this concern in terms of UNESCO's 1968 resolution, which invited its member states and other organizations to participate in Auroville "as an international township designed to bring together the values of different cultures and civilisations in a harmonious environment with integrated living standards which correspond to man's physical and spiritual needs. . . ." The fourth purpose spoke of UNESCO's third resolution in 1970 that directed its director-general to promote, within its budget, the development of Auroville "as an important international cultural programme. . . ."[19] The Act clearly was a response to concerns about possible international opinion as a result of such attention to the project.

The fifth stated purpose of the Act was the concern for funds Auroville had received from Indian governments, as well as from organizations within and outside of India. The sixth and seventh stated purposes indicated that the Act was a response to government allegations of "serious irregularities in the management" of the Sri Aurobindo Society, allegations of the "misutilisation of its funds and their diversion to other purposes," and the need to manage the township itself. The Act, then, stated that the government would hereby become a promoter of "the interests and objectives of Auroville."[20] The full strength of the "secular" state of India would now promote Auroville and its purposes.

Through the Act, the management of Auroville was vested in the central government for a period of two years. Neither the Sri Aurobindo Society nor any other organization could exercise powers of management, and all resolutions by Aurovillians or the Society required approval by the central government. The government would appoint an administrator to manage the project on its behalf and under its control and would constitute the "Auroville International Advisory Council" to encourage "the ideals for which Auroville has been established" and to ensure that the "members of Auroville are allowed freedom to grow and develop activities and institutions for the fulfilment of the aspirations and programmes envisaged in the Charter of Auroville."[21] Finally, the government would appoint a former or present judge of one of India's high courts as a tribunal with legal power to settle disputes.[22]

Parliamentary debate over this commitment to Auroville's success in terms of the purposes of its Charter indicated that there were members supportive of the Society while others supported the Aurovillians. Information and misinformation flew through the air. Aurobindo's role as a "freedom fighter" and an internationally renowned sage was invoked on all sides. Some members of Parliament were reluctant to act until Court challenges had been settled.

The debates also furthered the continued ambiguity of the term *religion* and the nature of its relationship to the Indian "secular" state. Members of Parliament debated over whether or not Auroville was actually a religious institution and, therefore, beyond a "secular" state's interests. The continuing ambiguity over terms such as *religious, secular,* and *spiritual* was evident throughout Parliamentary discussions.

One group of members of Parliament outside of the Congress Party, however, was less concerned with the religious status of Auroville than with the ineffectiveness of government intervention. In the Lok Sabha, Harikesh Bahadur of Gorakhpur argued that no matter what the religious status of an organization, government takeover was "wrong."

Fundamentally, I am very much against this concept of taking over any cultural, spiritual or religious organization. It is also some sort of spiritual or cultural organization. This Government, after taking over, after grabbing the political power, they want to capture almost all the cultural and religious organizations also.[23]

In the Rajya Sabha, a supporter of the Sri Aurobindo Society's stance, Narasingha Prasad Nanda from Orissa, claimed that some of those in the current debate were hypocritical because they had actually gone to Sri Aurobindo and the Mother when they were alive, "seeking their blessings for achievement of political objectives." He pondered how government takeover of Auroville could possibly promote "through a bureaucratic machinery" the Mother's three ideals of individual perfection, social transformation, or "human unity in rich diversity through service to the Divine."[24] Whether one calls Auroville "religious" or "spiritual," he said, it is outside of government concerns.

It is a voluntary organisation and it had a purpose with which certainly the Government is not so much concerned. The Government deals always with mundane affairs and not with spiritual affairs. It does not interfere with the spiritual or religious affairs of the people. The basic purpose for which this institution was founded is said to be spiritual. If that is so, how is the Government, which deals with mundane matters only, concerned with spiritual matters.[25]

N.P. Nanda's strict interpretation was that the state should keep its hands off of organizations not dealing with the "mundane." It certainly had no business interfering in anything "spiritual."

Dr. Bhair Mahavir even questioned whether "the Government, which claims to be secular (sekyūlar)" should take over an institution that is designated "cultural (sāṇskṛtik)," but he defined neither term. His speech presented, rather, an opportunity to criticize the government generally. "The Government's taking over Auroville is based on the presumption that the law and order situation there is worse than it is in the rest of the country. Thus rampant violence, police corruption and atrocities, and general turmoil across the nation is considered to be the ideal situation by the Government."[26]

Other members of the debate thought it important to define "religion." Some definitions included Auroville as a religious institution. N.K. Shejwalkar, Lok Sabha member from Gwalior who supported the Sri Aurobindo Society's position, argued that Aurobindo's thought must be seen as the background for Auroville, particularly its foundation in "Yogic consciousness," and its claim that all "belongs to the divine and all one has belong[s] to the divine." He quoted the Mother's statement, that Auroville's purpose is "the discovery and practice of the Divine Consciousness" and cited the goals of the Charter as religious. Thus, he noted, Auroville complied with "the dictionary meaning of religion [which] is: Belief in, recognition of, or an awakened sense of, a higher unseen controlling power or powers with an emotion and morality connected therewith." With these facts and this definition in hand, he had enough information to conclude that "actually it is a sort of religious body."[27]

Lok Sabha member Mool Chand Daga of Pali understood Auroville as religious on the basis of a definition of "religion (*rilijan*)" he quoted from the *Oxford Dictionary*: "System of faith and worship; human recognition of superhuman controlling power and especially of a personal God entitled to obedience." The requirement that an Aurovillian is to live as "the willing servitor of the Divine Consciousness" found in its Charter is evidence of this, he pleaded.[28] He also added, "There are countless religious (*dhārmika*) institutions in India. . . . Will the Government nationalize them all and send an administrator to each?"[29]

A number of members assumed it was a religious institution, without explicitly offering their definition of "religion." They therefore argued that Auroville was constitutionally protected from state interference. Lok Sabha member Ram Vilas Paswan from Hajipur pointed out that though Auroville's religion is not the religions of Islam, Sikhism, or Buddhism, "there are many other religious (*dharma*) sects in India." He had recently visited Auroville and found, "Performance of religious rituals by individuals is as much a part of Auroville as are schools and places for maintaining physical fitness."[30] He agreed that such a takeover was part of the government's larger intention to control the "religious (*dhārmika*) and spiritual (*spirchual*) institutions" of the country and that the move would in reality not only destroy Auroville but threaten other religious institutions through fear of government control. "Whenever the Government makes such a move, it leaves other communities such as the Sikhs, the Muslims, and the Buddhists, wondering if their religious institutions are safe from the hands of the Government." He joined other members who had little faith in the government's ability to effectively manage anything, he said, and thus expected inevitable disaster. "Besides, anything that the Government undertakes has been known to be a failure."[31]

In the Rajya Sabha debates, Lakhan Singh of Uttar Pradesh, who supported the position of the Sri Aurobindo Society, agreed. He defined Auroville as both a "cultural" (sāṇskṛtik) township as well as a "religious (dhārmik) institution." "Auroville is a religious institution," he asserted, "and the Government cannot interfere in its affairs."[32] Without arguing the point or giving an explicit definition, he noted the need to look carefully at Articles 25 and 26 of the Constitution and the insecurity among religious minorities that the "takeover of religious (dhārmik) institutions by the Government" promotes.[33]

Other speakers argued that it is not "religious." S.B. Chavan, the minister of education and social welfare, spoke in both houses and concluded that it is "not a religious institution" on three grounds. He argued first that in the past the Society itself declared that it was not religious when it approached the government for funding. To him this seemed an obvious point for consideration by the members of Parliament, and yet, he said in frustration, his opponents refuse to consider it while raising fear in those bodies that actually are "religious."

> . . . the organisers themselves say that it is a non-political, non-religious body. They approach the Education Ministry with an application to sponsor the resolution in which the UNESCO clearly states that it is a non-religious body. They approach the Finance Ministry for getting help under section 80(g) and section 35 of the Income-Tax Act asking for exemptions. They themselves have applied and said that "we are a non-religious body, a non-political body and we are interested merely in furthering the noble objectives of Sri Aurobindo" and still the hon. Members continuously go on saying "No, no, it is a religious body and we do not know how many religious bodies are going to be taken over by the Government." I think it is not correct. I would like to make it absolutely clear that the Government does not believe in interfering in anybody's religion.[34]

Second, "Aurobindo and Mother have categorically stated that this Auroville has nothing to do with religion and there are no rights [sic for rites] and other things involved; this is a new concept of eternal yoga as they call themselves."[35] The rights accorded to religion, he said, are available to "the conventional religions" but they are not protectors of Aurobindo's "eternal yoga" because even its founders denied that this "eternal yoga" was "religious." Third, Auroville is a place where people who belong to "different religions" come together. Since people of different religions and those who claim no religion can come together there, Auroville must not be one of the "religions" and, hence, not "religious."[36] In other words, the Minister's argument was that the government is legally able to control and promote Aurobindo's "eternal yoga," because "eternal yoga" is not one of the religions, nor is it a religious institution.

Jagannath Rao of Berhampur, who told his fellow members of the Lok Sabha that beginning in 1962 he had visited the Mother in Pondicherry annually for *darshan*, asserted that Auroville was not a "religious organisation" but a "voluntary" one. Without putting forth a definition of "religion" or arguing how "religion" cannot be voluntary, he argued on the basis of his own past activities in promoting Auroville to the state. "I know it because I myself persuaded the Finance Ministry to give exemption under section 80 of the Income-Tax Act for donations that were collected." The UNESCO, he asserted, also gave aid, "because it is a voluntary organisation."[37]

Bhogendra Jha, Lok Sabha member from Madhubani, agreed that Auroville was not religious and cited a definition of "religion." However, the argument he gave to show that Auroville was not "religious" was based on the very same definition of "religion" used by Mool Chand Daga to argue that it was "religious," that of the *Oxford Dictionary*. Focusing on the last phrase of that definition, that religion may include belief in "a personal God," he argued that since this is not a part of the Charter of Auroville, and, in fact, is lacking in all ancient Indian philosophy, Auroville is not a "religious" institution.[38] Thus, as one side argued that the Charter proved Auroville was a "religious" institution, Jha argued that it proved it was not. Era Anbarasu, Rajya Sabha member from Chengalpattu, agreed that this was obvious. "If the hon. Members of the Opposition go though the Charter of Auroville, they will find that it is not a religious institution."[39]

It is true that Auroville is not "religious," according to Pratibha Singh, Rajya Sabha member from Bihar, who, in just the opposite manner of R.V. Paswan, confined the word "religion" to "the well-defined religions of India such as Hinduism, Islam, Sikhism, Christianity." Actually Auroville, she said, is "secular" *par excel-*

lance. "In fact, Auroville has been conceived on lines that fulfil the highest ideals of secularism as understood in India under our Constitution."[40] For, like "secularism," it stands, she said, for human unity irrespective of "religion." Auroville, then, is a paradigmatic definition of true "secularism."

P. Ramamurti of Tamil Nadu expressed a third position during the debate in the Rajya Sabha. He did not care at all whether Auroville is "religious" or not, for he believed that in any case "secularity" allows the government to dissolve an institution, religious or not, when it allows within it such crimes as he believed were practiced in Auroville. ". . . we know that all sorts of activities, all sorts of malpractices, all sorts of immorality is going on in the so-called religious societies."[41] It is Ramamurti who argued that the government on this basis has not only the right but the responsibility to protect the integrity of the nation from "all sorts of anti-national and antisocial activities."

> My advice to the Government would be not to take over but to dissolve this society once and for all. Dissolve it once and for all. Let not the soil of our country be used in the name of religion for the importation and residence of spies, of people who spread a completely decadent culture. Let it not be used as a soil in the grandiose name of building up of humanity, spiritualism, this, that and all sorts of other things.[42]

Other members agreed. M. Kalyanasundaram of Tamil Nadu, commended Ramamurti, asking, "But why should we shed tears over this? If the Auroville is dissolved, the people will be happy and I do not see any other solution. . . ." In fact, he recommended that though Auroville may have been conceived for good reasons, "Please admit that your philosophy has failed, your ideals have failed." It is not that Kalyanasundaram does not respect Aurobindo the cultural hero. It is because he respects him that the project must be abandoned. "I feel that the existence of Auroville is an insult to the name of Aurobindo, and the earlier it is dissolved, [the] earlier the name of Aurobindo will be saved."[43]

In the Lok Sabha, Sunder Singh of Fillore took a similar position, commending the government's move and adding "that Auroville and all others that are exploiting and thus destroying India in the name of religion *(majahab)* should be treated similarly." Throw the "religious *(majahabi)* bums" out, he cried. In fact, "Wherever there are religious *(majahabi)* centers, wherever the troublemakers have polluted the environment, all should be taken over by the Government."[44]

A fourth position agreed that the term *religious* is an inappropriate designation, but that the designation "spiritual" is accurate. The government can and should be involved in legislation regarding the "spiritual," asserts Dr. Karan Singh, minister from Udhampur. Singh, who called himself an Aurovillian and was a member of the Sri Aurobindo Samiti and an Auroville benefactor, rejected the idea that Auroville is a religious institution. Instead, he said, it is a "spiritual" institution. His speech began with the assumptions of a full-fledged believer that Aurobindo's concept of "spiritual evolution" is a universally accepted fact. "The greatest miracle that surrounds us at every moment of our being is the fact of the evolution of consciousness on this planet."[45] On this basis, Auroville is the ground for a new supramental consciousness that the government should support.

Unlike Rajya Sabha member N. P. Nanda, who argued that the "secular" state should have nothing to do with the "spiritual," Lok Sabha Minister Karan Singh saw no contradiction between the ideas of the "spiritual" and the "secular." He thus found no problem with a "secular" state supporting a "spiritual" institution through legislative control.

In fact, Karan Singh went on to declare that even this Parliamentary action itself could be a "spiritual" activity. Accepting the *Weltanschauung* of Aurobindo and the Mother, he announced that the passage of this act could and should be seen as the action of the Divine Power of which Aurobindo spoke. Granted, he said of the Lok Sabha, that "very often, we do not act in a supramental manner," he recommended that Parliament itself should boldly act in that "supramental manner" in this case and pass the "Auroville Bill."

> I know, there are reservations and fears among some genuine followers of Sri Aurobindo. Apart from the legal aspects, which the Minister [of Education] has no doubt dealt with, there is a fear as to whether a spiritual township can come into being under an Act of Parliament. When some people spoke to me about this, I said, "if the supramental power is all-pervasive, there is no reason why occasionally, once in a while, it cannot pervade this Chamber also." I agree that, very often, we do not act in a supramental manner in this House. But if the Power is there, surely, it can also act through the elected representatives of the people, through this highest tribune of the nation.[46]

For Singh, then, India can both be "secular" and promote both the realm of the "spiritual" in general and the evolution of Divine Consciousness as envisioned by Aurobindo in particular.

In fact, Singh says, there is no other way at this time for the "spiritual" project called Auroville to be rescued from "the present deadlock of what can only be called 'disharmonious, undivine forces.'"[47] Parliament must promote what is beyond human consciousness, trusting the Divine evolution and not colluding with the "undivine." If it does this, realizing that it is doing something to promote "spiritual" and material evolution, Singh said, then Parliament is justified in passing a bill to take over Auroville.

> This is now a leap into the unknown, as it were. It could conceivably be the most important single Bill ever passed by this House because it deals not simply with material manifestation, not even with the collective human manifestation, but it deals with something which is still beyond the ken of human consciousness, it deals with an idea which is an arrow into the future. If, in that capacity, and in that spirit this House accepts this Bill, and if it is implemented in that spirit by the hon. Minister, the Ministry and the Government, we will be justified in doing this.[48]

Ratansinh Rajda, member from Bombay South, agreed with Singh, saying, "We were on the wave of sublimity when Dr. Karan Singh was addressing this house."[49] In a model of understatement, Chavan, representing Indira Gandhi's government, responded that it is unlikely that his government "will be able to come to the expectations which Dr. Karan Singh has expressed here."[50] However, as minister of education and social welfare, Chavan's expression of the nature of the government's interest in Auroville, which appealed to the majority of members of Parliament, did presume that Auroville is not a "religious" institution.

The key to India's interest in Auroville, Chavan said, is the interest India has had in Auroville all along, the reason India recommended it to UNESCO, and the reason it participated in the funding of Auroville. India's interest is not in Auroville as a fulfillment of a particular philosophy, religious position, or yoga, even Aurobindo's. The key is that the government sees Auroville as "an international cultural township." When it desires "to secure that the ideals for which Auroville has been established are encouraged," and when it seeks to assure the freedom of the members of

Auroville "to work out the programmes which have been envisaged in the Charter of Auroville,"[51] the State is thinking of promoting Auroville as a model community on Indian soil that will become an example to the world of the unity of peoples. There is no hint that the *Weltanschauung* of Aurobindo himself or the Mother is necessary for this goal.

> Keeping in view the international character of the Project and considering the Government's involvement in actively sponsoring the project through UNESCO, the growth and management of the project has [be]come the primary responsibility of the Government of India. The ideals of the project confirm India's highest aspirations, which could not be allowed to be defeated and frustrated.[52]

Going a step further in the Rajya Sabha debates, Chavan said that it is the very fact that Auroville is "an international cultural township," that makes it a "non-religious organization."[53] This, he said, must be kept in mind in all deliberations in order to understand the government's position.

In this regard, the government argued that it had a commitment to UNESCO to implement its resolutions, and this commitment became a major concern. To let Auroville fail would reflect badly on the prestige of India, and that prestige was a goal of the Act.

Some members of Parliament questioned the need for such a commitment, given the relatively small, total monetary contribution UNESCO had made, and others objected to the use of such an argument as the basis for the takeover. Lakhan Singh, who believed Auroville was a religious institution, argued that citing the UNESCO resolution was a means of circumventing the real issue and was a move that "is highly improper and will have serious consequences."[54] N.P. Nanda, who also objected to the takeover, questioned the argument regarding India's commitment to UNESCO. Such a commitment, whatever the government claimed it was, does not recognize the real issue, how best to promote the purposes of Auroville itself, purposes, he believed, the state by its very nature could not promote. Parliament should, therefore, reject the entire Act. Otherwise the alternative was bleak. "The bureaucrats will take control of the management of the Society. They will start a den of favouritism. They will bring in all kinds of people and it may not be in the national interest. My point is that it should not be done."[55] Ramakrishna Hegde, who declared the takeover "immoral and unconstitutional," was one who felt the UNESCO contribution was too small to matter.

> What is the total amount received from UNESCO? Is he [Minister Chavan] not aware that it is hardly Rs. 40,000? And he takes the name of UNESCO to justify the issuing of an ordinance and taking over the management saying—by quoting articles of the Constitution—that if a decision of an international body or organisation has to be implemented, then the Central Government has the jurisdiction.[56]

In spite of these objections, the government and the majority of Parliament were convinced that this project must succeed. It was important for India's international reputation. The world is watching. Minister Chavan was clear.

> It is not as to how much amount has been given by UNESCO. I am really surprised that hon. Members of this House . . . should say that they have just contributed Rs. 40,000. I do not think that UNESCO's contribution can be measured by us in terms of money. The international goodwill and the support that they gave made this a really international township.[57]

Others on both side of the argument over government management agreed that Auroville must succeed to maintain India's place in world opinion. K.P. Unikrishnan, who questioned the takeover, noted the international level of the issue and labeled Auroville's problems "an international difficulty."[58] E. Anbarasu, who supported the bill, reminded the House, "The world is looking at this legislation. If the interests of the Aurovillians—individuals belonging to different countries—are not protected properly, that will tell upon the international policy of our country."[59] V.P. Manusamy supported the government because, ". . . it is the responsibility of the Indian Government to maintain the fair name of this country in the eyes of the world."[60] Siv Chandra Jha argued that its success would bring respect from the international community,[61] while Pratibha Singh called it the government's duty to implement the decisions of UNESCO.[62] The UNESCO's endorsement thus gave Auroville legitimacy as an international phenomenon, while it reminded India's leaders that the project's failure would reflect negatively on India's international reputation, particularly in the area of international cooperation, an area where India prides herself as a leader.

In summary, in the process of the debate, members of Parliament indicated that they held a variety of understandings about how an institution like Auroville related to their definitions of "religion" and the "secular," and to their own concerns, ultimate and penultimate. The positions they affirmed included the following: (1) It is "religious" because it is based on the thought of Aurobindo which claims "all belongs to the divine." (2) It is not "religious" because Aurobindo and the movement claim it is not. (3) It does not have to be one of the "religions" to be "religious." (4) It must be one of the "religions" to be "religious." (5) It is "religious" based on a dictionary definition of "religion." (6) It is not "religious" based upon the same dictionary definition of "religion." (7) It is "religious," but a "secular" government can control or dissolve a "religious" institution. (8) It is "spiritual" but not "religious" and, therefore, the government can control it. (9) It is "spiritual," and, therefore, the government has no business with Auroville. (10) It is not religious because it is an international cultural institution.

Those positions that define Auroville as nonreligious and legally manageable by a "secular" government win the day since, of course, the Congress Party is the majority party. The tenth position, however, was most in keeping with the government's interest in Auroville. More transcendent justifications and goals may be ignored. Auroville is valuable as a city that will promote understanding among nations. It will bring together cultures in the hope that they will live in harmony and that a growing understanding will follow. There are in some cases concerns among individual members of Parliament that Auroville may be a place where Aurobindo's philosophy will ring true or be worked out. But whether "human unity" to the government meant acceptance of the insights of Aurobindo's *Weltanschauung*, the promotion of the evolution of Supermind, and the "Triple Transformation" he envisioned, rather than a general notion of the acceptance of all peoples in a spirit of togetherness, is another question. For most, however, Auroville will show before the other nations that India is a pioneer in the promotion of human unity. For India, it will provide prestige in the world community.

As in other countries, the courts, and, in this case particularly the Supreme Court, will provide an authoritative decision about whether an institution is "religious" or not and how the Indian secular state can relate to such an institution. But it is clear that though the members of Parliament may all say India is a "secular" state, there was no more agreement about what this meant in the Auroville debate than there was in the Constituent Assembly, and no clear guarantee, given this position, that an institution which sees itself in religious terms, or which others may see as religious, will not be a part of legislative action or government takeover for its own purposes.

Six

Auroville in Terms of India's and UNESCO's Mutual Goals

T he leaders of the Indian state viewed the endorsement of Auroville by the United Nations Educational, Scientific, and Cultural Organization in terms of the long history of positive mutual cooperation between India and UNESCO. The UNESCO resolutions commending Auroville provided further legitimacy and support for the project internationally, while they solidified India's commitment to the success of a venture India had first recommended to UNESCO. The history of Indian–UNESCO interaction, particularly in the area of international understanding and cooperation, had evidenced India's leadership. As early as Nehru, independent India saw herself as a force to mediate and ameliorate the various power blocks in the world. But even before independence, he and other modern Indian thinkers, not the least of which was Aurobindo, had proclaimed the future independent India as the world's spiritual leader, promoting international cooperation, the end of national egoism, and the emergence of what was often a Neo-Advaitin concept of world perfection.

From the earliest conceptions of the world city that would be Auroville, the Mother and her followers thought of it in global terms. It was appropriate that it be located geographically in India, not only because India was the home of Aurobindo and the Ashram but because Aurobindo and the Mother both envisioned India as the spiritual guru to the nations, a modern embodiment of what was, in reality, they believed, the nation's long traditional line of innovative spiritual experimentation, teaching, and leadership. But though it was located in India, Auroville was to be the world's city, belonging, as the Charter said, to no group, individual, or nation in particular, but to "humanity as a whole."[1]

It was both practical, financial assumptions and ideological ones that led to the solicitation of support from overseas followers and the world community as a whole. This of course meant soliciting support from devotees of Aurobindo and the Mother throughout the world, particularly in North America and Europe. Visits to Sri Aurobindo Centers abroad from representatives of Auroville and the Sri Aurobindo Society, especially its chairman, Navajata, garnered financial and moral support.

The Mother often told of visions she had of the world powers. On September 21, 1966, she told a disciple that a vision had shown her how the nations were continuing to proceed down a path of activities that were what she called acts of "Falsehood." They appear to be bent on bringing destruction through their futile attempts to respond to the world's problems, such as atomic war. Further development of military, political, and economic systems, she taught, will bring on the catastrophe, not save us from it. In spite of her own psychic attempts as "the Mother" to influence the nations otherwise, they continue, she said, to make "the psychological error of believing that fear can save you from danger."[2]

> For other reasons I was in the process of seeing the sorry state in which all countries are, the conditions of the earth which are truly difficult and dangerous, and there was a sort of overall vision showing how nations (men as nations) have acted and more and more act in a growing Falsehood, and how they have used all their creative power to create such formidable means of destruction, with the really childish idea in the back of their minds that it would be so terrible that no one would want to use them. But they don't know (they should know, but they don't) that these things have a consciousness and a force for manifestation, and that all these means of destruction press to be used: even if they don't want to use them, forces stronger than themselves would press for their use.[3]

Auroville, she said, is the answer to this escalating cycle of destructiveness. It is a chance for the nations to create a solution based on "Truth" instead of Falsehood. If they would collaborate in the creation of Auroville, the nations themselves would greatly benefit.

Support from the United Nations and particularly UNESCO, therefore, made much sense toward the attainment of Auroville's ends, but in 1966 the Mother had little faith in the world body. She was convinced that the United Nations and its organizations were slow to grasp the evolutionary forces of the Spirit. For example, whereas from her own visionary heights she had seen the need to officially encourage India to fight Pakistan to full victory in the September 1965 border conflict, the United Nations pressured India to surrender its advantage and end the conflict at Tashkent. She saw India's side in the skirmish as "the forces of Truth" that would create an "Asiatic Federation" to counterbalance the influence of the People's Republic of China. But U.N. intervention was "Falsehood."[4]

Her sayings portrayed little faith in the United Nations and UNESCO unless they begin to evidence some vision through their support of Auroville. She, for example, critiqued an initial response of U.N. representatives to an Auroville brochure as no better, no more enlightened, than that of any other people.

> What appears to be most recalcitrant (and this is wonderfully ironic) is . . . the United Nations! Those people are so old-fashioned, oh! . . . they are still at the stage of the "materialist anti-religious movement," and they've made a disparaging remark about the Auroville brochure, saying it is "mystical," with a "religious" tendency. The irony is lovely![5]

Here the Mother criticized the United Nations for being "anti-religious," not arguing that they misunderstood Auroville to be "religious" when it was not. It was their anti-religious prejudice that indicated that they were unevolved and, thus, actually a hinderance to the progress of the Truth, the Spirit, in the world's evolution. This also was further evidence that their actions are based in Falsehood at this time.

She told some of her followers that she recognized, however, that without UNESCO endorsement there would be others who would withhold support, particularly financial support, from Auroville. Thus, though she felt UNESCO was "200 years behind the earth's progress," and there was little hope that UNESCO would understand the goals and purposes of the city, she would not discourage them from seeking UNESCO's support for Auroville.[6]

So in 1966, two years before the official founding of Auroville, the Sri Aurobindo Society approached the government of India to gain official international support for the city by recruiting the support of UNESCO. The sense that such a request was appropriate and would be positively received was based upon India's long relationship with UNESCO.

India's Relationship to UNESCO

India had been a founding member of UNESCO. Mahendra Kumar argues that the purposes of UNESCO were in keeping with those of India's modern leaders, particularly in light of India's earlier support for the League of Nations while still a colony and the mutual interests India and UNESCO have in "intellectual cooperation" and "international understanding."[7] At the San Francisco Conference, which was convened to establish UNESCO in April 1945, and at the London Conference in the following November, Indian delegates participated fully as one of forty-four delegations. The leader of its delegation to the London Conference, Rajkumari Amrit Kaur, was elected as one of its vice presidents. In her speech to the Conference, she told the delegates that international cooperation must find its roots in the moral and spiritual values of life. Therefore, she said, UNESCO must do all that is in its power to promote these values through education in the cultures, histories, and religions of all the countries of the world.[8] Sewell's analysis of the Conference is instructive. "The London constitutional conference served as the first of immediate postwar occasions at which governmental and nongovernmental actions showed who was engaging, and why, in the organization of educational, scientific, cultural, and related international activities."[9]

The UNESCO's early years were characterized by member states seeking to define its ideals, but also, as Singh has said, by "a surprising degree of pessimism."[10] India was one of the thirty delegations at the First General Conference in Paris in November 1946 and pushed ahead in support of UNESCO's goals enthusiastically, endorsing the principles set forth in the preamble to UNESCO's constitution.

> Since wars begin in the minds of men, it is in the minds of men that the defences of peace must be constructed; that ignorance of each other's ways and lives has been a common cause of suspicion and mistrust between people of the world. . . . That the wide diffusion of culture and education of

humanity for justice and liberty and peace are indispensable to the dignity of man and constitute a sacred duty which all the nations must fulfil in a spirit of mutual assistance and concern.

Kumar argues that from the very beginning India stressed the idea that international trust and cooperation rests on what happens in "the minds of men."[11] At the first session, Radhakrishnan, leader of the Indian delegation, a member of the UNESCO's first executive board, and chairman of the board during the period 1948–1949, argued that UNESCO must create "a world brain, a world mind, or a world culture." He told the delegates that this meant UNESCO must stand for a new philosophy that is "devoted to spiritual values."

> The present perilous condition of the world is due to its positivist attitude to life, to its aversion from metaphysics, to its flight from spiritual values. To improve the world we have to return to an idealist view, to philosophic thought, to spiritual values.[12]

"We are a priesthood of the spirit," he told the delegates. "I am concerned that we in this body should stand above politics and for universal values."[13] Though India would be both an advocate and a recipient of scientific and other cooperation and aid, what Radhakrishnan labeled this "spiritual" element would be central to India's interest.

The close and supportive relationship between India and UNESCO is represented in the fact that India has been one of the few countries that has always had representatives on UNESCO's executive board, including two presidents of India, Radhakrishnan and Zakir Husain, and a prime minister, Indira Gandhi. In this early period, India would also provide three chairpersons for UNESCO's executive board. Besides Radhakrishnan, during the period 1948–1949, Dr. Arcot L. Mudaliar chaired the board during the period 1954–1956 and educationist Dr. Prem N. Kirpal during the period 1970–1972. The Ninth General Conference of UNESCO in 1956, the last to be held outside of UNESCO Headquarters in Paris, was held in New Delhi.

Likewise, as early as 1948, the Central Advisory Board of Education of the Government of India set up a committee to create a National Commission for UNESCO. A permanent Commission was set up by the government on October 16, 1951, which soon became one of the oldest and more active national commissions.[14] It was to serve as the liaison agency between UNESCO and national bodies and institutions (governmental and nongovernmental), acting as an advisor to the government in all matters related to UNESCO and promoting understanding of the goals of UNESCO to the Indian people. But it was closely tied to the government. The union minister of education and social welfare served as the chairman of its steering committee and as the *ex-officio* president of the Commission, and the ministry of education and social welfare also provided other officers.

In the field of intellectual cooperation and international understanding, UNESCO's work was usually done through subsidies to international nongovernmental organizations. These resulted in major conferences that dealt with a variety of subjects regarding education, literacy, scientific research, standardization of documentation, and the mutual appreciation of Eastern and Western cultural values. A number of conferences and symposia centering around cultural values were held in New Delhi, including a conference on "The Concept of Man and the Philosophy of Education in East and West" in December 1951, an international seminar on Gandhi's contribution and relevance in 1953, a symposium on "Education and Traditional Values" on September 28, 1962, and a "Round Table Conference on Jawaharlal Nehru" from September 26 to September 29, 1966, which Radhakrishnan inaugurated.

Other projects also reflected UNESCO's concern for cultural cooperation. At the New Delhi Conference in 1957, UNESCO developed the "Major Project on Mutual Appreciation of Eastern and Western Cultural Values," popularly known as the East–West Major Project. For a period of ten years, its goal was to promote a better mutual understanding of Eastern and Western cultural values consisting of three parts: studies and research, teaching, and educational programs for adults. In 1958, India created a national advisory committee for the project, and in 1960 research institutions called "Associated Institutions for the Study and Preservation of Cultural Values" were established. The Ramakrishna Mission Institute of Culture in Calcutta organized an East–West Cultural Conference in collaboration with UNESCO and the Indian National Commission in November 1961. The Conference called for the further promotion of the study of intercultural relations. These were highlights of India's enthusiastic participation in UNESCO's call for international intellectual cooperation.

In 1964, a "National Advisory Committee" was set up by the Indian National Committee to enhance the East–West Project. It recommended that the UNESCO East–West Project be continued even after the 1966 terminus, beginning with an international meeting of eminent thinkers assembled to evaluate the success of the project thus far. India proposed this to UNESCO at the 1964 General Conference. The proposal was accepted and a seminar sponsored by UNESCO was held in New Delhi in 1966. The UNESCO also continued its larger emphasis on international understanding, declaring 1965 as the International Cooperation Year.

Auroville as a UNESCO Project

By the fourteenth session of the General Conference of UNESCO in 1966, UNESCO was caught up in the momentum of international cooperation and understanding, and India was at the heart of that thrust. At the 1966 session, UNESCO unanimously adopted the "Principles of International Cultural Cooperation." In March 1971, the Indian National Commission was to organize a national seminar in New Delhi under the leadership of the then-chairman of the UNESCO executive board, Prem N. Kirpal, to consider ways to implement the declaration.

With this enthusiasm for the promotion of international cooperation on their mind, the Sri Aurobindo Society's proposal to the Indian government to bring the Auroville project before UNESCO as an "International Cultural Township" was in keeping with both UNESCO's thrust and India's leadership in this area of international affairs. In response to the Society's request, the Indian government took an active part in the international promotion of the project, as evidenced by its history of activity in UNESCO. The Indian delegation was headed by Kirpal, whose influence in UNESCO, as we have seen, was considerable. During the 1966 Conference, he was a member of the executive board on which he served from 1964 to 1972 and which he chaired from 1970 to 1972.

Kirpal presented a draft resolution to the Programme Committee of UNESCO, of which Kirpal was also the chair, telling the delegates that Auroville, "a community devoted to peace, contemplation and co-operative work," was to be the means by which India "plans to mark the twentieth anniversary of Unesco. . . ."[15] The resolution portrayed the desire to observe the anniversary of UNESCO as a major reason why the proposal itself was brought by

India before UNESCO, as well as the major reason why the project was originally conceived by the Sri Aurobindo Society. As a result, to the UNESCO Conference, Auroville's purpose would be closely identified with UNESCO from the very beginning. References to the Mother and her goals were missing from UNESCO's discussions. The project was that of the Sri Aurobindo Society, promoted by the government of India to mark UNESCO's anniversary and accomplishments. The UNESCO's interests in the promotion of international cooperation and understanding were thereby truncated from the fuller, transcendent interests of the Mother in Auroville.

The final draft of the resolution, approved basically unchanged by UNESCO, then requested support for Auroville as a community to be created in India by the Sri Aurobindo Society to mark UNESCO's twentieth anniversary. Both the 1966 and the 1968 resolutions, therefore, read as if Auroville were conceived as a project for this UNESCO commemoration. The first resolution was adopted on November 29, 1966, as follows:

> *The General Conference,*
>
> *Being appraised* that, in connection with the commemoration of the twentieth anniversary of Unesco, the Sri Aurobindo Society, Pondicherry India, a non-governmental organization affiliated to the Indian National Commission for Unesco, proposes to set up a cultural township known as Auroville where people of different countries will live together in harmony in one community and engage in cultural, educational, scientific and other pursuits,
>
> *Noting* that the township will have pavilions intended to represent the cultures of the world, not only intellectually but also by presenting different schools of architecture, painting, sculpture, music, etc. as part of a way of living,
>
> *Appreciating* that one of the aims of Auroville will be to bring together in close juxtaposition the values and ideals of different civilizations and cultures,
>
> *Expresses* the belief that the project will contribute to international understanding and promotion of peace and commends it to those interested in Unesco's ideals.[16]

A careful look at the resolution indicates the difference between UNESCO's interests and those of Aurobindo and the

Mother. The Mother was right. The UNESCO did not understand the basic importance or full intentions of Auroville. There was no mention of the thought and assumptions of Aurobindo or the Mother. The project had been severed in the process of its presentation by the Sri Aurobindo Society to the government and then to UNESCO, at least explicitly, from the Integral Yoga of Aurobindo. The UNESCO defined Auroville as "a cultural township," and that meant a place where UNESCO's more general ideals of living together in harmony and community could be attained. It became one of the projects of its member states to support its push for world understanding and cooperation. Therefore, UNESCO commended Auroville to the world "to those interested in Unesco's ideals," not the ideals of Aurobindo or the Mother. One could hardly expect more from a body that did not share, and would not affirm as ultimately true, the convictions of Sri Aurobindo or any of the multitude of specific religious/philosophical/metaphysical positions represented in the world of which Sri Aurobindo's was one.

The means UNESCO affirmed for attaining the goals of Auroville as UNESCO defined them are described vaguely but are consistent with UNESCO's interests, in terms of pursuits that are "cultural, educational, scientific and other. . . ." Its official interest in the project and the basis for the proposal was set forth as the fact that pavilions representing the variety of world cultures, thought of mostly in terms of the arts ("architecture, painting, sculpture, music, etc."), were to be constructed. Auroville's aim, UNESCO understood, was "to bring together in close juxtaposition the values and ideals of different civilizations and cultures" to "contribute to international understanding and promotion of peace."[17]

These general goals were not out of touch with some of the ideal results of Integral Yoga as proposed by Aurobindo and the Mother, but they were goals most people would affirm from a variety of *Weltanschauung*, and they certainly do not contain the full content of Aurobindo's and the Mother's position. One would not expect UNESCO to affirm Aurobindo's view of the evolution of the Spirit, the existence of the supramental, or the priority of Aurobindo's and the Mother's experiences, over those of others. What it would affirm were the assumptions embodied in its own charter about the promotion of cooperation and unity in the general terms that are expressed in the Auroville resolution.

In October and November 1968, eight months after the founding of Auroville, UNESCO approved a second resolution. The Sri

Aurobindo Society was now being treated by the government as the official overseer of the finances and administration of Auroville. It was the official channel for gifts to Auroville, including those from the Indian government and UNESCO. The Society was pursuing the project, assuming permanent authority.

In UNESCO's 1968 Session, the second resolution from India's delegation, again headed by Kirpal, and approved by the full body, invited "Member States and international non-governmental organizations to participate in the development of Auroville as an international cultural township. . . ."[18] The resolution began by again reinforcing the understanding that Auroville's initial purpose and conception were tied to UNESCO. "*Recalling* that in connexion with the commemoration of the twentieth anniversary of Unesco, the Shri Aurobindo Society, Pondicherry (India), had taken steps to establish an international cultural township known as Auroville where people will live together in one community. . . ." However, this second resolution brought before UNESCO by the Indian delegation and approved by the Conference, tied the project even further to UNESCO by identifying it with three U.N. declarations: "*Taking account* of the Universal Declaration of Human Rights, the United Nations Declaration on the Promotion among Youth of the Ideas of Peace, Mutual Respect and Understanding between Peoples, and the Declaration of the Principles of International Cultural Cooperation, adopted by the General Conference (1966), . . ." In this resolution there was, then, further identification of Auroville with UNESCO's purposes, while ignoring any reference to Aurobindo or the Mother.

The generic ideological notion that formed the basis for UNESCO support was that Auroville is "designed to bring together the values of different cultures and civilizations in a harmonious environment with integrated living standards which correspond to man's physical and spiritual needs." The resolution speaks of Auroville as a place "where people of different countries will live together in one community and engage in educational, scientific and cultural pursuits." It hopes for the elimination of "ignorance of the way of life and customs of peoples" and affirms Auroville as a symbol of "the coming together of nations in a spirit of human unity." Though the original draft proposed by the Indian delegation asked the director general to consider the possibility of financial assistance to the project, the final resolution included no financial commitment, and, again unlike Auroville's Charter, UNESCO's resolution neither assumed Aurobindo's and the Mother's analysis of Reality, nor did it mention the names of Aurobindo and the Mother. It did, however, use the term *spiritual* for the first time, without defining it. Humanity, it agreed, had needs that were not exclusively "physical."

The Mother's response to UNESCO's resolutions was functional. She interpreted them as official recognition that Auroville is an international community not tied to any single nation. The UNESCO recognition, she told a disciple, now meant that "everyone becomes an Aurovillian, no separate nationality." Passports, therefore, no longer mean anything in Auroville, she felt, as if UNESCO's recognition had eliminated national sovereignty over its citizens in this matter.[19]

In 1969, the Mother wrote to a UNESCO committee explaining her own goals for Auroville and making it clear that Auroville was her project and one that also was inspired by Aurobindo.

> The task of giving a concrete form to Sri Aurobindo's vision was entrusted to the Mother. The creation of a new world, a new humanity, a new society expressing and embodying the new consciousness is the work she has undertaken. By the very nature of things, it is a collective ideal that calls for a collective effort so that it may be realised in the terms of an integral human perfection.
>
> The Ashram founded and built by the Mother was the first step towards the accomplishment of this goal. The project of Auroville is the next step [, more exterior,] which seeks to widen the base of this attempt to establish harmony between soul and body, spirit and nature, heaven and earth, in the collective life of mankind.[20]

Her statement declared that she was the one in charge of the project on the basis of the fact that she had been "entrusted" with it by the Divine. Just as she was the founder of the Ashram, in the same way she was the founder of Auroville.

She also sought to clarify what the vision behind Auroville and the proposal for world support actually was. Though the terms of this explanation may be taken in a more general sense by those unfamiliar with Aurobindo's position, the Mother expected UNESCO to support that particular vision and its particular view of Reality. Auroville would be the next step in giving "concrete form to Sri Aurobindo's vision." And this was not merely an external unity of nations and peoples but a unity in terms of Truth, a

True Unity, as expressed in the position of Aurobindo. This position, taken as true, as not just merely one of the variety of options for humanity, in the eyes of the Mother, was to be promoted by all. She certainly did not see this as the promotion of one religious vision among many.

From the Mother's vantage point in 1968, UNESCO was still behind the Spirit's progress in the world, promoting lesser goods than those the Divine sought in the Auroville project. The UNESCO, she said to a disciple, was still at the level of "tolerance," not integration.[21] In her eyes, it was out of touch with the progress of the Spirit. This was, of course, because it was out of touch with the complete position that she espoused. In a message for UNESCO on February 1, 1972, she welcomed its help and that of anyone, but did so in terms of the "supramental."

> Auroville is meant to hasten the advent of the supramental Reality upon earth.
> The help of all those who find the world is not as it ought to be is welcome.
> Each one must know if he wants to associate with an old world ready for death, or to work for a new and better world preparing to be born.[22]

She placed less emphasis on UNESCO's help as a major legitimation of the project and used the opportunity to welcome anyone, including UNESCO's members, if they were ready to participate in the hastening of the manifestation of the Supermind on earth.

We have no record of these messages reaching the world body. The first resolutions, therefore, establish the pattern of UNESCO's understanding. First, Auroville is a project of the Sri Aurobindo Society. Second, Auroville was established to commemorate the twentieth anniversary of UNESCO, not as the result of a vision or revelation to Aurobindo or the Mother. Third, Auroville is meant to further UNESCO's general ideals of international understanding and cooperation. Auroville's goal is to eliminate "ignorance of the way of life and customs of peoples," which is "an obstacle to friendship among the nations, to peaceful co-operation, and to the progress of mankind."[23]

In the following resolutions, UNESCO continued to interpret the project without reference to Aurobindo's or the Mother's actual vision, but in general terms regarding global tolerance and cultural understanding, something Aurobindo and the Mother would have seen as quite superficial. There was no interest in the Supermind, higher consciousness, or any of Aurobindo's references to the Spirit.

By UNESCO's Sixteenth Session in 1970, the Sri Aurobindo Society had become an institutional member of the Indian National Commission. In addition, the director of the Sri Aurobindo Society, Navajata, attended UNESCO's Sixteenth Session as an advisor to the Indian delegation, which was headed by the union minister of education and youth services, Professor V.K.R.V. Rao, and continued to include P.N. Kirpal, who was also vice president of the UNESCO executive board. In his speech before UNESCO, Rao emphasized India's interest in "peace research" in the spirit of Mahatma Gandhi, the importance of establishing an enduring peace, and the promotion of international understanding and goodwill. He then invited the conference to turn its attention to the Auroville Project, which he described in terms of goals India and UNESCO share as "a unique effort to establish a cultural township where people of different countries will live together in harmony in one community and engage in cultural, educational, scientific and other pursuits."[24]

The resulting third Auroville resolution, passed by UNESCO in 1970, was consciously built upon the first two, beginning, "*Recalling* resolutions 4.36 and 4.02 concerning Auroville, adopted by the General Conference at its fourteenth and fifteenth sessions respectively, . . ." It recognized Auroville's progress and referred again to the justification that Auroville was "in keeping with the spirit of the Universal Declaration of Human Rights and of the Declaration of the Principles of International Cultural Co-operation." It concluded by instructing its director–general "to take such steps as may be feasible, within the budgetary provisions to promote the development of Auroville as an important international cultural programme."[25]

In the 1970 resolution, the General Assembly assumed the intent of the two previous resolutions, but for the first time it made reference to Auroville's Charter. It focused on two phrases from the Charter that were of particular interest to UNESCO programs. Auroville was to be "a place of unending education, of constant progress, of youth that never ages," and "the living embodiment of an actual human unity." There was again, however, no mention of the transcendent justification that is found in the Charter. Instead, the resolution was especially concerned with "youth." Even the minutes of the Programme Commission speak only of this intention. "One delegate submitted draft resolution 16 C/DR.45 on the development of Auroville as a cultural centre for young people."[26] Thus the final resolution referred to what seemed to be the prevalence of university student and other youthful protests in the world of the late sixties and early seventies. It spoke of the "growing unrest among youth from almost every part of the world," and "the urgent need to welcome the 'newly vocal young as allies in the search for a better world'. . . ." Auroville, the resolution affirmed, would be a chance "to promote among youth ideas of peace, mutual respect and understanding between peoples," and would, as UNESCO envisioned it, welcome the "newly vocal young." This 1970 resolution further declared as well that Auroville's legitimacy as a UNESCO project was tied to another UNESCO project. It was declared a "follow-up" to UNESCO's "Major Project on the Mutual Appreciation of Eastern and Western Cultural Values."

How different this was from the statement in the Charter that Auroville was to be a place of "a youth that never ages." In the second paragraph of the Charter, "youth" refers not to young people but to the concept of continual progress, freshness, newness, the "youthfulness" of the Universe, as the Supermind unfolds itself in the development of a city beyond the confines of the current and tired earth consciousness. Young and old are equally a part of this vision. The Mother made no references to youthful protests around the world in this context, but the reinterpreted reference did suit UNESCO's more general interests while helping identify it as a UNESCO project, and the government of India so presented it.

With UNESCO's endorsement, the government of India grew more and more interested in Auroville. For India's leaders, its success as a showpiece of international cooperation brought prestige to the nation, as was argued in Parliamentary debates over the Auroville bills. The UNESCO's endorsement all but assured that the government would see that Auroville was successful, but, of course, in its own terms. In his report, the secretary–general of the Indian National Commission indicated the limits of its interest in Auroville. The Sri Aurobindo Society, he reported, was an institutional member only "in so far as its educational and cultural activities are concerned." The report emphasized the pavilions governments would set up there and Auroville's "cultural, educational, scientific, and other pursuits." But what is conspicuous by its absence is the "spiritual," and the emphasis upon "divine consciousness," which was important to the Mother. Auroville's goal in the mind of the director–general is generic and stated carefully in terms of UNESCO's resolutions. "The aim of 'Auroville,'" he reported officially, "is to bring together in close juxtaposition, the values and ideals of different civilisations and cultures. The project is intended to contribute to international understanding and promotion of peace and to help demolish cultural and linguistic barriers by encouraging cultural exchanges between people of the world."[27] The UNESCO's financial commitment, he reported, was only $3,000 for equipment.

On October 26, 1974, at UNESCO's Eighteenth General Conference in Paris, India introduced a fourth resolution calling for UNESCO to invite member states and nongovernmental organizations to establish national pavilions in Auroville to commemorate the project's tenth anniversary. The draft resolution was amended in a Programme Committee but not passed by the full body.[28] The Indian pavilion, Bharat Niwas, was already under construction in one of the four principal zones, the International Zone, in which the nations of the world were to have pavilions displaying their culture, arts, and technology. The support of its own pavilion and the proposal to UNESCO continued to show the Indian government's commitment to the project, viewing it as serving their goals.

In 1983, following government takeover, the Indian delegation brought yet another Auroville resolution before UNESCO. The original was stripped of any budgetary implications during the Programme Commission's deliberations and passed by the General Conference of UNESCO as its fourth Auroville resolution. It noted in particular that, first, "the Government of India has taken an active interest in Auroville and has fully supported its ideals of international understanding and the unity of mankind"; second, that "an International Advisory Board" has been set up to advise the Government, and, third, that Auroville is being promoted throughout the world by "Auroville International Centres."[29] India's support was crucial, UNESCO said, but it noted that that support was with the goal of making Auroville international. India and Auroville were again explicitly linked together in the success of the project.

The references to "youth" found in the 1970 resolution were dropped. The resolution made reference again to Auroville's Charter, especially the declaration that Auroville is ultimately above nations, quoting the phrase that it "belongs to nobody in particular but to humanity as a whole. . . ." It spoke in general terms of Auroville as "the living embodiment of an actual human unity," and of both "material and spiritual research" carried out there, using the term *spiritual* again without defining it.

Unlike the previous resolutions, which emphasized only international cooperation and understanding in general terms, the 1984 resolution enumerated Auroville's "material" programs to restore the ecological balance of the area and its experiments with alternative sources of energy and economic development. Yet when it noted Auroville's aims, it further emphasized, repeating the words "moral and spiritual," Auroville's explicit ties to UNESCO's goals. "Recognizing that Auroville seeks to ensure international understanding, peace, innovative education, a learning society and all-round material and spiritual development for harmonious individual and collective growth and that such aims contribute to the advancement of the objectives of Unesco, . . ."

For UNESCO, Auroville was a project that promoted its own goals. The resolutions affirmed that its conception was to mark UNESCO's twentieth anniversary and referred to its aims as the advancing of UNESCO objectives. The Indian government brought Auroville to UNESCO as part of its enthusiastic, openly committed leadership of UNESCO nations in matters of "international understanding," "intellectual cooperation," and the overcoming of cultural barriers. The UNESCO was ready for the project because it was in the midst of an ongoing program to promote these aims, and the resolutions seemed to indicate that India was promoting the project for UNESCO and its programs. For the Indian government, Auroville would further strengthen the bonds between India and UNESCO. Thus national prestige and moral leadership in the organization was a matter of concern, because the extent to which Auroville was tied to UNESCO, to that extent Auroville was tied to India's reputation in UNESCO and the world. In fact, however, beyond issues of national reputation, the government's stated interests in Auroville (defined in the resolution as "international understanding and the unity of mankind") were more in line with UNESCO's goals than the intricacies of Sri Aurobindo's thought and practice.

Seven

Auroville in the Court's Opinion

T he passage of "The Auroville (Emergency Provisions) Act" of 1980 put the Indian state in control of Auroville to promote the interests of the nation internally and externally, but it did not finally settle the issue debated in Parliament of whether or not this was the interference of a "secular" state in matters of "religion." It was clear from the Parliamentary debates that there was still much disagreement over the definitions of these terms and their application to the case at hand. The ambiguity continued. Since it was up to the courts to come up with legal definitions of "religion" and the "secular," which would embody what they believed the Constitutional model to be, one issue to come before the Supreme Court of India with the challenge of the Auroville Ordinance and the following Act would be whether the Court would declare the Act unconstitutional or find it in accordance with other actions by the state and the union governments in matters related to "religion," which the Court had previously judged constitutional.

On November 8, 1982, the Supreme Court of India ruled in the case of S.P. Mittal, the Sri Aurobindo Society and others versus the Union of India, that "The Auroville (Emergency Provisions) Act" of 1980 did not violate constitutional provisions for freedom of religion. This decision was another in a line of judgments the Supreme Court was called upon to set down on the issue of religious freedom in India. That this has been difficult, and that even the categories "religion" and "secular" themselves have proven to be inadequate, Baird has already argued.[1]

Even before Parliamentary action on the Act, the Sri Aurobindo Society responded to "The Auroville (Emergency Provisions) Ordinance," signed by the president of India by filing a civil suit in the high court of Calcutta, contending that the Ordinance upon which the Act would be based was in conflict with the West Bengal Societies Registration Act, 1961, and that it was interfering in a religious institution and thus violating Articles 25 and 26 of the Constitution in particular. This and other petitions were transferred to the Supreme Court of India, which issued a partial injunction but ordered that the International Advisory Council provided for in the Act be constituted by the government. In December, 1980, over 90 percent of the Aurovillians represented by K. Tewari filed a petition in support of the government. The Court accepted the petition on December 19, and the Aurovillians were accepted as a party to the case. In January 1981, these Aurovillians followed with a Counter Affidavit.[2] The Court agreed to hear the case in January 1981, but the hearing was postponed a number of times.

In May 1981, the Court issued several orders regarding the case. On May 8, it ordered the government-appointed administrator, L.P. Nigam, a retired judge of the Allahabad High Court, to value the 37,000 shares belonging to the Society in Geo Industries and Insecticides, India, Ltd.; ordered the Executive Committee of the Society to report the assets of the Society that relate to Auroville; directed that the executive committee of the Society "will not interfere in any manner with the construction of the Matrimandir, the charge of which has been given to the Aurovillians"; and ordered the residents of Auroville to "submit to the Administrator a detailed list of the respective day to day activities which are conducted on the property called Auroville. . . ." One result of this order was that the Society could no longer block cement permits and funds for the Matrimandir.

On May 13, the Supreme Court ordered that "none should attempt to create fixed assets in Auroville property without prior permission in writing of the Administrator." All property that is created will be under "the collective ownership of the community residing in Auroville." On July 9, the local Tindivanam Court magistrate ordered that proceedings regarding ownership of Auroville cashew plantations be dropped. The Society had claimed ownership of most of the plantations. On August 7, the Supreme Court turned down two applications from a group of paid village workers and

German visitors led by Shyamsunder, a leader in the Society, which sought to add their names "as party–respondent in the writ petitions." The rejected petition had called for their inclusion under the term *Aurovillians* in the Court's May 8 order, for the rejection of the government takeover of Auroville, and for a revival of the old committees of the Society to manage Auroville. Finally, a group of Europeans working to raise support for Auroville in Europe added a petition to the Court endorsing the standpoint of the government of India.

The Arguments

The Court eventually heard arguments and on November 8, 1982, set down its decision. In doing so it was deciding "religious/secular" issues in a new realm. In past cases, the Court was dealing with what it agreed was a religion or religious community for which it was required to decide whether a practice or other component was "secular," and thus capable of regulation, or "religious," and thus protected by Articles 25 and 26 of the Constitution.

In those cases, the Court was required to answer questions such as, Was a religion's right to manage the properties of a temple secular or religious? Was the Swaminarayan religious sect Hindu? Is it a secular matter to decide what rituals and ceremonies of a religion are essential? Is the appointment of a priest a religious or secular matter? In all those cases, a community the Court had presupposed was a part of a "religion" or was "religious" was attempting to define which of its activities were "religious."[3] In the Auroville case, however, the Court was asked to determine whether or not a whole community, a thought system, and the resulting institutions actually constitute a religion and its components.

The petitioners in the Auroville case had argued that the followers of Sri Aurobindo accept his beliefs and thus form a religious denomination in the same manner that the followers of Ramanuja, Madhva, and other religious teachers do. Since in a 1954 case, Commissioner, Hindu Religious Endowments, Madras v. Sirur Mutt, the followers of Ramanuja and Madhva were viewed as religious denominations by the Court, they argued, the followers of the religious teacher Aurobindo also constitute a religious denomination. They share a common faith and organization and have a distinctive name.

Quoting Sri Aurobindo and the Mother and the opinions of others, the petitioners argued that though Sri Aurobindo and the Mother rejected "religion," "religiosity," and "religionism," they were not averse to "True Religion." The petitioners also submitted their own definition of "religion" and "religious denomination":

the ingredients of religion are:

(1) A spiritual ideal;
(2) A set of concepts or precepts on God-Man relationship underlying the ideal;
(3) A methodology given or evolved by the founder or followers of the religion to achieve the ideal; and
(4) A definite following of persons having common faith in the precepts and concepts; and in order to constitute a 'religious denomination' two further ingredients are needed;
(5) The followers should have a common organisation;
(6) They should be designated and designable by a distinct name—This may usually be the name of the founder himself.[4]

The petitioners then pointed out that in the case of Sri Aurobindo and his followers, one can identify an ideal, concepts, a methodology, a definite following with organizations such as Ashrams, as well as practices such as the chanting of mantras and the offering of flowers, the use of symbols for identification, and the existence of places of pilgrimage such as the Samadhi, and the burial place of Sri Aurobindo and the Mother in the Pondicherry Ashram. Thus according to the petitioners' definition, Aurobindo had set up a religion.

The contention of the respondents and the solicitor–general of India was that the teachings of Sri Aurobindo do not constitute a religion and that neither the Society nor Auroville are religious denominations. They submitted that membership in the Society requires only that one must subscribe to its aims and objects. In fact, rule nine of the "Rules and Regulations of the Sri Aurobindo Society" states that "The membership is open to people everywhere without any distinction of nationality, religion, caste, creed or sex." Since by the Society's self-definition membership is universal, they argued, the Society cannot be a religious denomination. One must lose one's previous religion to join another and that is not required here. Under this definition of "religion," then, a religious denomination cannot encompass others in an inclusivistic manner; it must require the abandonment of other religions for one to join it.

Further, they argued, a religious denomination must be new and distinctive. But, though Aurobindo may have introduced some innovations, his view is substantially "a part of the Hindu philosophy." Whereas others might have argued thus to claim that Aurobindo's views are a part of the religion of "Hinduism," the petitioners argue that this identification with "Hindu philosophy" makes it nonreligious.

Finally, they argued that since Aurobindo claimed insights from meditation, his teachings cannot be religious. Because scientists using scientific methods have been able to study meditation's effects on the body, meditation must be a science, they said. The Supreme Court itself has previously declared meditation "secular" in Hiralal Mallick v. State of Bihar in 1977, referring to claims made in the West in studies of Transcendental Meditation. "Modern scientific studies have validated ancient vedic insights bequeathing to mankind new meditational, yogic and other therapeutics, at once secular, empirically tested and trans-religious."[5] "Religion," the Court seems to be saying, must be something whose effects cannot be measured by science. Similarly, in a 1977 criminal case, the Court recognized the use of meditation as appropriate when discussing a "spiritual dimension" of the Indian Constitution, which may be projected into penology. "Indian courts may draw inspiration from Patanjali sutra even as they derive punitive patterns from the Penal Code (most of Indian meditational therapy is based on the sutras of Patanjali)."[6] Therefore, the respondents argued that Aurobindo's Integral Yoga is a science, not a religion.

The Decision

Though there were both majority and minority written opinions, the Court was unanimous in its rejection of the writ petitions. The Auroville Act, the justices said, did not violate either the West Bengal Societies Registration Act or Articles 25 and 26 of the Constitution. The justices' discussion of the definitions of the categories "religion" and "secular" in the Auroville case are particularly of interest. On this discussion the majority view was written by Justice R.B. Misra and the minority view by Justice Chinnappa Reddy.

Both opinions agreed that historically, Aurobindo, the Mother, and the Society had claimed that the Sri Aurobindo Ashram, the Society, and Auroville were nonreligious institutions. The Court was clear that it was the nation of India's goals that were the most important considerations. In bringing the Auroville project to the government and then to UNESCO, the project was proposed as a "cultural township," which was in "full consonance and conformity with India's highest ideals and aspirations."[7] The reason the government of India took the project to UNESCO was "for the development of Auroville as an international cultural township," not a religious institution. Likewise, the Memorandum of Association of the Society speaks of it as a "scientific research organisation," as does the application for exemption under the Income Tax Act. In the majority opinion, the Society cannot first say that it is secular and that Auroville is a secular undertaking and later claim that both are religious institutions. The government of India had accepted the former claims and acted upon them for its purposes.

The majority opinion accepted the Charter of Auroville as given by the Mother as evidence that Auroville is not a religious institution. Though the Charter requires each one who lives in Auroville to be "the willing servitor of the Divine consciousness," though it calls for the use of "all discoveries from without and within," and though it describes Auroville as the site of both "material and spiritual research," the majority of the justices had no trouble seeing these by its own definition as nonreligious. Thus they took the Charter as proof that Auroville is a secular institution.[8]

As expected, the majority opinion began with a discussion of the meaning of the term *religion*. Reviewing the fact that the words "religion" and "religious denomination" are undefined in the Constitution, and quoting one of the traditional epics, the *Mahabharata*, regarding the term *dharma* to support the ambiguity of the term *religion*, it asserted that the term has no clear meaning. "It is a term which is hardly susceptible of any rigid definition."[9] The opinion then delineated as its basic definitional assumptions five "propositions of law" that it distilled from the judgment of the Court in the 1954 case Commissioner, Hindu Religious Endowments, Madras v. Sirur Mutt. The Court, it claimed, has "consistently followed" this definition of "religion" in later cases.

(1) Religion means "a system of beliefs and doctrines which are regarded by those who profess that religion as conducive to their spiritual well-being."

(2) A religion is not merely an opinion, doctrine or belief. It has its outward expression in acts as well.

(3) Religion need not be theistic.

(4) "Religious denomination" means a religious sect or body having a common faith and organisation and designated by a distinctive name.

(5) A law which takes away the rights of administration from the hands of a religious denomination altogether and vests [it] in another authority would amount to violation of the right guaranteed under Clause (d) of Art 26.[10]

The majority opinion went on to examine the teachings of Sri Aurobindo "to see whether they constitute a religion." Its summary recognized that Aurobindo professed "a divine consciousness pervading the whole universe"; an evolution of this Divine which will lead humanity "back to all pervading divine consciousness" in which humanity and the universe "are destined to become divine"; a path leading to "union with Brahman," which will free "the individual from the hands of individuality and by exclusion of all mankind, will eventually achieve Mukti or liberation"; and a universality of appeal and explanation in terms of "the subtle worlds working behind" the surface and a "spark of divinity within which is one everywhere." The opinion made no attempt to relate these to its own definition of "religion" but concluded that Aurobindo's beliefs constitute a philosophy of "cosmic salvation through spiritual evolution" with its "distinctive feature" being that it is universal.

The claim that Aurobindo's teaching and method can include people from all the religions, its inclusivism, is what the majority opinion was convinced is its "distinctive feature." Though this was similar to the claim of inclusivism made by "Hindu" apologists who espouse a Neo-Advaita position, that position particularly made popular by Swami Vivekananda and S. Radhakrishnan, the majority of the judges accepted Aurobindo's claim of universality and thereby assumed his position to be one encompassing all religions. By such an assumption, it cannot be one of the religions. "Any one born in any part of the world, born of parents professing any religion can accept his yoga."[11] Among the modern Hindu apologists, however, this all-inclusive characteristic is a claim made of "Hinduism," even giving it superiority over the other religions that are exclusivistic.

Though their summary of persuasive evidence referred to the totality of the arguments in a general manner, the acceptance of the claim of universality made by Aurobindo and the Mother seems to constitute the most crucial element for the majority of the justices as they side with the respondents. In fact, the majority opinion does not comment on any other doctrine it cites. It is only the claim to universality that is discussed as being important in the Court's actual citation of evidence for its judgment that Aurobindo's view is nonreligious and that the Society is not a religious denomination.

This would seem to be the end of the discussion on the basis of what the Court considers now an established definition of religion with "propositions of law laid down" by the Court. However, in his minority opinion, Justice Chinnappa Reddy did not feel compelled to accept any previous definitions given by the Court. In his opinion, judicial definitions are "explanatory not definitive." They are not statutory in themselves, deciding what the only legal definition of a term is, but merely attempts to explain what was meant in a particular statute. Thus, a new statute by its very intentions may include new definitions.

Unfortunately, he said, judicial definitions often are mistakenly taken as statutory themselves.

> Law has a tendency to harden with the passage of time and judicial pronouncements are made to assume the form of statutory pronouncements. So soon as a word or expression occur[ing] in the statute is judicially defined, the tendency is to try to interpret the language employed by the judges in the judicial definition as if it has been transformed into a statutory definition. That is wrong. Always words and expressions to be interpreted are those employed in the statute and not those used by judges for felicitous explanation.[12]

With this assumption as his starting point, he was free to reexamine the intended meaning of the term and to range through the problems involved in defining "religion" with the intention of struggling anew with the matter.

His opinion began with a reminder to the Court similar to that of the majority, though in more precise terms. The issue surrounding the term *religion* is that different people define the word differently, not that the word cannot be defined or cannot be given a rigid definition. "Religion like 'democracy' and 'equality' is an elusive expression, which everyone understands according to his preconceptions. What is religion to some is pure dogma to others and what is religion to others is pure superstition to some others."[13]

But, he said, the appropriate approach to the question of definition here is explanatory, to explain what was and is meant. One must not only ask what the experts say, but what do the people of "the Socialist, Secular, Democratic Republic of India" mean by "religion" and "religious denomination"? On the basis of the fact that India is a democracy, the appropriate approach to the question then is to determine what the people of India mean by "religion." Since the Constitution says this involves the conscience, "religion" must be taken in "no narrow, stifling sense but in a liberal, expansive way."

Though he called for a broad definition, Justice Reddy had definite limits in mind. Thus, he said, etymology is of no help because it provides too broad a meaning, "to bind." Every bond would be called "religion" on that definition. On the one hand, for Justice Reddy one cannot "obviously" confine "religion" to the traditional religions (Hinduism, Islam, Buddhism, Christianity, etc.). "A religion may not be widespread. It may have little following. It may not have even a name, as indeed most tribal religions do not have." But few would doubt that these unnamed activities are "religions" as well.

On the other hand, there are further limits to the definition, for, he said, groups may be dedicated to "secular" tasks but may lack "the 'spiritual connection.'"

> Again, a band of persons, large or small, may not be said to be adherents of a religion merely because they share some common beliefs and common interests and practise common rites and ceremonies; nor can pietistic recitation and solemn ritual combine to produce religion on that account only. Secret societies dedicated to secular tasks and indulging in queer oaths and observances, guilds and groups of persons who meet but to dine and wine but who subject their members to extravagant initiation ceremonies, village and tribal sorcerers and coven of witches who chant, rant and dance in the most weird way possible are all far removed from religion. They appear to lack the 'spiritual connection'.[14]

Justice Reddy's opinion assumed that one can distinguish secular tasks; indeed, past Supreme Court decisions have done this through the imposition of a new religious model that conflicts with traditional models in which religion encompasses all of life. And the Courts have shown that these "secular" activities can be associated with "religion." But for Justice Reddy, in the question of whether or not a community constitutes a religion, what cannot be lacking is "the spiritual connection." That "spiritual" element is what would distinguish a "religious" group from a "secular" one. He moved on without offering a definition of that element.

Justice Reddy surveyed the Constitutional discussions of religion by examining the language surrounding it in Articles 25 and 26 of the Constitution itself. He concluded that "the Constitution considers Religion as a matter of thought, expression, belief, faith and worship, a matter involving the conscience and a matter which may be professed, practised and propagated by anyone and which may even have some secular activity associated with it." He then surveyed past court decisions, and concluded that they also evidence that "religion" is "incapable of precise judicial definition. . . ." Yet, based upon the Constitution and these past decisions, he summed up, "So, religion is a matter of belief and doctrine, concerning the human spirit, expressed overtly in the form of ritual and worship."[15]

Armed with this definition distilled from the Constitution and, thus, representing the view of the people of India, he found that the definition is easily applied in some cases. In others, a religion may not be easily identified by the definition. As a result, for these exceptional cases he recommended that the Court fall back upon the claims of the community and the viewpoints of outsiders about the institution in question.

> There is no formula of general application. There is no knife-edge test. Primarily, it is a question of the consciousness of the community, how does the fraternity or sodality (if it is permissible to use the word without confining it to Roman Catholic groups) regard itself, how do others regard the fraternity or sodality.[16]

Justice Reddy proposed that in cases where a community does not clearly fit into a general definition of religion, the community itself and the perceptions of outsiders should be the test of whether or not a community constitutes a religion.

He suggested that a community may be a religion, even if the founder of the community did not intend to found a religion.

> In origin, the founder may not have intended to found a religion at all. He may have merely protested against some ritu-

als and observances, he may have disagreed with the interpretation of some earlier religious tenets. What he said, what he preached and what he taught, his protest, his dissent, his disagreement might have developed into a religion in the course of time, even during his lifetime. He may be against religion itself, yet history and the perception of the community may make a religion out of what was not intended to be a religion and he may be hailed as the founder of a new religion.[17]

Regarding the phrase "religious denomination," Justice Reddy rejected the Oxford Dictionary definition borrowed by Justice Mukherjea in the Sirur Mutt case, "a collection of individuals classed together under the same name; a religious sect or body having a common faith and organisation and designated by a distinctive name."[18] Since judicial definitions are explanatory not statutory, he said, the Court is under no obligation to continue to use previous definitions. In fact, many accepted groups possessed no "distinctive name" or special organization.

In applying these thought to what Justice Reddy called "Aurobindoism," the justice did not cite Aurobindo's followers but outside experts who have observed Aurobindo and the movement. He discovered numerous cases in encyclopedias and other secondary literature to support the contention that "the world and India treated and respected Shri Aurobindo as a religious teacher and the founder of a new religious movement whose principal thesis was the evolution or transformation of humanity into divinity through the practice of Integral Yoga."[19] Of course, like other great religious teachers, Aurobindo denied that he was founding a religion. But his disciples and religious leaders all over the world thought he was. Arguments then that Aurobindoism is not a religion are unconvincing, and he concluded that there is no reason why "'Aurobindoism' cannot be classified, if not as a new religion, as a new sect of Hinduism and why the followers of Shri Aurobindo cannot be termed a religious denomination."[20] Since the Society stands before the Court making the same claim to religious status, he allowed them their claim. Past claims by the Society that it was a nonreligious organization notwithstanding, the fact is these merely indicate that a religious denomination was engaged in nonreligious activities.

Though the two opinions differed over the nature of "Aurobindoism" as a religion, they agreed that the Act was constitutional. The majority opinion, "even assuming but not holding the

Society or Auroville were a religious denomination," followed the standard procedure of the Court for dealing with such matters. The Act, it said, only takes over "the management of the Auroville by the Society in respect of the secular matters."[21] The Act deals with the administration of property, and property management is "a purely secular matter," as consistently held in previous decisions.

The minority opinion agreed. It held that the Sri Aurobindo Society is a section of a religious denomination. But the Act provides for the management of Auroville, and that is a secular institution.

> Auroville is a township and not a place of worship. It is a township dedicated not to the practice and propagation of any religious doctrine but to promote international understanding and world peace, surely a secular and not a religious activity.[22]

Promotion of international understanding and world peace is defined as a secular undertaking, "by no means a religious ideal." Since that was Auroville's purpose, the government of India and UNESCO had adopted the project. In the minority opinion then, this was another example of a secular activity of a religion, hence it is not protected by the Articles 25 and 26 of the Constitution.

Furthering the "Secular"

As the Supreme Court made the final judgment on what is meant by the "religious," the assumption that there are two realms designated "religion" and "secular" was taken for granted, though Aurobindo himself would have disagreed. The idea is not argued, but in the process it is the Court's duty to define both terms. No one approached the bench questioning this assumption. It is clear that it was accepted by those on both sides of the case, even those who approached the Court to argue that an action of the state is interference with religion.

As pointed out in chapter 1, the Supreme Court of India fully accepted the responsibility of determining what falls within these two categories, and at times even declared the determination difficult. It emphasized that the Constitution allows the state to regulate and even administer economic, financial, and political activities carried on by religions. Therefore, when the state stepped in to administer properties of a religion, that was clearly acceptable. The

Court acts thereby as the authority that promotes religious change. If the "secular" is a new category, its progressive definition is an expansion of the power of the state to make what from a traditional view are "religious" pronouncements.

In its history of defining "religion," the Court has introduced further categories such as "essentiality" and said it was important to decide whether an activity was "essential to a religion." After first stating that what was essential would be determined in terms of the religion itself, when a religious institution explicitly attempted to do so by claiming that how temple income is spent was a religious matter, the Court rejected the claim. The religious community's explicit statement of "essentiality" was not taken as a basis for accepting whether an activity was religious or essential to a religion. Later, the Court declared that the scale of expenses and the provision of proper materials for rituals, the determination of which priestly duties are "religious," and the appointment of a priest are "secular" matters that are done by "religious" institutions.

By 1980 and the Auroville case, the majority of the Court had adopted a definition of "religion," which it said it would use in this new case to decide whether an entire system that is professed, practiced, and even propagated is a religion. There is nothing, however, in the majority opinion itself that actually argued in terms of a comparison between the Court's definition of religion and Aurobindo's beliefs and practices. The opinion proposed that the Court examine "the teachings of Sri Aurobindo to see whether they constitute a religion."[23] Though the teachings were given by the Court as a "system of beliefs or doctrines" that are meant to produce "spiritual well-being," though these beliefs also involve "outward expression" in meditation and devotion, and though "religion need not be theistic," there was no attempt to address these specific elements of the accepted definition. Aurobindo's beliefs were presented without argument or comment except for one element, a reference to what the majority of the Court calls "the distinctive feature" of these beliefs: its universality.

This characteristic, however, is unhelpful. Universality is, as noted earlier, an important characteristic of "Hinduism" in the minds of modern Hindu apologists who argue that universality often sets "Hinduism" apart from the other religions. The Court itself had actually identified this as a characteristic of "Hindu religion" in Sastri Yagnapurushadji v. Muldas Bhudardas Vaishya (1966), quoting Radhakrishnan. It even repeated that quotation from Radhakrishnan in the Auroville case when referencing the 1966 decision. "Universality," it would appear from the Court's own discussions, can therefore be a claim of a religion as much as a claim of a nonreligious institution. The justices did not, however, notice the contradiction in Court definitions.

The introduction of the category "spiritual" by Justice Reddy in the minority opinion without further explanation draws attention to another ambiguous term that often has been used in the discussion of the definition of "religion," including the Parliamentary debates concerning the Auroville Act. The manner in which Justice Reddy used the term in the writing of his opinion seems to assume that all people understand the meaning of the word "spiritual." In other legal contexts, however, "the spiritual dimension" seems to be taken as "secular." For the Supreme Court in its 1977 decision, "spiritual" was "secular." There the Court referred to a "spiritual dimension to the first page of our Constitution. . . ."[24] The secular state's founding document that protects its secularity had, the Court said, a "spiritual" dimension. In the majority opinion in the Auroville case, the use of the term *spiritual* in Auroville's Charter was not considered an indication of religion, just as in the Parliamentary debates some minsters saw no problem with a secular state supporting a "spiritual" institution.

The ambiguity of the term *spiritual* is also, therefore, clear. And Justice Reddy offered no help in the definition of it either. He had noted that the category "superstition" was inadequate as well, though the Court used it in Yagnapurushdasji v. Muldas[25] to attempt to distinguish nonreligious beliefs from religious ones. "What is religion to others is pure superstition to some others," Justice Reddy noted. Yet his use of the term *spiritual* assumed that it is somehow less ambiguous, and so, without definition, he moved on as do others who use the term.

Finally, Justice Reddy reintroduced the notion of self-definition by the religious community. For the Court, the idea that a religious community itself can define which of its elements are religious is not new. In March 1954, in Panachand Gandhi v. State of Bombay, an institution the Court accepted as religious attempted to argue that activities to be regulated by the state of Madras were religious and, thus, protected. In an earlier case the same month, Commissioner, Hindu Religious Endowments, Madras v. Sirur Mutt, the Court had said that a religious institution has the right to determine its own affairs in matters of "religion," and that what constitutes "religion" is ascertained with reference to the doctrines of the religion itself. In spite of this statement, in Panachand Gandhi v. State of Bombay, the Court rejected the claims of an accepted "religious" institution that the activity in question was "religious." What this indicated was that given the Court's definition of "religious" and "secular," the religious institution was attempting to extend the "religious" into an area of its activities the Court already considered "secular."[26] It was, therefore, unacceptable to the Court, even if the self-definition of the community were otherwise.

A further question in any self-definition is who speaks authoritatively for the community when its members disagree? How does the Court, therefore, know which evidence is best in determining a community's self-definition? Two further complications arise. First, if the community identifies with a historical tradition of any length in which various opinions exist, which opinion is authoritative? Is it the position of the founder or one in a line of gurus? Is it the current community or a previous representative? Do previous statements of the same organization take precedence over present ones?

Second, if the community denies that there is such an authority, where does one seek the self-definition? Is there a pope or an authoritative religious leader to whom the members surrender? Is there a scripture upon which they agree, and is there an authoritative interpreter? According to members of the Aurobindo movement, following the Mother, authority is now left with the inner Spirit which indwells each individual. What if their individual perceptions of the direction of that inner Spirit apparently disagree? Do the members of the Sri Aurobindo Society or the Aurovillians now speak with that authority?

Justice Reddy did not mention those followers who would deny that "Aurobindoism" is a religion. In their Counter Affidavit to the Court, followers of Aurobindo in Auroville did not speak to the issue of whether or not "Aurobindoism" is a religion. Their claim was that Auroville was not a religious institution or denomination. Their petition spoke more in terms of the issue of previous Court judgments, whether or not an institution or activity of a "religion" was "religious." As their lawyer summarized their claim

It is in this most profound sense that I, speaking on behalf of the Auroville residents, feel this assertion by the Society that Auroville constitutes a religious denomination to be the perpetration of an immense fraud which falsifies the very reasons and understanding which led us all to come here and invest our lives towards the realization of Auroville as a research experiment for the "living embodiment of an actual human unity." And I pray that this false assertion will not be allowed to hinder the unfolding of the Mother's 'Dream.'[27]

Interviews with many followers of Aurobindo indicate that they deny that his viewpoint constitutes a "religion."

Justice Reddy did not ask who in a community speaks for the community on the issue of whether or not it is a religion. What if the whole community or its authoritative voices deny that it is a religion? Even within the accepted religions (Christianity, Islam, Hinduism, etc.), religious thinkers and others will often deny that their beliefs and practices constitute a religion.[28]

In the past, the Court has used reification, that is, treating as a single entity a collection of historical facts that are characterized by diversity and change, to its advantage to solve this problem. In 1958, in M.H. Quareshi v. State of Bihar, the Court treated Islam, a category that includes a multitude of varied communities geographically and historically throughout the world, as a reified entity. Instead of asking whether it is essential to the community of believers before the Court, the judges asked whether it is essential to "Islam." Surveying "Islam" as a reification, they found within that category an opinion that the sacrifice of a cow on Bakr Id Day was unessential.

> It has also been pointed out that from time immemorial the Indian Mussalmans have been sacrificing cows and this practice, if not enjoined, is certainly sanctioned by their religion and it amounts to their practice of religion protected by Article 25. While the petitioners claim that the sacrifice of a cow is essential, the State denies the obligatory nature of the religious practice. The fact emphasised by the respondents [the State], cannot be disputed, namely that many Mussalmans do not sacrifice a cow on the Bakr Id Day.[29]

Hence, accepting a reified notion of religious positions that have a similar designation, the Court determined that "Islam" taught that it was unessential, even though the members of the present community claimed it was an essential and traditional element of their faith. These Muslims simply misunderstood the essentials of their religion, the Court declared.

The Court has similarly thought of "Aurobindoism" as a rei-fied entity with an assumed unity. This method for the majority of the Court enabled the judges to refer to Aurobindo and the Mother. "There can be no better proof than what Sri Aurobindo and the Mother themselves thought of their teachings and their institu-tions to find out whether the teachings of Sri Aurobindo and his integral Yoga constitute a religion or a philosophy."[30] This and pre-vious declarations of the Society for purposes of government sup-port, the majority of judges concluded, mean that "there is no room for doubt that neither the Society nor Auroville constitute a reli-gious denomination and the teachings of Sri Aurobindo only repre-sent his philosophy and not a religion."[31]

In the minority opinion, reification enabled the conclusion that Aurobindoism is a religion. Founder's opinions are of little use, and the Society's past claims merely indicate "that it is engaged in several secular activities. . . ." However, the people of India and the world treated Sri Aurobindo as a religious teacher. Justice Reddy actually quoted no members of the movement *per se*, though some of the experts may have been members. In any case, he concluded, "We must hold, the Aurobindo Society is a section of a religious denomination within the meaning of the expression in Art. 26 of the Constitution."

The determination of a consistent basis for a definitive defin-ition of "religion" seemed no easier in the case of Auroville than it had in the earliest cases that came before the Supreme Court. The Court seemed to come easily to the conclusion that supported the government's takeover of the township. It thus agreed with those in the Parliament who argued that such government control was nec-essary to promote India's national interests and international pres-tige. But the Court's written records do not eliminate the ambigu-ity of the term, and the contradictory use of arguments in past cases and the present one make it unclear what arguments could per-suade the Court. The justices themselves might be seen as both "religious" and not. Behind the majority opinion were justices who were popularly identified with various contemporary gurus such as Sai Baba and Muktananda, gurus who would support various ver-sions of Neo-Advaita and a definition of inclusivism similar to Rad-hakrishnan's. The minority view was written by a justice more pop-ularly known as a theoretical Marxist.

What has been consistent is the expansion of the realm desig-nated by the category "secular" and the fact that in all but two of the cases that have come before the Supreme Court of India, one before and one after the Auroville case,[32] the Court has supported the state in legislation that limits the scope of religion and increases the realm over which legislation may be passed. The Supreme Court's disposition of Auroville, then, whether it is in fact a religious or secular institution, is consistent with the Court's preference for the expansion of the "secular" over the "religious." The judicial arguments also evidence that what appears to be a settled judicial definition of "religion" is still problematic for members of the Court. What is less problematic is not the arguments used for the definition of religion or even for supporting the state's regulations, but the preference the Court has for upholding state restrictions on what is either admittedly a "religious" institution, or what the Court must decide, in spite of the claimants, is not. A level of ambiguity regarding the "religious," the "spiritual," and the "secular" remained in the judicial discussion even though the Supreme Court justices had officially decided the issue.

Eight

⊂◈⊃

Auroville, the "Spiritual," and the "Secular" in the Post–Decision Debates

The "Auroville (Emergency Provisions) Act, 1980" had vested the temporary management of the Auroville township in the central government of India for a period of two years, beginning on November 10, 1980. When the Auroville case came before the Supreme Court, the Court issued directions that effectively let the heart of the Act's provisions proceed as the basis for management while it considered the case. Only with the Court's decision in November 1982 did the Act come into full force. This arrangement was extended on a year-to-year basis until November 1985, when the government brought before the Parliament the first of two Amendment Acts to extend its temporary control over the township.

When "The Auroville (Emergency Provisions) Amendment Bill, 1985," was introduced in the Rajya Sabha on August 14, 1985, Auroville had already begun its experience of management under a full-time state administrator, Justice L.P. Nigam, an International Advisory Committee consisting of eminent Indians and other international figures[1] had been constituted to manage the project, the Supreme Court had declared that Auroville was not a religious institution and, in its majority opinion, that Aurobindo's teachings were not religious, and investigations into "irregularities and financial improprieties" of the previous management of Auroville by the Sri Aurobindo Society were fully underway by India's Central Bureau of Investigation with the results in courts in Pondicherry and Orissa. The Amendment Act extended the temporary management of Auroville by the central government for two more years. It was passed and assented to by the president on September 2.

By the time the second amendment bill, which would become "The Auroville (Emergency Provisions) Amendment Act, 1987," was introduced into the Lok Sabha on November 9, 1987, an Act that extended temporary government management another year, the investigations had been completed and the cases against the Sri Aurobindo Society had been dismissed. Thus it would seem that a number of criminal and civil issues had been settled, especially since it had been judicially declared that in regard to Auroville the issue of the "secular" state's interference in "religion" was legally dead. There would appear to be no *legal* ambiguity, for the Court's decision was final, regardless of how it was made.

The Debate Continues

During the debates over these two amendment bills, the government and members of Parliament continued the discussion of a number of key issues relevant to the nature of Auroville and its ideal relationship to the state in a manner that indicated that some of these issues had, in fact, not been clearly settled in their minds by the ensuing events. Depending on whether they supported the Sri Aurobindo Society or the Aurovillians, they also rehearsed allegations, both real and unsubstantiated, against each side, such as the allegations of American CIA involvement among the Aurovillians.

It was most often the case that references to Auroville in the Parliament during these debates used the politically acceptable description, "an international cultural township." This was the Congress-I government's phrase from Minister of Education K.C. Pant, who introduced and explained the 1985 Bill, and Minister of Human Resource Development and Minister of Health and Family Welfare P.V. Narasimha Rao, who did the same for the 1987 Bill. Rao also was a member of Auroville's International Advisory Committee at the time.

The ministers and members also continued to justify their intentions with references to UNESCO's resolutions "commending Auroville to those interested in UNESCO's ideals, and inviting its Member States and international Governmental and non-Governmental organisations to participate in the development of Auroville as an international cultural township. . . ."[2] For Krishna Kaul, Rajya Sabha member from Uttar Pradesh, it should also be regarded as important that UNESCO had supported the government's actions to assume Auroville's management.

> . . . I would like to submit that in 1983, UNESCO passed a unanimous resolution—for the attention of one hon. Member on the opposite side who objected to it [the idea of Government management]—supporting the intervention of the Government of India and asking the Director General of UNESCO to support the programme of Auroville which, in fact, is a tribute to the government takeover of the administration of the Auroville and I congratulate the administration, the hon. Minister of Education, for its laudable achievement and for its continuing efforts in launching programmes towards all round development of the Auroville.[3]

India was doing something for the world. Thus, M.P Kaushik of Haryana told the Rajya Sabha that by the intermingling of cultures in Auroville "we can evolve an absolutely new culture for the benefit of humanity at large, for the peace and tranquility of the world."[4] But the members also continued to be aware of world opinion. Rajya Sabha Member V. Narayanasamy of Pondicherry interpreted the UNESCO resolutions as approval of "the said wishes of the Holy Mother,"[5] though, as we have seen, there was no actual acknowledgment of the Mother in any of the resolutions.

The emphasis upon the international nature and impact of Auroville caught up a number of members, inspiring them to speak. Priya Rajan Das Munsi of Howrah described Auroville to the Lok Sabha in terms of India's pride. "It belongs to India, it is a pride for Indians and the Indian civilisation."[6] V. Narayanasamy described Auroville as "an international city, with rich cultural heritage, not only internal integration but international integration will be affected in this international city." International understanding and unity, "to inculcate the impression that [the] world is one family," were what Rajya Sabha member V. Arunachalam of Tamil Nadu called the "glorious objectives and glittering generalities" acknowledged by UNESCO, which attracted "more than 60 nations . . . to donate liberally for this international township." So great was his impression of Auroville that, he said, nothing of cultural value would be omitted there. "It is also to absorb all values of civilisation and different cultures."[7]

The takeover was meant to "enforce the aims of the Charter," the key to which was its goal of "human unity," and no one put that more eloquently and identified it more fully with India's national goals than Minister P.V. Narasimha Rao in 1987.

> As is well known, Auroville was founded on the 28th February, 1968, on the basis of a Charter which declares that it is a place of perpetual education, that is dedicated to material and spiritual researches and that its aim is to realise human unity. In India we have held the ideal of the entire world as one family, and the aims and objects envisaged for Auroville by Shri Aurobindo and the Mother are in full conformity with that ideal.[8]

The members also framed these debates in terms of pride, even reverence, for India's own Sri Aurobindo and her adopted spirit, the Mother. Introducing the 1985 Bill, Minister of Education K.C. Pant set something of the tone for the discussion of the cultural hero and how Auroville must succeed as a tribute to him.

> It is now only fitting that Sri Aurobindo and the Mother should have pioneered such a concept, such a project, because Sri Aurobindo occupies a place of great dignity in the history of India of the last few decades. He has been an outstanding person. He has not only contributed to the freedom struggle, he at one stage had lighted a new flame in the hearts and minds of the young people . . . , and then bent his formidable energies, his powers of the spirit, his gigantic intellect to experiment with ideas to project his understanding of India's culture, his vision of the future of this concept he projected and projected in a manner of which we in this country can be proud. He projected them in a manner which was untremmelled [*sic*] by the narrow confines even of nationalism. Therefore, it is but fitting that the man who could think with his visions, whose horizons were almost limitless should have conceived of this nation, of an international cultural community.[9]

They agreed that Aurobindo was a renowned giant of a man from India. One member of the Rajya Sabha, Dharam Chander Prashant of Jammu and Kashmir, spoke passionately of the world-renowned Aurobindo as "the great Yogi, Philosopher and Spiritualist."

"Thoughts and writings of this yogi, Aurobindo Gosh are recognised all over the world." Those who come to Auroville, he said, therefore, do so "considering it a sacred place, a 'Tirath,' because the spirit of Aurobindo Ghosh still prevails there." Prashant was convinced this was appropriate, though he accepted this reverence on the testimony of others, for he had neither met Aurobindo nor personally understood his writings.

> I have not got a chance to meet, to see or to have darshan of Aurobindo Ji during his lifetime, but I have met those who visited Pondicherry Ashram and had his "darshan." They say after meeting Shri Aurobindo Gosh for five minutes they got spirit that remained with them for six months. Such personalities are rare in the country. And in this 20th century the country got this great yogi and philosopher.[10]

Similarly, he himself had tried to read Aurobindo's greatest writing, his "Mahakavya called Savitri," but he had to admit that he could not get anything out of it, "because it was very deep philosophy."[11] Yet both houses of Parliament agreed that the affirmation and prestige of Aurobindo the cultural hero and international personality, the nation's greatness, and the success of the Auroville project were inextricably intertwined.

It was not only Aurobindo revered as freedom fighter and sage whom they spoke of in reverential terms. The members spoke with almost equal reverence for the Mother as well. P.R.D. Munsi reminded his Lok Sabha colleagues that Aurobindo not only taught revolution to the young people of Bengal but after his realization of "the divine truth and the eternity of the human soul," Aurobindo told them "that ultimately it was the devotion to the Mother that would live long and not merely terrorism."[12] Chintamani Jena of Balasore responded in like reverence. Yes, "the Divine Mother" had died, but she is still active among us. "Though she is not with us now, she is always with us judging our activities in the mortal wor[l]d."[13] This reverence is quite appropriate for every Indian, Banwari Lal Purohit of Nagpur told the Lok Sabha. "Every citizen in the country owes reverence to the Aurobindo Ashram. The Mother of the Aurobindo Ashram is worshipped by lakhs of families in the country with devotion and reverence."[14] Such reverence continued to mean that if India allowed Auroville to fail it would bring disgrace on Aurobindo's memory, on the Mother, and on India herself.

Therefore, members of Parliament argued that it was the government's duty to promote the vision and ideas of Aurobindo and the Mother through Auroville. Lok Sabha member Narain Chand Parashar of Hamirpur not only believed it appropriate that, "The Government would like to see that Auroville emerge as a dream city or as a city of dawn, as was envisaged by the Holy Mother when it was inaugurated on 38th February, 1968." It was the very duty of the Indian "secular" state to ensure the opportunity for the realization of Aurobindo's and the Mother's dream. "But the Government owes it to the country that the vision of Sri Aurobindo and the Holy Mother be given the fullest possible opportunity to develop and to fashion the city as the City of Dawn, as the city of the future, as was envisaged."[15] B. Ramachandra Rao of Andhra Pradesh reminded the Rajya Sabha that this city, which he called "the fountain-head of India," is the result of contributions to the nation from two great individuals. For that reason, he said, it should be supported. "Let us remember that Auroville is the outcome of the great contributions made by the great personality, the Holy Mother. It is the outcome of the great contributions that were made by Shri Aurobindo, who was not only a freedom fighter but a great philosopher, who has given a new direction to the Indian spiritual heritage."[16]

To some members, the government's duty was not merely to promote Auroville, but the promotion of the theoretical position of Aurobindo and the Mother in and through Auroville. Chintamani Jena requested that the government promote the "ideology of Shri Aurobindo." "See that the thoughts of Shri Aurobindo and Divine Mother are implemented through our present Education Minister."[17] D. C. Prashant spoke further of the "need to spread the philosophy of Aurobindo all over the country."[18] Thinking more globally, Narain Chand Parashar spoke of promoting Aurobindo's thought to the world. In doing so, he tied such promotion to the modern Nationalist concept of India's unique mission to the international community.

> Linked with Auroville is the idea of India emerging as the mother of culture for the entire community and for this, the Government may do whatever is possible in its strength and capacity and ultimately the Government should not cling to it. This is not a child to be carried on wooden legs. It is a flower to be allowed to blossom in the fullest sense of the term and the fragrance of this garden of flowers must spread to the whole of mankind and enrapture humanity with a new spiritual order that transcends all differences.[19]

The idea that India could still be a leader, even a guru, to the nations, had not died. Thus, he recommended, we should look beyond the immediate policies and problems concerning Auroville to the promotion of Aurobindo's vision to save the entire world. To these members, it was appropriate that the Indian "secular" state not only ensure that Aurobindo's and the Mother's ideals succeed in Auroville, but that the state promote Aurobindo's thought throughout India and the world. Was not this the promotion of one person's thought above others? Apparently, inclusivism of the absorbing type was not a threat to these members as it might be to others. One could no longer legally claim this was the state promoting one "religious" position over others. After all, even the majority on the Supreme Court had declared that Aurobindo's system of thought and practice, Integral Yoga, was not "religious." Sankar Prasad Mitra from West Bengal agreed, and he told his Rajya Sabha colleagues confidently, "Sri Aurobindo did not preach any religion of any kind. Perhaps it can be said that his philosophy of evolution of the human mind based on the science of evolution was a glorious example of secular activism and of socialist humanism."[20] In spite of what those who disagreed might think, Aurobindo's inclusivistic thought was "secular" and the state ought to propagate it.

Though the Supreme Court had legally ended the debate over Auroville's religious nature, there were a few members, however, who persisted. Particularly outspoken was Communist Party of India member of the Lok Sabha, Sudhir Roy from Burdwan. During the debate over the 1985 Bill, he continued to speak of the situation as "religious" and the Sri Aurobindo Society as a "religious society," seeing the basic problem as one inherent in "religious" groups. He accused the Society of being typical of many new "religious" groups in modern India, and Auroville as just its means for reaching their usual goal—obtaining both government and outside money.

> Sir, in the post–independence period, a mushroom growth of religious missions and trusts have taken place. We often found that schools and colleges and charitable institutions were founded by them to get Government money and to seek donations from national and international agencies. We often found that in the secular State of ours, Babas and Matajis have had thriving growth. Also we have found that they have been setting up more and more institutions to grab more and more

money from the government. They have little intention of doing good to the people. Their only ambition is to get money—nothing else.[21]

There was no subtlety in Roy's argument. Though Auroville "started with a bang," he said, its leaders, whom he called "the Holy Men," tried to make money off the project and then did everything possible to complicate government investigations into their "irregularities." "But, Government should not lend any sort of respectability to any religious association or denomination whenever they profess some idea." The Sri Aurobindo Society and its Auroville "project" is just one example of how "secularism" is being eroded by "religious institutions and denominations, and often these registered Societies. . . ." No religious organization should be encouraged by "a secular State like India," he concluded. Thus, no matter what action the government takes, nothing should associate the government with this Society.[22]

During the debate in 1987, he continued, supporting the takeover of Auroville but critical of giving it further government funds. Auroville, he said, was a typical religious attempt at creating a utopian society, all of which fail. He compared it to another utopian institution, much less popular in India, the Ashram of the Guru Rajneesh and his notorious township which had failed in the United States.

> But those societies would not succeed. In an otherwise imperfect world, imperfect social system, we can never visualise that such a society should thrive. Often we find that such societies degenerate into some sort of Rajneeshpuram, that has earned notoriety in the world or they received so much money that quarrels started among the followers and they engage in fractional squabbles.[23]

The comparison offended Gopeshwar of Jamshedpur. Without mounting an argument, he merely asserted that, as opposed to that of Rajneesh, the Parliament should understand Aurobindo and the Mother's thought and its application as "great" philosophy with a workable application. "I very strongly object to any comparison with Rajneeshpuram, or anything of the kind. We should understand that a very great philosophy was enunciated by Shri Aurobindo and was put to practical system by the Mother."[24] On the basis of its "greatness," he argued, it should be promoted by a "responsible agency," but not by the government.

The vast majority of speakers rejected the idea that the Sri Aurobindo Society and Auroville were "religious." B. Satyanarayan Reddy of Andhra Pradesh reminded the Rajya Sabha that the evidence of this is its inclusivity, that "people belonging to different religions, people belonging to different faiths, and even people having no religion at all can come to and live at Auroville as human beings."[25] He did not refer to the Mother's statement that Auroville is a place for people to give up their religions. In the Lok Sabha, Minister K.C. Pant reminded Roy that the Supreme Court had already settled the matter and suggested the "if he is interested," Roy should study the decision.[26] Eduardo Faleiro of Mormugao was convinced, he told the Lok Sabha, that the society was "not a religious society" and that its malpractices were "very secular malpractices."[27]

For some, references to Auroville took on the words of sacredness and religious piety without treating it as "religious." P.R.D. Munsi's reaction to Roy was one of incredulity, but he was still willing to refer to Aurobindo's concept as "a divine truth."

> I am rather surprised to hear the speech of my hon. friend from the opposite Mr. Sudhir Roy belonging to the Marxist party. He tried to compare Aurobindo and Auroville and this Bill, in a religious manner and that, like other religions, it is merely a religious centre. . . . I could not understand on what grounds he tried to compare Aurobindo merely as a religious leader. Aurobindo's vision is not a concept of a particular narrow point of religion. His concept of a divine truth, the best spirit of the human life, how to live and let live, is a concept of not a particular religion but for all religions of humanity of the world.[28]

Accepting without argument a definition of "religion," which included its exclusive claims, he asserted that inclusivity was not a mark of "religion." "Religions" are narrow and exclusivistic. But Aurobindo's vision is the "divine truth" in and for all "religions," and therefore it cannot be one of the "religions." This unchallenged and apparently common assumption of Radhakrishnan and other Neo-Advaitins seemed too obvious for second thoughts.

Rajya Sabha member Pratibha Singh of Bihar, also declared that Aurobindo's and the Mother's teachings were nonreligious because they were not dogmatic. Their aim is human perfection by the realization of oneself through "Karma Yoga," which, she said, is different than the "dogmatism and ritualism" of "religion alone."[29] Minister K.C. Pant declared it basically "a vision in action."[30] M.S. Gurupadaswamy at one point was willing to cover all possibilities as he told his Rajya Sabha colleagues that the government should "be very careful in evolving any approach to religious institutions, quasi-religious institutions and spiritual institutions." He labeled Auroville, in contrast to the government, a "non-temporal institution."[31] Syed Shahabuddin of Kishanganj used a different set of terms when he told the Lok Sabha that there should be some screening process before people are admitted to what he called "the holy precincts of Auroville." Though he would not label Auroville "religious," he was concerned that the process ensure that applicants have a "religious and spiritual motive for coming there."[32] P. Shanmugam of Pondicherry preferred the term *divinity*, as he told his Lok Sabha colleagues that Auroville would not only be a place where "divinity became the bond between the residents" but "a place for realising the divinity propounded in all religions of the world."[33]

The most common term used in Parliamentary references to Aurobindo and Auroville was the term *spiritual*. The term may have been as ambiguous as "religion," but they agreed that "spiritual" did not mean whatever "religious" did. Many lauded the inclusion of "spiritual" elements, by which they meant something other than "material," which, in the end, was also an ambiguous term. However, its ambiguity allowed the term *spiritual* to function on both sides of the argument, just as the term *religious* had in the Constituent Assembly. Some believed that because it was "spiritual," the government should not be involved. N.C. Parashar praised Aurobindo's "attempt to synthesise the two aspects—the material and the spiritual," for, he said, that this synthesis "is the only hope for mankind and for the future." But he looked forward to the day when the government was out of Auroville.[34] Satyanarayan Reddy recommended that government management be terminated as soon as possible "as a spiritual project like this can be managed only by a team of dedicated and devoted persons."[35] Kailashpathi Mishra of Bihar, who believed Aurobindo had attained the highest levels of "spirituality (*ādhya-atmikā*)," rose to remind the government that it was not dealing with just any "factory, college or residence," but with an institution inspired by the "philosophy (*darshan*)" of Aurobindo and the soul (*ātmā*) and discipline (*sādhanā*) of himself and the Mother. The government should, therefore, see to it that Aurobindo's philosophy is the inspiration for those in charge.[36]

In some contexts, the term *spiritual* was hardly more than a replacement for previous usages of "religious," as an argument against the appropriateness of government involvement. The difference in the usage, however, was that one could not use the argument that the Constitution protected the "spiritual" as it did the "religious." "Spiritual" did not have guaranteed freedoms that "religion" did. M.S. Gurupadaswamy, who spoke of Auroville as "non-temporal," also praised it as "a live and dynamic synthesis of both spiritual and temporal affairs . . . a happy combination of materialism and spiritualism." For that very reason, he said, the government should have kept away, even if there was mismanagement. "If Auroville had been mismanaged, if there had been misappropriation of funds, misdirection of funds, the Government of India should have thought that Auroville being a spiritual institution, an important institution with a rich background, they should not interfere or invade the domain of spiritual and cultural activity." He went further and compared the takeover to what might be called a takeover of "religious" institutions as if there were no difference in his mind.

> Suppose tomorrow, a mosque is mismanaged, a gurudwara is mismanaged, a temple is mismanaged, are you going to take over the management? Certainly not. Therefore, I think, the Government committed a folly in taking over this institution. And it is committing a further folly in extending its control over Auroville.[37]

Gurupadaswamy's usage embodied the ambiguity. He could use the term *spiritual*, but distinguishing if from temples, mosques, and gurudwaras on that basis was difficult.

Others argued that the "secular state" should be involved in the promotion of the "spiritual." This, of course, was the government's position, affirming the Charter meant, as Minister P.V. Narasimha Rao said, that it was "dedicated to material and spiritual researches."[38] B. Ramachandra Rao, therefore, called Auroville not only a center for the application of science and technology but "above all, . . . a spiritual abode for the entire country."[39] Banwari Lal Purohit of Nagpur, in the Lok Sabha, went further, expecting any society and its institutions to make people aware of the spiritual. "It is certain that it is the duty of society and highly good institutions to create spiritual awareness among the people." Yet he was confident that Auroville needed an even stronger management structure set up by the government.[40]

Pratibha Singh put it cautiously when she praised Auroville for including spiritual, and not merely material, growth as its goal, and commended government promotion of it. She was certain that Aurobindo's dream was "the total spiritual direction given to the whole life of the whole nature." Likewise, she was sure that the problem was that some had "wanted to become mahants and wanted to turn the Auroville into a religious organisation which was never meant to be such." Yet she was unsure about the extent of the difference between "spiritual" and "religious." "Spiritual growth," she said, "is not exactly what we call religion; it is a little different."[41]

As in the discussion of the original Act, other members were against government management in principle, whether Auroville was religious or secular, and this became another occasion to criticize the government. Jaswant Singh of Rajasthan told the Rajya Sabha that given the "ennobling vision" behind Auroville, and no matter what the failures of the Aurovillians, the Ashram, and the Society, the idea that government could manage Auroville any better was questionable. Auroville was too ennobling a vision for the government to even presume that it comprehends it, much less successfully implements it.

> I, on fundamental grounds, oppose bureaucratic implementation where private individuals can be left to implement their visions, their dreams, their own aspirations. When it is a question of putting into practice such an ennobling vision, then, for the Government to arrogate to itself both the comprehension of that vision and the ability through bureaucrats to be able to put it into effect is a question which is seriously open to doubt.[42]

Though he could not argue that its "religious" nature put Auroville out of the government's reach, he argued that the nature of its "vision" did so. The continuance of government interference only perpetuated the government's claim over "such a vision."[43] Aurobindo's philosophy as it is practiced, Gopeshwar agreed, is not one that "any government machinery" can administer.[44]

The assurance was that government control would be temporary, in any case. Representing the government for the one-year extension, P.V. Narasimha Rao said, "All I can say is: if I cannot do it in the next one year, I do not think, I will ever be able to do it." Yet he admitted that Auroville was a unique case, blending "science, spirituality, and modern living" with "high thinking not quite compatible with other aspects of modern living as we find it." "We do not have any precedent to go by." He agreed that the "vision" behind the township had not been grasped by many, much less lived.

The union minister, however, concluded with a word that reminded one of the ambiguity of the terms involved. He used a phrase that distinguished the "spiritual" from the "secular." Had the word "religious" been substituted for "spiritual," it would have sounded much like the Constitutional distinction between the "religious" and the "secular," coupled with the fact that Articles 25 and 26 allow the state to restrict and regulate "secular activity" connected to "religion."

> But the point is if there is no one to manage the secular affairs of a spiritual institution, nothing will happen. There is a subtle difference between managing a temple and managing these secular aspects of a religious institution. This is a very well-recognised distinction accepted by the highest courts in the country and accepted by common sense more than anything else.[45]

The usage was interesting, though unnoticed at the time. The parallel between a temple and Auroville was made, as well as between "a religious institution" and "a spiritual institution." His argument was that the "spiritual/secular" distinction was like the "religious/secular" one, but the Courts had dealt only with the latter. The quotation, or verbal slip, illustrates, at least, that there continued to be ambiguity within the government representative's mind in the usage of the terms *spiritual* and *religious*, even in the midst of debates where he and others appeared to have the definitions settled. It could further mean that once declared "spiritual," an institution that may by definition fall outside of the "secular" can be under government control in a manner that a legally declared "religious" institution could not. In either case, once the affairs of a "religious" institution are declared "secular," the state can step in.

The Parliamentary debates over the Amendment Acts reflected similar concerns as those over the original Act. Though the Supreme Court's decision for the most part had precluded discussions of Auroville as "religious," for many there was still the sense that Auroville was something different, something unique, something holy. The term *spiritual* was the most common term still left to the discussion to label this difference, and the ambiguity of that term allowed its official use even though at times it seemed for some to merely take the place of past usages of the term *religious*. Auroville was officially an example, then, of the regulation of a "spiritual institution" or the "secular affairs" of a spiritual institution, that sounded at times no different than the regulation of a "religious" institution. In any case, the politically correct hope for members of Parliament who accepted government regulation at all, was that, regarding Auroville, the government was temporarily stepping in to regulate one of the following: (1) a secular institution; (2) a spiritual institution; or (3) the "secular" activities of a "spiritual" institution.

The Foundation Act

Contrary to previous statements, however, state control of Auroville would not be temporary. Minister of Human Resource Development P. Shiv Shanker told the Parliament in September 1988 that the Sri Aurobindo Society and the residents of Auroville were not cooperating with each other, that efforts at a solution had not succeeded, and that the government had, therefore, reached a consensus that it needed to impose a permanent solution. Thus, on August 31, a bill that would become "The Auroville Foundation Act, 1988" was introduced into the Rajya Sabha. Both Houses debated and passed the Bill in September, and on September 29, 1988, the president assented to it.

The Act cited the fact that funds to develop this "cultural township" had been received from organizations throughout the world and in particular the central and state governments of India, and that UNESCO "had, from time to time, reflected in its resolutions that the project on Auroville is contributing to international understanding and promotion of peace." It called for permanent government control through the establishment of "The Auroville Foundation." The Foundation would consist of three bodies:

1. A *Governing Board*, consisting of nine members nominated by the central government for four-year terms, two who are representatives of the central government and seven who have ren-

dered service to Auroville, "dedicated themselves to the ideals of life-long education, synthesis of material and spiritual researches or human unity," and contributed significantly to a broad list of activities envisaged or pursued by the township, which includes "integral yoga." The Board would be the ultimate authority within the Foundation, responsible for the general direction, supervision, and management of the Foundation's affairs, including promoting its ideals, developing its future plans, authorizing fund-raising, and approving the decisions of the Residents' Assembly.

2. *The Residents' Assembly*, consisting of all of the registered residents of Auroville that will advise the Governing Board on all activities related to the residents, organize activities relating to Auroville, develop a master plan for the Board's approval, admit new residents in accord with the Act's regulations, and make proposals to the Board for fund-raising.

3. *The Auroville International Advisory Council*, consisting of a maximum of five members appointed by the central government who, in its opinion, are "devoted to the ideals of human unity, peace and progress." It is an advisory body to the Governing Board and its purpose is to ensure that "the ideals for which Auroville has been established are encouraged, and the residents of Auroville are allowed freedom to grow and develop activities and institutions for the fulfilment of the aspirations and programmes envisaged in the said Charter of Auroville."

The Act ensured that the government was the final and permanent authority. At any time, the government, upon notification, could dissolve the Foundation and reconstitute it. All properties, funds, rights, and other items and projects related to Auroville and all that was related to Auroville and owned by the Sri Aurobindo Society, immediately became the property of the central government without the payment of compensation. The properties, the government reasoned, were acquired from donations given for the specific purpose of the realization of Auroville, the purpose at which the new Act aims. They would, when appropriate, be transferred to the Foundation. Finally, the central government also reserved the right to make additional rules for carrying out the provisions of the Act.

The Parliamentary debate was relatively muted. Much that could have been said had been aired in the debates on the earlier bills. In his speech to move the Bill, Minister P. Shiv Shanker spoke officially again of the "international cultural township" whose "aim is to discover a new life, deeper and more complete and to show the world that tomorrow will be better than today." Though he referred to the residents as people who come to engage in "material and spiritual researches," the official statements emphasized the material and scientific activities.[46] He spoke of the initial vision of Aurobindo and the Mother, reminding the Parliament that the "vision" was theirs while "the proposed Foundation is intended to provide the infrastructure for realisation of such a lofty endeavour."[47] He went into no detail regarding their "vision," and certainly did not include their accompanying particular views of Reality.

Members of Parliament again wanted to emphasize the importance of the message of Aurobindo behind the project as well as their own pride in the personality of the cultural hero who was both a revolutionary and an internationally renowned thinker. Aurobindo, Aziz Qureshi of Satna told the Lok Sabha, "kept the flame of [the] independence movement burning not only in India but outside the borders of India, in Canada, America, Japan, Afghanistan and Turkey." Aurobindo's burial place, the Samadhi, in the Ashram, Quereshi observed, "is a place of worship for the new generation and where they go to pay their homage."[48] He was a "freedom fighter" and a "Karma Yogi," Pratibha Singh, Rajya Sabha member from Bihar, told her colleagues, and his name should be made everlasting through support of the Bill.[49]

Najma Heptulla of Maharashtra went further and emphasized the theoretical position of Aurobindo and the Mother, the Charter as the embodiment of this position, and Auroville as the application of their ideology. She quoted the Mother regarding their theory of "an ascending evolution in nature," and of the future of that evolution beyond the current stage of humanity to "a being who will remain a man in its external form, and yet whose consciousness will rise far above the mental. . . ."[50] She had no problem with the idea that the State would be promoting this particular philosophy, but instead proudly placed it within the tradition of Indian thought represented by well-known religious texts. She considered Aurobindo and the Mother's position a new stage in the history of theoretical synthesis.

> In India, there have been four stages of synthesis. The Vedas, the Upanishads, the Gita, and the Tantrik. Now, we are passing through the fifth stage. In these days of materialism, let us

help to build such institutions like Auroville where spirituality and humanity is above all and where people from far and near come, of diverse religions, languages, castes, colour and creed. Let this institution be a beacon light for one and all to achieve divine consciousness for spiritual research and for a living embodiment of actual human unity. I recommend that this institution be made an institution of national importance like Visva Bharati, Asiatic Society, etc.[51]

Thus, she followed without question a consistent pattern of inclusivism that saw the theoretical position of Aurobindo and the Mother as a synthesis and integration of all other positions. It was, therefore, not merely one of the alternative viewpoints, call them religious or not, available to human beings, but the essence or affirmation of them all.

Using language borrowed from Western religions, Ram Singh Yadav of Alwar also thought it important to recommend that the government set up Auroville to "preserve the spirit and sanctity of his [Aurobindo's] gospel. . . ." Yet this Bill, he objected, did not make appropriate provision for the promotion of the study of Aurobindo's "gospel," so the state could guarantee that Aurobindo's "mission" would be accomplished.

We should make such a provision in the Bill which may inspire the young generation and coming generation to follow the principles of Shri Aurobindo so that they could lead a peaceful life, a life which Shri Aurobindo had dreamt of. It is absolutely necessary to embody these sentiments in the Bill. I am hopeful that the philosophy, the principles and teachings of Shri Aurobindo, will find berth [*sic*] in the Bill and the imaginations of this great sage will be fulfilled. It will provide soul to His soul and fulfil the mission he had started.[52]

N.G. Ranga of Guntur agreed. Auroville, he said, was a place where "students of philosophy and [the] Aurobindo Ghosh School of thought" come from "all over the world" to study Indian and other religious and philosophical traditions. "We are extremely anxious that government should go out of its way and afford them every possible physical facility for the gentlemen and women who gather there under the inspiration and the canopy of the philosophy of Aurobindo and the Mother."[53] With the legal decision out of the way, Aurobindo's position could no longer be considered a "religious" one. Therefore, the government could put its resources behind the promotion of his position and, some felt, that meant it could propagate it for all Indians and even the world. No one asked what this meant for positions that did not agree. Under the Neo-Advaitin and Aurobindo's definitions, which were accepted by the Court and by most in Parliament, the other positions were exclusivistic and, therefore, by definition, "religious." The state certainly could not promote them.

The debate over the religious nature of Auroville and Aurobindo's view was now legally over. No one stood to argue that it was "religious." Even references to its "spiritual" nature were less frequent. Ram Singh Yadav described Aurobindo's message as "spiritual" and added that his ideals also were "secular" and "inclusive": they were "the high ideals of secularism and equality of all religions of Pandit Jawahar Lal Nehru and Mahatma Gandhi. . . ."[54] V. Narayanasamy of Pondicherry used what could be called "religious" language when he described Aurobindo, the Mother, and Auroville to the Rajya Sabha. "The concept of Auroville was the vision of Shri Aurobindo, the divine personality of the world, and the Mother who is regarded as the goddess of the world." He quoted the Charter's call that Auroville was to be a willing servitor of the "divine consciousness," pointed out that the Mother had conceived Auroville "with a divine purpose," spoke of the Matrimandir as the result of a "divine design," described the duty of those who settle there as "to do service to God," noted that the International Advisory Council consists of "persons of eminence in spiritual matters," and even indicated his pleasure that, "The Government has considered the spirit of divine purpose for which it was created."[55] As one who had participated in the debates over both Amendment Bills as well, he apparently felt such facts and this language were consistent with "secular" purposes.

Likewise, free from the legal concern that "religion" was involved, in the Lok Sabha, Sriballav Panigrahi of Deogarh could speak of Aurobindo as "a rishi in the modern sense of the term" and a "great spiritual leader," refer to Aurobindo's inspiration in his experience of the god Krishna in the Alipore jail, explain that Aurobindo believed in "*Divva Jeevan* divine life," conceive of Auroville as the promotion of "Sri Aurobindo's philosophy which is to be looked upon as a vision," describe his vision of Auroville as a place that provides "the infrastructure for a better divine life for a better tomorrow for everybody," and recommend that the state take over Auroville and promote his thought.[56] In the Rajya Sabha,

Pratibha Singh could support the takeover in light of her understanding of its goal as the promotion of self-realization (*ātmatva*) and "karmayoga" and of what is said about both in "Vedic Vedanta."[57]

In the debates that took place after the Supreme Court had decided that legally neither Auroville nor Aurobindo's thought and practice were "religious," the designation was soon dropped. In the process, Aurobindo's views were further thought of as being different from "religions" on the basis of his perceived universalism, and the term *religion* was used of exclusivistic and parochial systems of thought and practice, antithetical to what the speakers believed was the Truth and the "spiritual."

The term *spiritual* further took the place of "religious," with some noticeable direct parallels in its ambiguous usages. The Supreme Court had not defined "spiritual." The judges' written opinions indicated the term's ambiguity, for they too had not agreed on a definition of the term. Yet the difference was that a "secular state" could regulate the "spiritual," whether or not they or the members of Parliament agreed that the term referred to something other than the "secular" or something within the realm of the "secular." The "spiritual" did not have Constitutional protection.

The majority of the members of Parliament came to agree that it was "spiritual," not "religious." Some hoped for that reason the state would soon turn Auroville over to a more appropriate body that could better take the "spiritual" into consideration. Some argued not only that the state should promote Auroville, but that it should promote Aurobindo's thought and yoga. It would do so, they believed, through these Acts, not merely by ensuring the success of the township as the embodiment of Aurobindo's thought, but by state-supported propagation of his thought to all Indians and into the world.

Seldom did the ministers of government get caught up in such enthusiasm, however. They were not always clear about the distinction between "spiritual" and "religious," though they affirmed it. Their attention, as well as that of other members, was most often fixed on the interests of the state: India's historic commitment to universalism and world unity, its commitment to UNESCO and possible embarrassment if the project it had brought before UNESCO with India's full backing should fail, its commitment to the fame of its honored son, hero, freedom fighter, and world-renowned thinker, and to the Mother, with her international reputation and following, and its need to ensure the proper use of state and federal funds already committed to the project. And these commitments must be "secular" ones for the "secular state" to promote them. With the state in control, and with these as the dominant state interests in their minds, whether they accept or merely tolerate the system of thought and practice taught by Aurobindo and the Mother, these interests that are now in place through legislation and judicial approval will have the power to decide the activities and status of the "City of Dawn."

Nine

Clarity and Ambiguity in the Discussion of Auroville's Status

This early history of the "City of Dawn" saw the township begin as a "divine vision" in the mind of the Mother, which was based upon the *Weltanschauung* of a modern Indian visionary, Sri Aurobindo, who called his theory a "religion," and end as a project of a "secular" state. This transformation took place in the midst of a larger, ongoing process—the definition of the relationship between the "Indian secular state" and theories and institutions that some designate "religion." In the process, it was clear that key terms that were used by participants, as if everyone understood them, were ambiguous. Often the fact that the principal participants in the discussions could agree on a term, without explicitly discussing its definition, actually enabled the process to proceed unabated. People felt there was agreement where it may not have existed. Such a process might actually appear successful, until the implications of the different implicit definitions that are behind the terms later raise correlative issues or even reveal themselves in actual practice. The case of the Indian state and Auroville is one example where these implicit differences continued to exist without their full force being apparent, but where, even before they became apparent, the case was legally, if not actually, resolved. Such cases are resolved legally, either by accepting an apparent consensus or agreement based on the fact that the differences remain implicit, or by the explicit imposition of one of the implicit definitions by an institution or individual of sufficient authority. In this case, in the constitutional democracy that is India, that sufficient authority is the Supreme Court, though it could also have been the legislative process of amending the Constitution.

One means to openly analyze the process that took place is to stand apart from the practical need to provide immediate political or legal solutions and clarify the discussion and debate by offering stipulative definitions of the ambiguous terms within it. Since stipulative definitions are not "real" definitions, that is, they do not make claims about the true relationship between a word and a thing, or they do not tell one what an entity really is—they can clarify a process without making claims to truth. Yet defining terms in such a manner to indicate to others what is meant when a term is used makes their meanings sometimes painfully explicit. It is possible, as a result, to compare and contrast the meanings and thereby uncover actual disagreements where previously agreement merely seemed to exist. Therefore, the use of stipulative definitions in itself, while clarifying communication, may raise issues some would rather leave buried. It may not often lead to immediate agreement, but although similar symbols—words—for things might have been used, through this clarification the participants in the process can better compare the *various things* to which the participants' *similar words* point.

This is not to enter the philosophical and theological arguments about some inherent relationship between words and things, such as whether words are "signs" or "symbols," assuming even that these two words also refer to different things. What is clear to the historian is that words do have histories and that the definitions to which one has become accustomed have a comfortable fit within the words one uses.[1] Though, as Robinson has argued,[2] it is difficult to argue that words have inherent or real meanings from which they cannot be extracted without damaging Reality, the importance of stipulating what one means when one uses a term with a history of meanings is that the process of stipulating the definitions of ambiguous words begins also to make explicit the assumptions and corollaries of the term as the person uses it. In sum, while improving verbal communication, the process of stipulating a definition also makes disagreements explicit.

It is certainly no revelation to say that few terms are more ambiguous than the English term *religion*. The literature on the subject is vast, with contemporary religious writers continuing to add definitions which, in spite of their hopes, have resulted in no more agreement about its meaning. Wilfred Cantwell Smith's classic work, *The Meaning and End of Religion*, traced the history of the term while arguing that there is no useful reason to continue to use the term *religion* to understand "religious" people. He suggested that the term *faith* would be more accurate, but gave no credence to its parallel ambiguity. Likewise, Smith noted how leading thinkers may on the one hand identify with a religious tradition, while, on the other, reject the term *religion* as a designation of their own beliefs and practices. His list is impressive, including, Karl Barth's declaration that "Religion is unbelief . . . and unbelief . . . is sin"; Deitrich Bonhoffer's reference to "religionless Christianity"; Nehru's claim that "It is hardly possible . . . to say whether [Hinduism] is a religion or not"; and Said Ramadan's statement that "Islam is not merely a 'religion' in the sense in which this term is understood in the West."[3]

This flight from the use of the term *religion* to designate one's own beliefs, practices, and self-defined traditions is not confined to the great thinkers. It is common to hear believers rush to claim that they have no "religion," while substituting what are apparently more comfortable terms such as *spirituality, a faith, a personal relationship, a tradition, a way of life, a philosophy*, and *a civilization*. Without much doubt, popularly the term has fallen on hard times. A history of its demise would include not only the view that it is inadequate to express what many believers experience, as Smith argues, but that it is identified by believers with organizations and structures that they feel have been institutionally oppressive, personally destructive, or legalistically judgmental, and, therefore, are rejected by the believers. Some prefer to say that they have rejected "organized religion."

The Mother and many of her followers constitute one example of those who most often use the term *religion* to designate what they considered negative entities and, thus, not an appropriate designation of their own beliefs, practices, and institutions. "Religion," the Mother believed, referred to organizations and traditions that had three characteristics that she rejected. First, they inculcate dogmatic beliefs and expect a response that some have called "blind faith," whereas she believed that her teachings and institutions came through her own direct and personal experiences. Even Auroville, she declared, was "given" to her by the Divine. Aurobindo's own claims, she felt, were validated not only through his experiences but through her own. The model for such a standard was the "scientific" experimentation that takes place in a science laboratory. Through Aurobindo's and her own experiments with consciousness, both believed they had "learned" these truths personally, not merely accepted them because they were taught by "religious" authorities. This was, however, a standard claim about true "religion" among Neo-Advaitins. Radhakrishnan, who did not hesitate to use the term *religion* positively, spoke of "Hinduism" as a religion based on experience and his own "religion of the spirit" as "scientific."[4]

The second characteristic of the entities the Mother referred to as "religions" and thereby criticized was that they are exclusivistic. They believe that those outside of their purview are "heathens," "the lost," or "infidels," and they engage in conversion and propagation. Again, as it was just pointed out, the standard claim of Neo-Advaita is a universalism, and that is the Mother's position as well. Neo-Advaitins also consider this the teaching of true "Hinduism" as well, but by the Mother's definition its universalism is additional proof that Aurobindo's and her beliefs are not "religions."

This is not to say that all positions, "religious" or not, are actually considered equal. The position held by this universalism is considered superior, for it is the position that understands correctly, whereas "religious positions," which are by definition in disagreement, do not understand the higher truth of universalism. The higher truth of universalism either believes some version of inclusivism, or it rejects these other *positions* while believing that the followers of the positions will "make it," variously defined, either because their understandings are partially helpful, or in spite of their beliefs.

This is closely allied with the third characteristic of "religions" as the Mother defined them. They do not understand the "Truth" defined in terms of the spiritual/material evolution of the Divine. The Mother, as we have noted, regularly spoke of her view as "Truth." From the Mother's view of "Truth," the "religions," instead of realizing the temporary nature of their beliefs and practices, egoistically cling to their positions as if they are absolutely and eternally true. But in the light of her view of Reality, these "religious" positions are temporary, at best only finitely valuable. Since the position of Aurobindo and the Mother is believed to transcend these limited understandings, it is, therefore, not "religious" by definition. Again, we see an affirmation of Neo-Advaitin inclusivism.

Thus, the definition of "religion" used by the Mother is tied to her assumptions about Reality. Her intention, however, was not a stipulative definition. She was not merely attempting to clarify her use of the word "religion"; she was defining the true nature of the very thing religion, as if her definition were the true definition of the thing. She was working with a real definition. Aurobindo, as we have seen, also criticized "religions" but did not fully reject the term as if there were something *inherently* wrong with "religion." From his perspective, he could criticize the exclusivity, egoism, misunderstandings of Reality, and dogmatism of most religions, while still using the term for his own Integral Yoga.

To choose a stipulative definition for the term *religion* is at most a minimal statement about the nature of Reality. As an attempt to improve communication, it functionally, if not ultimately, assumes the possibility of verbal, human communication. Yet, for example, its activity can take place even within a world-view that believes the world is ultimately unreal. The process in such a view becomes a part of the temporary reality of a level of consciousness that is appearance, which some traditions have called *maya*. In such a worldview, clarity of communication may be seen as ultimately unimportant, but, in the meantime, stipulating definitions is a way of functioning in the ultimately unimportant. In the end, to stipulate a meaning for a word is not a statement about Reality in itself, but an arbitrary activity. It is not a claim about the truth of the definition or the nature of Reality. Though others might object to the stipulative definition of "religion" one offers, they can do so only because they do not accept it as a stipulative definition, or because it does not aid communication, that is, it is not functional. To disagree with the definition because they do not believe it designates what "religion" really is is to misunderstand the definition's intention. In any case, a stipulative definition of "religion" is not a statement about a thing. It is a semiarbitrary choice made for purposes of communication and analysis.[5]

"Religion" as Ultimate Concern

Using the stipulative definition of "religion" as "that which is of greatest concern to individuals and communities," proposed by Robert Baird as a variant of Paul Tillich's real definition of "religion," provides a basis for the analysis of the nature of the conflict of "religions" in cases such as Auroville. One asks what the ultimate concerns of the individuals and groups are and notes the nature of their potential conflicts. Baird has noted that "religion" so defined can be analyzed on two levels: the ideal level as explicitly proclaimed or implied by the individuals and recommended as what should be of ultimate concern, and the real level that involves "the empirical indications of what in fact is ultimate . . . regardless of what they profess."[6] Understanding the former level is preliminary to studying the latter.

Ultimate concern, interestingly enough, is apparently how the Mother used the term the one time it is recorded that she did so in a positive light. As noted previously, once in response to a devotee's question, she defined religion as what a human being believes is "the most precious thing in life," as "something which may seem to be worth consecrating one's life to" or as "the centre for one's existence." The believer might not even be conscious of this ideal, and it may be an inferior one, but in the ordinary, unexamined life, she said, an individual "always has a religion."[7]

Using this stipulative definition to ask what the ultimate concerns of the participants in the Auroville case are is enlightening and clarifying even on the ideal level and opens up discussion of the variety of interests the parties expressed in the project. Aurobindo's own religion in one phrase was "the perfection of the world." What "perfection" meant, of course, was defined by his *Weltanschauung*, the most important features of which were his belief that Reality was both eternal Being and eternal Becoming and that the world was a movement of the previously involuted Spirit or Divine in evolution to higher levels of consciousness and manifestation. Therefore, for him, the "perfection of the world" was the manifestation of the Supermind in all levels of reality, spiritual and material. Without the acceptance of this accompanying view of Reality, one might have "perfection" as the goal, but miss what Aurobindo sought to achieve. Should some other definition of "perfection" be achieved, other people might be satisfied, but not Aurobindo. He had already declared that "all human systems have failed in the end," because they did not understand the true nature of the Divine Becoming and, therefore, clung to reason as their ultimate guide.[8] True "perfection," "human unity," and other common terms and phrases others might use were to be defined in terms of Aurobindo's view of Reality. He taught that what he proclaimed as the theory and practice of Integral Yoga with all the variety of paths it encompassed was the sufficient and necessary means for the individual to promote this Divine evolution toward true perfection.

The Mother's "religion" was, of course, similar, for she had accepted Aurobindo's *Weltanschauung* with few modifications. She emphasized the experiential and practical aspects of Integral Yoga and Auroville as a living laboratory of the active elements of that Yoga. Auroville was a means to this perfection, along with all of the other activities she oversaw in the Ashram. The descriptions she gave of Auroville's purpose, including those in her messages to UNESCO—"to hasten the advent of the supramental Reality upon earth," "the attempt toward collective realisation," "for a progressive superhumanity," "for the creation of a new world, the supramental, expressing the divine perfection"[9]—were neither hyperbole nor casual usage. They reflected her unwavering understanding of the project in terms of the Divine evolution. She was entrusted by the Divine, she told them, with the task of "giving concrete form to Sri Aurobindo's vision." Her apparent impatience with governments and international organizations such as UNESCO was a result of the fact that their visions were too limited and did not include the broader definition of the "Truth" she and Aurobindo assumed. She could not believe UNESCO understood the "Truth," for they were relatively unevolved. Rightly, she knew they would not comprehend what she believed were the real intentions behind Auroville and would likely promote it for inferior reasons.

One might assume that the "religions" of the Aurovillians and the members of the Sri Aurobindo Society were the same as the Mother's. That is clearly the ideal they preached and recommended to the world and each other. How each understood their place in the promotion of the project as interpreters of the Mother's intentions differed. Without a clearly designated charismatic successor, leadership and management became an issue, and "real" concerns such as money, power, and control apparently clashed, while the attempt to unite the world broke down into factions. One of the Aurovillians' most articulate members and a twenty-one-year resident, Savitra, looked back in 1994, honestly and openly observing the encroachment of the "real" in the late 70s: "We were at this point a community under siege, growing more and more paranoid, more and more stressed under the intensifying madness."[10] The actions of the Sri Aurobindo Society betrayed an encroachment of other concerns as well. Yet, the ideal "religion," the ultimate concern, was still accessible in the words of the Mother and proclaimed in the writings of both sides.

This "religion" was in contrast to the "religion" of the state, the ultimate concern embodied in the Constitution and interpreted by influential national leaders. The ultimate concern of the Constitutional model, including the additional Forty-Second Amendment Act, 1976, is stated in the Constitution's Preamble. It gives its purpose as

. . . to constitute India into a SOVEREIGN SOCIALIST SEC-
ULAR DEMOCRATIC REPUBLIC and to secure to all citizens:
>JUSTICE, social, economic and political;
>LIBERTY of thought, expression, belief, faith and wor-
ship;
>EQUALITY of status and of opportunity;
>and to promote among them all
>FRATERNITY assuring the dignity of the individual and
the unity and integrity of the Nation. . . .

Threats to national unity and integrity since the initial implementation of the Constitution translated into an emphasis on national
unity above individual freedom, as reflected in Supreme Court decisions about "religion." The 1976 Amendment, however, further
expressed this emphasis by adding "integrity" to the original Preamble and a list of "Fundamental Duties" to the "Fundamental
Rights" in the original Constitution after "Part IV." These ten
duties described a national ethic with concern for the integrity of
the nation in the foreground throughout the list.

Part IV-A
FUNDAMENTAL DUTIES

51–A. It shall be the duty of every citizen of India—
>(a) to abide by the Constitution and respect its ideals and
institutions, the National Flag and the National Anthem;
>(b) to cherish and follow the noble ideals which inspired
our national struggle for freedom;
>(c) to uphold and protect the sovereignty, unity and
integrity of India;
>(d) to defend the country and render national service
when called upon to do so;
>(e) to promote harmony and the spirit of common broth-
erhood amongst all the people of India transcending religious,
linguistic and regional or sectional diversities; to renounce
practices derogatory to the dignity of women;
>(f) to value and preserve the rich heritage of our compos-
ite culture;
>(g) to protect and improve the natural environment
including forests, lakes, rivers and wild life, and to have compassion for living creatures;

(h) to develop the scientific temper, humanism and the spirit of inquiry and reform;
(i) to safeguard public property and to abjure violence;
(j) to strive towards excellence in all spheres of individual and collective activity so that the nation constantly rises to higher levels of endeavour and achievement.

This list of the duties of citizens includes a curious mixture of traditional ideas such as "compassion for all creatures," along with the duty to set aside or "reform" traditions that might hinder national unity and integrity, such as is found in the duty "to develop a scientific temper, humanism and the spirit of inquiry and reform." Though it calls individuals to personal achievements by pledging them "to strive for excellence," it maintains that the nation is the ultimate concern behind personal and collective excellence, for the motivation for excellence is "so that the nation constantly rises to higher levels. . . ."

Enacted during a declared emergency in which the government perceived threats to national unity and integrity, but also in the same period in which Auroville was being presented by the government to UNESCO for funding, the duties provide a further clue to the "religion" as the ultimate concern, expressed in the amended Constitution. As the state approached Auroville, then, in terms of its own ultimate concern, the unity and integrity of a "Sovereign, Socialist, Democratic Republic," the state's interest in Auroville was ultimately in how it would promote its own "religion," which Baird has called the Constitutional religious model. This model, he points out, ignores completely certain traditional concepts such as karma and rebirth or the inequalities in the theory behind the caste system.[11]

Likewise, the Constitutional model does not assume either the traditional or the more modern concepts espoused in Aurobindo's and the Mother's theory of Reality as the evolutionary Becoming of the Supermind. Beyond a general and nineteenth and twentieth century liberal sense of human progress, its world is limited to the present and the material, with what may be an implicit recognition that human beings have something more to them that remains ambiguous and might be called "spiritual," though others might call it "psychological," "emotional," "intuitive," or even "religious." By definition, the state's affirmation of this "spiritual" element, however, would only be in the context of its own interests, of how the "spiritual" promotes its ultimate concern. General and ambiguous terms such as *spiritual* can be accommodated by the state to the extent that they serve the ultimate concern. Thus, when the state agreed that it would ensure that the goals of Auroville's Charter would be achieved, there was no indication that it understood the Charter in terms of Aurobindo's and the Mother's views of Reality in spite of the adulations that were heaped upon them both. The government understood the Charter in terms of its own more limited definition of Reality and its own ultimate concern, effectively ignoring the more specific and "spiritual" view of Aurobindo.

The government's "religion" can be seen as the basis for its proposal of the Auroville project to UNESCO and, as the project ran into difficulties, as an explicit reason why India needed to guarantee Auroville's success. India's standing among the nations and its reputation as a nation that prides itself as a world leader in the history of the promotion of international cooperation, even its aspirations as a light or "guru" to the nations, were invoked by government and Parliamentary members as reasons for ensuring Auroville's success.

Whether or not the Supreme Court had declared Auroville a "religious" organization, such an ultimate concern had almost guaranteed some government action. Yet given the history of the activist decisions of the judges of the Court in the tradition of Chief Justice Gajendragadkar and the spirit of supporters of such activism, including legal experts such as Professor Baxi, given the Court's history of supporting "progressive" government actions to "reform" religious institutions and its expansion of the realm of what is defined as "secular," given that the justices most often come from "progressive" understandings of Reality that value the modern, and given that they are sworn to promote the Constitutional model, the decision was no surprise. We hear these ideas of reform in the influential Chief Justice Gajendragadkar's plea that, "A secular rationalist who alone can help the progress of democracy is never a slave to any dogmas or reasons and he does not readily believe that any principle is absolutely true for all times, in all situations, and in all places."[12] Or, "Democracy, like the rule of law, must test every problem rationally, and scientifically, and decide upon the solution which would be to the general good of society and will help the achievement of socio-economic justice."[13] Justice P.N. Bhagwati, who sat on the Auroville case, put the ideal clearly: "The constitution makers did not wish to allow freedom of religion to become an instrument for thwarting the progress of the nation to a new social order. . . ."[14] In sum, as Dhavan has pointed out, in religion as in a number of areas, "the declarations of judges correspond very greatly to the general value orientations presented by other agencies of the government."[15] The Auroville case was no exception. The Court was clear that the nation was the ultimate concern behind its decisions, for it affirmed with the government that Auroville was in "full consonance and conformity with India's highest ideals and aspirations."

When the Indian government turned to UNESCO for support on the basis of the state's "religion," it turned to an organization with yet another "religion." Nations participated in UNESCO for a variety of reasons, but none that would compromise their own sovereignty and their own "religion." The explicit purpose that the original member states hammered out and embodied in UNESCO's Constitution made UNESCO's ultimate concern on the ideal level universal justice, liberty, peace, and human dignity. To quote its preamble again

> Since wars begin in the minds of men, it is in the minds of men that the defences of peace must be constructed; that ignorance of each other's ways and lives has been a common cause of suspicion and mistrust between the people of the world. . . . That the wide diffusion of culture and the education of humanity for justice and liberty and peace are indispensable to the dignity of man and constitute a sacred duty which all the nations must fulfil in a spirit of mutual assistance and concern.

These terms also are general enough to be ambiguous and, again, their ambiguity may also have enabled the founding nations to agree on the UNESCO Constitution, only to raise later issues in UNESCO. However, general issues relevant to UNESCO's interest in Auroville are found here, such as an emphasis on the promotion of the mutual understanding of different cultures and cooperation and education to dispel ignorance and end the denigration of others. The Preamble designates these as no less than "a sacred duty." Article 1 put its ultimate concern and the means for attaining it succinctly, "to contribute to peace and security by promoting collaboration among the nations through education, science, and culture in order to further universal respect for justice, for the rule of law, and for the human rights and fundamental freedoms which are affirmed for the people of the world, without distinction of race, sex, language or religion by the Charter of the United Nations."

The UNESCO's ultimate concern was, then, not the sovereignty, unity, integrity, or reputation of the nation of India or any nation— though the stability of India and its other members would be a penultimate concern for UNESCO's purposes—nor was it the promotion of "perfection," as Aurobindo and the Mother defined it. Even if it were true that the only way to attain UNESCO's "religion" of permanent peace and security would be to devalue the nation states, as some idealists, including Radhakrishnan, have argued, UNESCO could not consciously threaten the sovereignty of its members. That would produce a clash of ultimate concerns. Its members would not allow that, and the integrity, unity, and very existence of UNESCO would be jeopardized.[16]

For the nation of India to bring the Auroville project to UNESCO and receive its endorsement, the explicit statement of the project's intentions would have to conform to both "religions" involved, India's and UNESCO's. Ambiguity of language might have also enabled agreement, but that was not solely the case. India brought Auroville before UNESCO in terms that fit UNESCO's ultimate concern. The UNESCO endorsed the project, then, because what it heard and saw did not include discussions of the specific theories of Aurobindo and the Mother. The Mother had clearly envisioned Auroville as a chance to express Aurobindo's ideals, but India's own official interest in Auroville had already ignored their importance, except in the use of general and ambiguous terms such as *human unity, spiritual, international cooperation,* and *an international cultural township.*

Using this stipulative definition, then, at least three "religions" as ultimate concerns are represented in the Auroville case: Aurobindo's and the Mother's, India's, and UNESCO's. Ambiguity in the use of terms functioned to enable these three "religions" to bring Auroville to its status as a "project," managed by the "secular state" and endorsed by UNESCO. The "religion" of the "secular state" was the triumphant one. As the "sovereign," the state has the power and the authority officially given to it by the people of India to legally dispose of institutions within it by defining the nature of those institutions ("religious" or not, legal or not, worthy or not). The state also includes the institutions for doing this (the Parliament and the courts) and the means to enforce its decisions (the military, police, courts, educational institutions, etc.). Auroville thus became the property and project of the state, functioning to the extent that it supports the state's "religion." The other "religions" could function within the state's ultimate concern, to the extent that they promote it or, at least, did not threaten it.

Real, Legal, and Civil "Religion"

As with any nation, the state of India and its organs cannot settle for stipulative definitions. By necessity, government decisions must do more than clarify communication. They must decide issues that have practical consequences, while doing so in light of the "religion," that is, the ultimate concern, of the state. One can hope this will take place with clarity of communication as well, but that is not an absolute requirement. Ambiguity may function to support, at least temporarily, the integrity and unity of a nation.

Thus, the Supreme Court was required to decide whether or not the government takeover was constitutional. This could have resulted in a number of solutions within the Constitutional model. Auroville could have been legally declared a "religious institution," with the state exercising its constitutional right to regulate and restrict "any economic, financial, political or other secular activity which may be associated with religious practice." The Court could decide that legally what was being regulated or restricted by the state was the "secular, etc." activity associated with "religion." As we have seen, this was, in fact, the minority opinion of Justice Reddy in the Auroville case. Auroville, he said, was a "secular" activity of the Sri Aurobindo Society, which was a "religious organization." The burden for the Court under this approach is to legally define the activity in question as "secular" rather than define the institution as such, a task the Court frequently has done before.

The majority opinion expressed a second option. It declared that Auroville was not a "religious institution" and the Sri Aurobindo Society was not a "religious organization." On that basis, the state could fully regulate both. However, the majority opinion went further and legally defined the very *Weltanschauung* of Aurobindo and the Mother as "secular," calling it a "philosophy" and citing as proof that it was not "religious," the fact that it was inclusive and universalist.

Legal definitions, like stipulative definitions, are thus functional, but their purpose is to enable a state to establish and maintain its ultimate concern. It is the fact that their goal is to promote an ultimate concern which differs from the purpose of stipulative definitions, and which, in particular legal, political, and national circumstances, may decide a term's and its designates' fates. To declare Auroville or "Aurobindoism" a "religion" stipulatively may clarify analysis, but to declare them legally so will have economic, social, legal, and managerial ramifications, as declaring them legally "secular" did for Auroville, the Sri Aurobindo Society, and the "philosophy" of Aurobindo. Ideally, one could hope that the result of such a legal decision would be a legal definition in agreement with the corresponding "real" definition, but whether or not that ought to be expected would depend on how one defines such relationships. It moves one into discussions of the relationships between what is legal and what is moral, which are only settled in terms of one's own "religion," defined stipulatively as ultimate concern again.

In the case of Auroville, we see a definitional pattern that could have national consequences. Larson's helpful discussion of Indian "civil religion" as "Neo-Hindu" and credited to Gandhi and Nehru as "the loose conglomeration of Neo-Hindu notions and liberal-democratic-cum-socialist ideas"[17] that we have seen is particularly embodied in the speeches and writings of Radhakrishnan, is apparent in the Auroville case. Is the problem then not the term *secular* in itself, but its use without clear definitions while expecting agreement because the ambiguous term is used? Of the two strands of meaning represented by Nehru and Radhakrishnan, the Nehruvian definition appears to be taking a back seat to that of Radhakrishnan and, thus, the legal definition of "secular" defines it more as "Neo-Hindu," or more precisely, "Neo-Advaitin," rather than as state "neutrality" toward all religious positions.

In the process of defining the state, one of the interesting challenges the Indian courts, particularly the Supreme Court, have taken up, is to define "Hinduism" as a legal category. Article 25 of the Constitution has required this. It refers to "Hindu religious institutions" in particular, and in "Explanation II" defines "Hindu" for legal purposes "as including a reference to persons professing the Sikh, Jaina or Buddhist religion." Baird argues that this Constitutional language "suggests that *as religions* these are distinguishable from 'Hinduism' *as a religion*, but that *before the law* they *are* to be included within the category of 'Hindu.'"[18] Baird traces two general challenges the Indian courts have accepted regarding the definition of a "Hindu." First, they have been required to decide whether certain movements fall within the legal definition of "Hinduism" so that laws for "Hindus" apply to them, without the Courts attempting to determine whether or not the movements are actually Hindu religiously. Second, however, he also looks at cases where both the high courts and the Supreme Court have attempted to determine if a movement is part of religious "Hinduism."[19]

Baird observes that the key to the definition of "Hinduism" in judicial discourse is the characterization and now legal declaration that it is inclusive. "That which had been the obstacle to constructing a model of Hinduism which would fit the concrete data is turned into one of its major characteristics—it is inclusive."[20] As we have seen, this is one of its distinctive features according to Radhakrishnan's "Neo-Advaitin" model. And, as Derrett has shown, the Court relies on Radhakrishnan and other authorities, as well as on texts such as the *Bhagavad-gita*, which are interpreted by "Neo-Hindus" as "inclusive" to discuss Hindu religion.[21] Elsewhere, in an article appropriately entitled "'Hindu': a Definition Wanted for the Purpose of Applying a Personal Law," Derrett argues that it is the Court that has "given voice" to this characteristic. "In a sense the State has put its weight behind the *Gita* itself."[22] And in doing so it has taken one position within the variety of historical options subsumed under the label "Hinduism," the "Neo-Advaitin" definition of "Hinduism," and legally enforced it as "the Hindu" position. Galanter sees this redefinition of "Hinduism" as Constitutional as well. As he puts it, "In crucial respects the Constitution *is* a charter for the reform of Hinduism."[23] And, he argues, the process of "reforming" "Hinduism" was, and continues to be, accepted freely by Gajendragadkar, as by other judges, "because he is confident of his grasp of the 'true teachings' of Hinduism" to which all who call themselves "Hindus" might not agree.[24]

Yet, the legally defined characteristic of "Hinduism" as inclusive in the Neo-Advaitin sense has not universally been a successful argument before Indian courts when other issues related to the state were concerned. Baird points to the specific use of such an argument in the case of "Mahab Chandra Bandopadhya and others v. State of West Bengal," in which the Ramakrishna Mission argued successfully that it was not "Hindu" and, thus, it was a minority religion not subject to state restrictions placed on educational appointments by "The West Bengal College Teachers (Security and Service) Act, 1975." As a result of the decision, the Mission fell under Article 30 (1) of the Indian Constitution: "All minorities, whether based on religion or language, shall have the right to estab-

lish and administer educational institutions of their choice." The
state argued specifically on the basis of inclusivism and that the
teachings of Ramakrishna and Swami Vivekananda were inclusivist. The Court rejected the argument by citing a grander inclusivism. Ironically, after quoting a previous Supreme Court judgment, which in the original case actually cited Ramakrishna and
Swami Vivekananda's teachings as "Hindu religion flowered in its
most attractive, progressive and dynamic form," the Justice passed
on to other issues of teaching and practice, declaring "Ramakrish-
naism" a "World Religion." Other interests entered into the
Court's deliberations, which even set this mark of "Hinduism"
aside as a definitive characteristic.[25] Baird, concludes, however, "in
the light of Supreme Court statements on Hinduism as a religious
category, it is difficult to see the Supreme Court affirming this decision."[26]

Whether it will reach the Supreme Court is unclear. Yet the
Auroville case indicates that "inclusivism" can be used on both
sides of the argument over whether a system of thought and practice is in itself a "religion." The majority opinion declared that the
inclusiveness of Aurobindo's thought and practice indicates it is
not a "religion." Certainly it could not be a section of "Hinduism"
for which inclusivism is a defining characteristic in other cases. In
the Auroville case, such inclusiveness put Aurobindo's thought and
practice in the realm of the legal definition of the "secular," but in
other cases the characteristic of "inclusivism" would have included
it under the legal definition of "Hinduism."

Because of this ambiguity around inclusivism, the Court
agreed with Radhakrishnan's definition of a "secular state" as a
state that can promote a "religion of the spirit." Not only does this
promote the "reform" of Hinduism as Derrett and Galanter argue,
but it declares the "Civil Religion" of the state as "Neo-Hindu," as
Larson points out. The definition of "secularism" is not that of
"religious neutrality," as credited to Nehru. The predominant discourse of "secularism" then is the discourse of a "Neo-Hindu"
state. The problems with the term *secularism* thus are problems
not of "tolerance" but of the identification of such with the "inclusivism" that is "Neo-Hindu." Nandy's objection would not be
against "secularism" as a term, but against this particular "Neo-
Hindu," even "Neo-Advaitin," definition of it.[27]

Though Aurobindo's and the Mother's thought is not
"Advaitin," many in influential government positions as good
"Civil Religionists," or possibly even as "Neo-Advaitins" them-

selves, see it as so. It shares with the "Neo-Advaitin" position the belief in the Divine within and the inclusivism and universalism that Radhakrishnan's position espouses. It is a subordinating form of inclusivism that accepts other positions when they are understood in its own terms. Thus, a state that defines "secularism" in terms of this "Neo-Hindu" position can ensure the success and even promote the *Weltanschauung* of Aurobindo, particularly if there is ambiguity about the relationship of Aurobindo's and the Mother's teachings to the "Neo-Advaitin" position. When members of Parliament recommend that the Integral Yoga of Aurobindo be propagated by the state throughout India and the world, they are assuming this definition of the "Indian secular state." Since they may not be interested in, find significant, or even be aware of the distinctions between the thought of Sri Aurobindo and the "Neo-Advaita" of Radhakrishnan, it is the promotion of the Civil Religion that is in mind. If they fully accept Radhakrishnan's position, any differences would be insignificant, or unreal, just as Radhakrishnan believed were those between himself and Nehru.

As we have seen, Aurobindo, however, would not have ignored the differences between himself and others. He had no compunctions about criticizing Indian and "Neo-Hindu" cultural heros. Though Radhakrishnan interpreted "Buddhism" as being in essential agreement with "Hinduism," and the Buddha as a crypto-Vedantin,[28] Aurobindo criticized "Buddhism" for its negative valuation of the world and accused it of "disturbing the balance" of Indian thought by emphasizing world negation. He also taught that the Buddha's teachings indicate the Buddha himself had not attained "a complete realization." Aurobindo criticized the eighth-century thinker Shankara, who has become another Indian cultural hero in the modern period, especially for "Neo-Advaita" and Indian Civil Religion. Shankara, he said, "weighed the tradition down" with his teaching of world negation, a position Shankara came to by an overemphasis on reason. He criticized Civil Religion's modern saint, Mahatma Gandhi, because, he said, *satyagraha* was merely a limited "mental theory," hardly worth attention. He rejected the emphasis of another modern cultural hero and evangelist for "Neo-Advaita," Swami Vivekananda, on active service as a "universal ideal."[29] As such, Aurobindo expressed what he believed was his higher understanding of these positions and was clearly not hesitant to criticize other viewpoints. The subordinating nature of his inclusivism was in the foreground.

Radhakrishnan's "Neo-Advaita," therefore, was being used in

the discourse of national governmental, legislative, and judicial leadership to define both "Hinduism" and "secular." Radhakrishnan himself did so. He could speak of "the Hindu view" and the "secular" one with the same definition for both. Such a discourse could be used passively, or it could be used aggressively, as it is by Hindu nationalist groups to apparently subsume other positions while believing that what is actually happening is helping these other positions see the truth in them.

In the midst of this discourse, a township named Auroville became another means through which the government promoted its "Civil Religion," its ultimate concern. Beginning with a cultural hero and freedom fighter who was taken to represent India and its ideals, who was known throughout the world as a "Maha-yogi," and who, with the Mother and the resultant institutions, was seen as an advocate of "secularism" as "Civil Religion," the state established its role in the promotion of an institution meant to further his vision. The apparatus of the state declared that Auroville coincides with the purposes of "secularism" and the state's ultimate concern. The UNESCO, on the basis of the State's interpretation of these goals, legitimized the state's interests, and many of the followers of Aurobindo and the Mother have rejoiced in that process, even declaring that state management ultimately happened at the Mother's direction, though they had hoped it was temporary.

On the one hand, it appears that the state has agreed to promote one position above the many that exist in India. The state had declared that this position, as well as its resulting institutions, was not a "religion." It was, in some ambiguous way, more than material or physical, however. The politically correct designation was another ambiguous term, *spiritual*. The Mother had used this term to refer to those teachings that accepted Aurobindo's *Weltanschauung* and were, therefore, not "religious." The term had been used freely with full ambiguity in Parliamentary discussions and by the Supreme Court, and at times it functioned as the term *religion* had previously, before the Supreme Court declared that "religion" was an inappropriate designation for both Aurobindo's thought and Auroville. Many speakers went further and encouraged the government to promote Aurobindo and the Mother's teachings beyond Auroville. Accepting them as the Civil Religion, assuming their agreement with that "Neo-Advaita," enabled their excitement for what others might see as the promotion of one position over others.

On the other hand, the ambiguities that accompanied the process thus far may continue, though one hopes the result will at least and in spite of the naysayers in Parliament be human unity, international cooperation, and peace, even if not that envisioned by Sri Aurobindo. As for the Indian "secular state," the Auroville case indicates that the meaning of the phrase for India is whatever the state and its institutions define it to be, though the Civil Religion called "Neo-Advaita" is currently the key to that definition.

Notes

Chapter 1

1. The Amendment was criticized, and in some circles continues to be, because of its timing and its multiple, and some say questionable, intentions. For one sustained criticism, see Rajeev Dhavan, *The Amendment: Conspiracy or Revolution* (Allahabad: Wheeler, 1978).

2. The Amendment, which covered twenty-two printed pages and consisted of fifty-nine clauses, was actually longer than the Indian Constitution itself.

3. Section 2 of the Amendment read as follows:

2. *Amendment to the Preamble.* In the Preamble to the Constitution,—

(a) for the words "SOVEREIGN DEMOCRATIC REPUBLIC," the words "SOVEREIGN SOCIALIST SECULAR DEMOCRATIC REPUBLIC" shall be substituted; and

(b) for the words "unity of the Nation," the words "unity and integrity of the Nation" shall be substituted.

4. Robert D. Baird, "'Secular State' and the Indian Constitution," in Robert D. Baird, *Essays in the History of Religions* (New York: Peter Lang, 1991), p. 157.

5. V.P. Luthera. *The Concept of the Secular State and India* (Calcutta: Oxford University Press, 1964), pp. vii–viii.

6. *Ibid.*, p. 15.

7. *Ibid.*, p. 155.

8. Donald Eugene Smith, *India as a Secular State* (Princeton: Princeton University Press, 1963), p. 110n.

9. *Ibid.*, p.4.

10. *Ibid.*, p. 500.

11. See his full discussion in Baird, "'Secular State,'" pp. 147–55. See also his other essays on this subject brought together in *Essays in the History of Religions* and "On Defining 'Hinduism' as a Religious and Legal Category" in Robert D. Baird, ed., *Religion and Law in Independent India* (Delhi: Manohar, 1993), pp. 41–58.

12. *Ibid.*, p. 142.

13. *Ibid.*, p. 147.

14. Gerald James Larson, *India's Agony over Religion* (Albany: State University of New York Press, 1995), p. 191.

15. Upendra Baxi, "Secularism: Real and Pseudo," in M.M. Sankhdher, ed, *Secularism in India: Dilemmas and Challenges* (New Delhi: Deep & Deep Pub., 1992), p. 93.

16. *Ibid.*, p. 107. Baxi sees the courts as social and political entities, not as elite legal institutions, and thus urges the courts to promote distributive and populist justice. This is more fully argued in Upendra Baxi, *The Indian Supreme Court and Politics* (Lucknow: Eastern Book Co., 1980).

17. H.V. Seshadri, "Secularism: An Insight," in M.M. Sankhdher, p. 149.

18. *Ibid.*, pp. 150–52.

19. K.S. Sudarshan, "Secularism and Distortions," in M.M. Sankhdher, p. 189.

20. The full text of Articles 25 and 26 of the Constitution is:

25. (1) Subject to public order, morality and health and to the other provisions of this Part, all persons are equally entitled to freedom of conscience and the right freely to profess, practise and propagate religion.

(2) Nothing in this article shall affect the operation of any existing law or prevent the State from making any law—

(a) regulating or restricting any economic, financial, political or other secular activity which may be associated with religious practise;

(b) providing for social welfare and reform or the throwing open of Hindu religious institutions of a public character to all classes and sections of Hindus.

Explanation I.—The wearing and carrying of *kirpans* shall be deemed to be included in the profession of Sikh religion.

Explanation II.—In sub-clause (b) of clause (2), the reference to Hindus shall be construed as including reference to persons professing the Sikh, Jaina or Buddhist religion, and the reference to Hindu religious institutions shall be construed accordingly.

26. Subject to public order, morality and health, every religious denomination or any section thereof shall have the right—

(a) to establish and maintain institutions for religious and charitable purposes;

(b) to manage its own affairs in matters of religion;

(c) to own and acquire movable and immovable property; and

(d) to administer such property in accordance with law.

21. Robert D. Baird, "Religion and the Secular: Categories for Religious Change in Independent India," in Baird, *Essays in the History of Religions*, p. 98.

22. In *Ibid.*, pp. 95–118.

23. *Ibid.*

24. Gerald James Larson, pp. 191–203.

25. Jawaharlal Nehru, *Toward Freedom: The Autobiography of Jawaharlal Nehru* (Boston: Beacon Press, 1958), p. 71. This was first published in 1941.

26. For sustained arguments regarding the nature and working of Radhakrishnan's position and its understanding and treatment of other religious positions, see Robert N. Minor, "Sarvepalli Radhakrishnan on the Nature of 'Hindu' Tolerance," *The Journal of the American Academy of Religion*, L, No. 2 (June 1982), 275–90, and Robert N. Minor, "Sarvepalli Radhakrishnan and Religious Pluralism," *Studia Missionalia*, XLII (1993), pp. 307–27.

27. I have argued fully this and the arguments that follow with complete citations in Robert N. Minor, *Radhakrishnan: A Religious Biography* (Albany: State University of New York Press, 1987), pp. 101–27.

28. Note, for example, the words of Rajendra Prasad, the Assembly President, about Radhakrishnan when Radhakrishnan resigned from the Constituent Assembly: *Indian Constituent Assembly Debates. Official Report* (Delhi: Manager of Publications, 1946–1950), IX, p. 676.

29. Quoted in Minor, *Radhakrishnan: A Religious Biography*, p. 92. See the full discussion there for the basis of this analysis.

30. *Indian Constituent Assembly Debates*, IV, p. 772.

31. For a full discussion, see Minor, *Radhakrishnan: A Religious Biography*, pp. 115–27.

32. On how Radhakrishnan progressively changed the designation of his own religious position without changing the position itself, see Robert N. Minor, "Sarvepalli Radhakrishnan and 'Hinduism' Defined and Defended," in Robert D. Baird, ed., *Religion in Modern India*, 3d rev. ed (Delhi: Manohar, 1995), pp. 480–514.

33. Minor, *Radhakrishnan: A Religious Biography*, p. 121.

34. S. Radhakrishnan, *President Radhakrishnan's Speeches and Writings. May 1962–May 1964* (New Delhi: Ministry of Information and Broadcasting, Government of India, 1965), p. 146.

35. S. Radhakrishnan, *Recovery of Faith* (Delhi: Hind Pocket Books, 1967), pp. 186–87. This was originally published in 1955 when he was vice president. For fuller discussions, see note 26 earlier. Robert N. Minor, "S. Radhakrishnan and Religious Pluralism," refers to various analyses of his inclusivism, which scholars have called "inclusivism of the hierarchic, subordinating type," "a form of religious self-assertion," and "that of a superior who tolerates the weaknesses of an inferior." (pp. 309–10)

36. See Minor, *Radhakrishnan: A Religious Biography*, pp. 71–73.

37. K.S. Sudarshan, "Secularism and Distortions," p. 191.

38. H.V. Seshadri, "Secularism: An Insight," p. 150.

39. K.S. Sudarshan, "Secularism and Distortions," pp. 190–91.

40. Rajeev Dhavan, *The Amendment*, Appendix VI, gives their full "new" proposals. See p. 199.

41. Minor, "Sarvepalli Radhakrishnan and Religious Pluralism," pp. 326–27.

42. R. David Kaylor, "Radhakrishnan as Proponent and Critic of Religion," *Indian Philosophical Annual* XII (1977–78), p. 63.

43. Minor, "Sarvepalli Radhakrishnan and Religious Pluralism," p. 327.

44. Gerald James Larson, p. 199.

45. See, for example, Robert D. Baird, "Religion and the Legitimation of Nehru's Concept of the Secular State," in Baird, *Essays in the History of Religions*, pp. 119–39.

46. Nehru, *Toward Freedom*, p. 72.

47. *Ibid.*, p. 240. See also his comments on p. 237.

48. *Ibid.*, p. 292.

49. Jawaharlal Nehru, *Independence and After: A Collection of Speeches, 1946–1949* (New York: The John Day Company, 1950), p. 122.

50. Baird, "Religion and the Legitimation of Nehru's Concept of the Secular State," p. 133.

51. Jawaharlal Nehru, *The Discovery of India* (New York: The John Day Company, 1946), p. 254.

52. Robert N. Minor, "Radhakrishnan as Advocate of the Class/Caste System as a Universal Religio-Social System," *International Journal of Hindu Studies* I, No. 2 (August 1997), pp. 386–400.

53. One could, for example, find no position more clearly opposed to any form of monism or Advaita than that of the well-known thirteenth-century South Indian Dvaita philosopher and outspoken critic of Advaita, Madhva, but Radhakrishnan either ignores Madhva or subordinates him in his inclusivism. See Minor, "Sarvepalli Radhakrishnan and Religious Pluralism," pp. 317–18.

54. See Minor, *Radhakrishnan: A Religious Biography*, pp. 111–13.

55. Marc Galanter, "Hinduism, Secularism, and the Indian Judiciary," in Marc Galanter, *Law and Society in Modern India* (Delhi: Oxford University Press, 1989), pp. 237–58, argues that the Supreme Court's judgments are attempts to actively reform "Hinduism."

56. Rajeev Dhavan, "Introduction," in *ibid.*, xxv. "However, his ideas were never critically assailed or evaluated. Gajendragadkar's status as Chief Justice of India, his jurisprudence and his extra-judicial pronouncements acquired an *ex cathedra* status and character."

57. Robert D. Baird, "Mr. Justice Gajendragadkar and the Religion of the Indian Secular State," in Baird, *Essays in the History of Religions*, pp. 225–47.

58. P.B. Gajendragadkar, *Secularism and the Constitution of India* (Bombay: Bombay University Press, 1971), p. 120. Gajendragadkar was

familiar with Smith's *India as a Secular State*, but prefers to think of Smith's definition as the product of "Western," not "Indian," traditions (pp. 4–23).

59. *Ibid.*, p. 42.

60. *Ibid.*, p. 101. Note that Gajendragadkar accepts the thought of Radhakrishnan as the basis for his definition of "Hinduism" and "Hindu thought," but that the only relevant concept for his own purposes of defining "secularism" is the concept of "tolerance."

61. *Ibid.*, p. 55.

62. *Ibid.*, p. 89.

63. *Ibid.*, p. 49. This is what Baird ("Mr. Justice Gajendragadkar and the Religion of the Indian Secular State," p. 226) identifies as Gajendragadkar's ideal view of "religion": "relegated to personal experience and metaphysical speculation severed from political and economic expressions."

64. V.R. Krishna Iyer, *Law and the People: A Collection of Essays* (New Delhi: People's Publishing House, 1972), p. 19. See also his *Indian Secularism: Proclamation Versus Performance and a Viable Philosophy* (Delhi, 1975); *Law and Religion* (New Delhi: Deep and Deep, 1984); and *Social Mission of Law* (Bombay: Orient Longman, 1972).

Chapter 2

1. For biographies of Sri Aurobindo, see especially Peter Heehs, *Sri Aurobindo: A Brief Biography* (Delhi: Oxford University Press, 1989) and K.R. Srinivasa Iyengar, *Sri Aurobindo: A Biography and a History* (4th rev. ed., Pondicherry: Sri Aurobindo Ashram Trust, 1985).

2. For an analysis of his thought in the various periods of his life, see Robert N. Minor, *Sri Aurobindo: the Perfect and the Good* (Columbia, Mo.: South Asia Books, 1978).

3. Sri Aurobindo, *Birth Centenary Library* (Pondicherry: Sri Aurobindo Ashram Trust, 1971) I, p. 47 ("New Lamps for Old," *Indu Prakash*, February 5, 1894). Hereafter, this set will be abbreviated *BCL*.

4. Quoted in Minor, *Sri Aurobindo*, p. 54.

5. *BCL.* I, p. 66.

6. *Ibid.*, p. 902.

7. *Ibid.*, p. 653 (*Bande Mataram*, January 19, 1908). For studies of the theoretical basis of his political activity, see Minor, pp. 44–99 and, among

numerous others, especially David L. Johnson, *The Religious Roots of Indian Nationalism: Aurobindo's Early Political Thought* (Calcutta: Firma K.L. Mukhopadhyay, 1974), who shows that Aurobindo's language was not merely a technique for arousing the people but flowed directly from his beliefs.

8. *Ibid.*, IV, pp. 257–97 (*Kara-Kahini*).

9. *Ibid.* II, p.7.

10. *Ibid.*, p. 10.

11. *Ibid.*, p. 386.

12. *BCL.* XXVI, p. 36. Aurobindo often spoke of himself in the third person.

13. *Ibid.*, pp. 432–33.

14. *Ibid.*, p. 430 (Letter to Joseph Baptista, January 1920).

15. See Minor, *Sri Aurobindo*, pp. 103–56. Numerous introductions to Aurobindo's fully developed thought are available. Particularly insightful are Stephen H. Phillips, *Aurobindo's Philosophy of Brahman* (Leiden: E.J. Brill, 1986); Beatrice Bruteau, *Worthy is the World: The Hindu Philosophy of Sri Aurobindo* (Rutherford, N.J.: Farleigh Dickinson University Press, 1971); and Haridas Chaudhuri, *Sri Aurobindo: Prophet of the Life Divine* (San Francisco: Cultural Integration Fellowship, 1973).

16. *BCL.* XIX, p. 1,031.

17. See Robert N. Minor, "Sri Aurobindo and Experience: Yogic and Otherwise," in Baird, ed., *Religion in Modern India*, pp. 452–79.

18. *BCL.* XVIII, p. 323.

19. *Ibid.*, p. 312.

20. *Ibid.*, pp. 464–65.

21. *Ibid.*, p. 377.

22. See Minor, "Sri Aurobindo and Experience," pp. 452–79.

23. *BCL.* XXIII, p. 509.

24. See Minor, *Sri Aurobindo*, pp. 119–21.

25. For a full discussion of the place of the guru, see Robert N. Minor, "The Guru in Vedanta: The Case of Aurobindo," in *Studies in Vedanta*, edited by S.S. Rama Rao Pappu (Delhi: Indian Book House, forthcoming).

26. *BCL.* XIX, 1,062–63.

27. *Ibid.*, p. 1,062.

28. *Ibid.*, XV, p. 127.

29. For a full discussion of Aurobindo's position toward "religion" and "the religions," see Robert N. Minor, "The Response of Sri Aurobindo and the Mother," in *Modern Indian Responses to Religious Pluralism*, edited by Harold Coward (Albany: State University of New York Press, 1987), pp. 85–104.

30. *BCL*. XIV, pp. 123–24.

31. *Ibid.*, XV, p. 543.

32. *Ibid.*, XVIII, pp. 416–17.

33. *Ibid.*, XV, p. 164.

34. *Ibid.*, XXII, p. 139. Cf. XIX, pp. 1,022, 1,023; XV, p. 249.

35. See also Robert N. Minor, "Sri Aurobindo's Integral View of Other Religions," *Religious Studies* XV, pp. 365–77.

36. *BCL*, XXII, pp. 490–91.

37. *Ibid.*, pp. 447, 483.

38. *Ibid.*, XXII, p. 150. Aurobindo approves of Vivekananda's teaching on "service" as a counterbalance to religions that only emphasize personal salvation (*BCL.*, XX, pp. 257–58), but thinks that Vivekananda goes too far by making it a universal requirement, thereby committing the usual error of religions, absolutizing one side of the truth for all.

39. *Ibid.*, XV, pp. 166–67.

40. Minor, "Sri Aurobindo's Integral View of Other Religions," p. 373.

41. *Ibid.*, p. 377.

42. *BCL*. XV, p. 554.

43. *Ibid.*, p. 214.

44. *Ibid.*, p. 555.

45. *Ibid.*, p. 544.

46. *Ibid.*, XIX, pp. 872–73.

47. *Ibid.*, pp. 865–72. Cf. XV, p. 215.

Chapter 3

1. See Minor, "Sri Aurobindo and Experience: Yogic and Otherwise," p. 473.

2. See Minor, *Sri Aurobindo*, pp. 108–12. Though he apparently kept a diary of his yogic practices before this experience, which has been published in serial form in a semiannual journal published by the Sri Aurobindo Ashram, *Sri Aurobindo: Archives and Research*, beginning in 1986 with volume 10, there is little similar documentation after this date.

3. In a letter to the Maharani of Baroda, Aurobindo speaks of his desire "to create a centre of spiritual life which shall serve as a means of bringing down the higher consciousness and making it a power not merely for 'salvation' but for a divine life upon earth." Though he may have hesitated to use the word because the traditional concept of a "retreat" seemed to be a place to escape the world permanently, he calls this "centre" an "Ashram in Pondicherry (so called for want of a better word, for it is not an Ashram of Sannyasins, but of those who want to leave all else and prepare for this rule)." *BCL* XXVII, p. 416.

4. Most of the information about the spiritual experiences of the Mother comes from Satprem's accounts of her personal conversations with him in the thirteen-volume *L'Agenda de Mere* (Paris: Institut de Recherches Evolutives). After the events described in the following chapter, not all of the Mother's followers have accepted the authenticity of all of these reports. Thus, for example, a biography of the Mother published by one party in the dispute related in the following chapter, the Sri Aurobindo Society, includes no references to Satprem's recollections: Wilfred, *The Mother: A Short Biography* (Pondicherry: Sri Aurobindo Society, 1986).
Satprem (1923–), a French disciple, was the "volatile and provocative" voice of the Aurovillians, the side opposed to the Sri Aurobindo Society side in the dispute. Allegations of an assassination attempt against him in August 1976 and eventually his expulsion from the Ashram for "anti-Ashram activities" in December 1977, as he attempted to publish *L'Agenda*, indicate his central place in the dispute as well as the negative reaction of the Society. After numerous unsuccessful attempts to get the thirteen-volume *L'Agenda* published by Ashram, Auroville, and Society presses, he founded "L'Institut de Recherches Evolutives" in Paris in July 1977 as a nonprofit organization to do so.
Without conceding anything to the Society, one major writer and member of the Aurovillian side who was a twenty-one-year resident of Auroville has later reflected on Satprem's approach. "He was not only speaking *in* Her [the Mother's] name but *for* Her. Imperceptibly, the 'for' became 'as.'" As for his later reflections on the Aurovillian's reception of Satprem's words, "Amidst the initial turbulence when the SAS [Sri

Aurobindo Society] attempted to dominate the Auroville experiment so soon after Mother's passing, Satprem became a rallying point for a confused community unprepared then to believe that those whom Mother trusted were actually doing this to us." See Savitra, "When Intensity Overtakes Integrality: A Personal Look at the Man and Myth called Satprem," *NexUS: Newsletter for the USA Centers of Sri Aurobindo and the Mother* (winter 1994–95), pp. 27–30. I, therefore, use selections from his recollections with caution when they purport to deal with issues directly related to the dispute between Satprem and the Society.

5. Some selections from a journal she kept during this period are published in "Prayers and Meditations," found in volume 1 of The Mother, *Collected Works* (Pondicherry: Sri Aurobindo Ashram, 1978).

6. See, for example, *BCL.*, XXV, pp. 55–57.

7. *Ibid.*, XXVI, p. 455.

8. *Ibid.*, p. 458.

9. *Ibid.*, p. 459.

10. *Ibid.*, XXV, p. 241.

11. *Ibid.*, pp. 229–30.

12. *Ibid.*, XXVI, pp. 511–12.

13. *Ibid.*, XXV, p. 48.

14. *Ibid.*, p. 49.

15. *Ibid.*, I, p. 65.

16. *Ibid.*, XXV, p. 48.

17. *Ibid.*, pp. 139–63.

18. The Mother, *Collected Works* IX, p. 354.

19. *Ibid.*

20. *Ibid.*, X, p. 96.

21. *Ibid.*

22. *Ibid.*, VIII, p. 147; III, p. 83.

23. *Ibid.*, XV, p. 31.

24. *Ibid.*, III, p. 76; III, p. 213. For one close disciple's account of her definition of "religion," see *Auroville References in Mother's Agenda* (Auroville: Auroville Press, n.d.), p. 200. On exclusivity as her main critique of "religions," see p. 161.

25. *Ibid.*, XV, p. 32; XII, p. 310.

26. *Ibid.*

27. *Ibid.*, II, p. 162.

28. *Ibid.* XV, pp. 33–34.

29. *Ibid.*, XI, p. 133.

30. Originally called the "Sri Aurobindo International University Centre," its name was changed to this in 1959.

31. The Mother, *Collected Works* XII, p. 93.

32. See, for example, Satprem's recollections in *Auroville References in Mother's Agenda*, pp. 7–10. This single volume contains all of the references to Auroville in both the original thirteen-volume French *L' Agenda de Mere* (Paris: Institut de Recherches Evolutives) and in those volumes translated into English as *Mother's Agenda* (New York: Institute for Evolutionary Research).

33. The Mother, *Collected Works* XIII, p. 257.

34. *Ibid.*, p. 202.

35. *Auroville References in Mother's Agenda*, p. 34. Emphasis in the original.

36. The Mother, *Collected Works*, p. 197. Cf. p. 207.

37. *Ibid.*, pp. 51–52.

38. *Ibid.*, p. 274.

39. The Mother, *Collected Works.*, XIII, p. 198. See also the Mother's discussion in *Auroville References in Mother's Agenda*, pp. 43–44.

40. *Auroville References in Mother's Agenda*, pp. 62–63.

41. *Ibid.*, p. 65.

42. The Mother, *Collected Works*, XIII, pp. 199–201.

43. *Auroville References in Mother's Agenda*, p. 79.

44. *Ibid.*, pp. 76–77. Note here and at p. 91, the Mother objects to these changes being made without her approval. Satprem, in The *Agenda*, indicates that she took the controversy over this term as a portent of the controversy to come after her death, "But that gave me a very accurate picture of what would happen if for some reason I weren't here any more. . . . Each one would speak in my name. . . . (*Mother laughs*) It would be dreadful!"

45. The Mother, *Collected Works* XIII, p. 208.

46. *Ibid.,* p. 224.

47. *Ibid.,* pp. 211, 194.

48. *Ibid.,* p. 207.

49. *Ibid.,* pp. 227, 228.

50. *Auroville References in Mother's Agenda,* p. 204.

51. The Mother, *Collected Works* XIII, p. 197.

52. *Ibid.,* p. 195.

53. *Ibid.,* p. 212. Satprem (*Auroville References in Mother's Agenda,* pp. 196–98) records that the Mother originally wrote "a life essentially religious." When a disciple suggested that she substitute the word "spiritual" for "religious" because the Mother also says "no religions," the Mother rejected the substitution because its connotation in French, she said, is the rejection of matter. "I used 'religious' in the sense of a 'life essentially preoccupied with the discovery of or search for the Divine.'" She settled, instead, on the word "divine."

54. *Ibid.* Emphasis is in the original.

55. *Auroville References in Mother's Agenda,* p. 90. Cf. p. 149.

56. *Ibid.,* p. 150. Emphasis is in the original. In a footnote to this quotation, the volume's editors are quick to point out in words that reflect the bitter struggle over the issue, that this remembrance substantiates their position against the Sri Aurobindo Society in the later court case discussed later. "Thus, after Mother's passing the 'owners' of Auroville declared, that they constituted a 'religious institution,' thus compounding spiritual fraud with financial double-dealing. Not a single voice was raised in the Sri Aurobindo Ashram when those people dared to declare in front of the Indian courts that Sri Aurobindo's was a 'religious' teaching."

Chapter 4

1. The Mother, *Collected Works,* XIII, p. 195.

2. *Ibid.,* p. 207.

3. *Ibid.,* p. 225.

4. These twenty-two meetings were tape-recorded and are in *ibid.,* pp. 317–53.

5. *Ibid.*, p. 234.

6. *Ibid.*, p. 202.

7. *Ibid.*, p. 203.

8. *Ibid.*, p. 206.

9. *Ibid.*, p. 208.

10. *Ibid.*, pp. 213–14. According to the account of the construction of this list recorded in *Auroville References in Mother's Agenda*, p. 207, the Mother commented, "The idea is this: 'We come to Auroville to escape from the social and moral rules that are practised artificially everywhere, but it is not to give license to the satisfaction of all desires: it is to rise above desires into a truer consciousness.'"

11. *Ibid.*, pp. 219, 223. See also *Auroville References in Mother's Agenda*, pp. 110, 187.

12. *Ibid.*, p. 354.

13. *Auroville References in Mother's Agenda*, p. 79.

14. The Mother, *Collected Works*, p. 242.

15. *Ibid.*, p. 245. See her 1970 reference to drug use in Auroville in *Auroville References in Mother's Agenda*, p. 181.

16. *Ibid.*, p. 267.

17. *Ibid.*, pp. 245–46.

18. *Ibid.*, pp. 275–76. Cf. p. 195. Cf. *Auroville References in Mother's Agenda*, pp. 82–84.

19. *Ibid.*, p. 277. See *Auroville References in Mother's Agenda*, pp. 84–85.

20. *Ibid.*

21. *Ibid.*, p. 317.

22. The full purpose of the Society as stated in the documents registering it as such an institution is the carrying out of the following in and outside of India:
(i) To make known to the members of the public in general: the aims and ideals of Sri Aurobindo and the Mother, their system of integral yoga and to work for its fulfilment in all possible ways and for the attainment of a spiritualised society as envisaged by Sri Aurobindo;
(ii) To train selected students and teachers from all over the world in the integral system of education, i.e. spiritual, psychic, mental, vital and physical;

(iii) To help in cash and/or kind by way of donations, gifts, subsidies and in also other ways in the all round development of Sri Aurobindo International Centre of Education and to help similar centres of education;

(iv) To establish study groups, libraries, Ashrams, and other institutions, centres, branches and societies for study and practice of integral yoga of Sri Aurobindo and the Mother and to help the existing ones;

(v) To establish centres of physical culture, sports and volunteer organizations for inculcating and promoting the spirit of discipline, co-operation and service to others and to undertake activities for promotion of health and bodily perfection;

(vi) To organise, encourage, promote and assist in the study, research and pursuit of science, literature and fine arts;

(vii) To acquire, purchase, build, construct or take on lease or in exchange or hire any movable or immovable property, or gifts or privileges; and

(viii) Generally to do all other acts, deeds and things necessary, conducive, suitable or incidental to or for the attainment of the above objects or any of them or part of them.

23. *Auroville References in Mother's Agenda*, p. 50.

24. See previous note 4.

25. See her deliberations, which she taught were actually revelations from higher consciousness, in *Collected Works* XIII, pp. 283–316.

26. Bill Sullivan, "On Matrimandir: What About this Watertank?," *Auroville Review*, no. 6 (summer/fall 1982), p. 3.

27. Ruud Lohman, *A House for the Third Millennium: Essays on Matrimandir* (Pondicherry: Ruud Lohman, 1986), pp. 62–63.

28. The Mother, *Collected Works*, XIII, pp. 229–33.

29. Ruud Lohman, p. 60. The emphasis is in the original. This coincides with my own interviews with foreign nationals who had lived in Auroville. The interest in and passion for the project continued among former and present residents into the 1990s.

30. Regarding the last year of the Mother's life, there is controversy among those who were on the scene. Both its degree and nature are difficult to verify objectively, given the highly emotionally charged claims and counterclaims. Allegations were made against Ashram authorities regarding their treatment of the Mother during this period, including that she was under virtual "imprisonment" by Ashram authorities. Satprem's accounts of her conversations with him picture her as being critical of the Ashram leaders and the heads of both the Sri Aurobindo Society, Navajata, and Sri Aurobindo Action. See *Mother's Agenda*, XIII. Members of the Society and the Ashram deny such allegations.

31. For an analysis of succession issues in terms of Max Weber's classic concept of charisma and its routinization, see Robert N. Minor, "Nonroutinized Charisma: The Case of Aurobindo and Auroville," in *Religion in South Asia: Essays in Honor of Robert Frykenberg* (Delhi, forthcoming).

32. Adilakshmi, *Mother Meera* (Thalheim, Germany: Mother Meera Publications, 1987), p. 14. For her accounts of similar visionary messages, see also pp. 20, 24, 29, 38.

33. For example, one devotee drawn to Mother Meera, Andrew Harvey, writes that one reason he followed her was "being a spiritual beginner, I needed a Master in the body. I prayed that I should meet Someone." (*Ibid.*, p. 115)

34. See "Germany's Meera," *Hinduism Today*, XI, no. 4 (April 1989), pp. 1, 18.

35. Larry D. Shinn, "Auroville: A Fragmented Mandala," p. 10; an unpublished paper that is a revision of a presentation to the Annual Meeting of the American Academy of Religion, October 30, 1976, based upon the author's two-month stay in Auroville in 1975.

36. Historical information for this chapter is taken from contemporary documents, government documents and records, court documents, newspaper accounts, eyewitness interviews, copies of documents obtained from participants, and published positions on the various sides of the controversies narrated here. One account from the side of the Aurovillians, which I have found to be accurate in its documentation, is Savitra, *Auroville: Sun-Word Rising* (Auroville: The Community of Auroville, 1980).

37. Navajata, "Auroville—A Model of Human Unity," in *All Indian Conference on the Relevance of Sri Aurobindo Today, 1975: Souvenir Volume*, (Calcutta: Sri Aurobindo Samiti, 1975), p. 99. "Human unity" is an often repeated phrase in the speech. See pp. 95, 96, 100, 102.

38. *Ibid.*, p. 87.

39. *Ibid.*, p. 99.

40. *Ibid*, p. 96. "Aurovillians are trying to find their own group soul— a group-soul of the people dedicated to realising and manifesting the Divine, the Truth, the Perfect Consciousness." (p. 100)

41. Savitra, *Auroville: The First Six Years, 1968–74* (Auroville: Auropublications, 1974), p. 4.

42. Savitra, *Auroville: Sun-Word Rising*, pp. 104–5.

43. UNESCO, *Records of the General Conference: Eighteenth Session* (Paris: UNESCO, 1974), II, p. 140; IV, p. 153.

44. Quoted in Savitra, *Auroville: Sun-Word Rising*, p. 123.

45. Quoted in *ibid.*, p. 127.

46. From the document, which is also quoted in *ibid.*, p. 148.

47. Sri Aurobindo Society Rejoinder Affidavit, December 2, 1975, filed in the Second Additional Munsiff's Court, Pondicherry. Excerpts are quoted in *ibid.*, pp. 150–51.

48. Quoted from the document. The business trust was formed by four individuals including Navajata, none of whom resided in Auroville.

49. From the letter to the Society from T.R. Thulsiram, Chartered Accountant and Auditor of the Sri Aurobindo Society, May 26, 1976, quoted in "S.P. Mittal vs. Union of India," Supreme Court, *The All India Reporter*, 1983, p. 36.

50. These charges were repeated in newspaper articles, apparently based upon the press releases of the Society. They were repeated as well by members of the Lok Sabha and Rajya Sabha in the debates over the various Auroville acts. For example, P. Ramamurti (Rajya Sabha Minister from Tamil Nadu) repeated them, "Sex crimes, smuggling and then what you call the drug-peddling are there. The students of the college there are getting corrupted. As a result of that, all sorts of things are emanating from that Society, from that particular spot. You go to Pondicherry and talk to people of Pondicherry. They will tell you these things." (*Parliamentary Debates, Rajya Sabha: Official Report*, XVI [no. 16], December 9, 1980 [New Delhi: Rajya Sabha Secretariat, 1980], p. 229).

51. Savitra, *Auroville: Sun-Word Rising*, pp. 172–74.

52. I was unable to interview any from this group. Some Aurovillians who opposed the Society felt the group's self-designation as "Neutrals" was hypocritical, for they provided an internal dispute in addition to the battle with the Society. See, for example, the articles on "The Neutrals" in the Auroville newsletter *Auroville Review*, December 1988.

53. See Savitra, *Auroville: Sun-Word Rising*, pp. 206–8, for the Aurovillian's position.

54. At different stages in the ensuing period international groups of followers responded in a variety of ways. For example, the Sri Aurobindo Centre in Bell Street, London, officially stopped contributing either to the Society or the Pour Tous fund. In their "Newsletter" of March 1981, they pointed out, "We have good friends on both sides of 'the fence.' So for the time being, and until both contenders come together in harmony which we feel must inevitably happen at some time, we remain neutral and loyal to *all* our friends, looking with admiration at all the undoubted miracles that

have happened in Auroville because of the hard work and courage of many people in both Pour Tous and the Sri Aurobindo Society."

55. Quoted in Savitra, *Auroville: Sun Word Rising*, p. 209.

56. *Bharat ka Rajapatra: The Gazette of India, Extraordinary*, no. 235 (December 21, 1976), I, p. 1,803.

57. From the Committee's report, which is also extensively quoted in "S.P. Mittal vs. Union of India," pp. 37–38.

58. See the reference to this in *Parliamentary Debates: Rajya Sabha*, p. 318.

59. The Aurovillian's position is presented in Savitra, *Auroville: Sun-Word Rising*, pp. 255–74.

60. For the Aurovillians' account of these incidents, see *Collaboration*, VII, no. 1 (Fall 1980), p. 21.

61. For one brief account of these protests, see Umashanker Phadnis, "Clean Up the Mess in Auroville," *The Overseas Hindustan Times* (July 12, 1986), p. 7.

62. See, for example, *Auroville Today*, no. 17 (May 1990), p. 1.

Chapter 5

1. *Parliamentary Debates: Rajya Sabha, Official Report* (New Delhi Rajya Sabha Secretariat, 1980), CXVI, no. 16 (December 9, 1980), p. 301. Hereafter cited as *Rajya Sabha Debates*.

2. *Toward Freedom*, p. 35.

3. *The Discovery of India*, p. 86. The omissions are in the original quotation by Nehru. Cf. p. 9.

4. *Ibid.*, p. 181.

5. *Ibid.*, p. 522. Cf. p. 99.

6. For example, see S. Radhakrishnan, *President Radhakrishnan's Speeches and Writings. Second Series, May 1964—May 1967* (New Delhi: Ministry of Information and Broadcasting, Government of India, 1967), p. 3; S. Radhakrishnan *Occasional Speeches and Writings. Second Series, February 1956—February 1957.* (New Delhi: Ministry of Information and Broadcasting, Government of India, 1957), p. 189.

7. S. Radhakrishnan, *President Radhakrishnan's Speeches and Writings. May 1962—May 1964*, p. 252.

8. "Appendix: Sri Aurobindo Samiti" in *All India Conference on the Relevance of Sri Aurobindo Today, 1975: Souvenir Volume*, p. 105.

9. Fakhruddin Ali Ahmed, "Inaugural Address," in *ibid.*, p. 4.

10. D.P. Chattopadhyaya, "Introductory Address," in *ibid.*, pp. 10–11.

11. *Ibid.*, p. 11.

12. A.L. Dias, "Address of Welcome," in *ibid.*, pp. 5–6.

13. Siddhartha Shankar Ray, "Chief Minister's Address," in *ibid.*, p. 7.

14. Navajata, "Auroville—A Model of Human Unity," in *ibid.*, p. 95. Deletions and emphasis in Navajata's original quotation.

15. *Ibid.*, p. 96.

16. *Ibid.*, p. 100.

17. *Bharat ka Rajapatra: The Gazette of India, Extraordinary*, no. 45 (November 25, 1980), II, p. 1,107.

18. "The Auroville (Emergency Provisions) Act, 1980: No. 59 of 1980," in *Acts of Parliament, 1980* (New Delhi: Ministry of Law, Justice and Company Affairs, Government of India, 1980), p. 412.

19. *Ibid.*

20. *Ibid.*, pp. 412–13.

21. *Ibid.*, pp. 414–16.

22. *Ibid.*, p. 417.

23. *Lok Sabha Debates, 4th Session* (New Delhi: Lok Sabha Secretariat, 1980), X, No. 11 (December 17, 1980), p. 397. Hereafter, *Lok Sabha Debates*.

24. *Rajya Sabha Debates* (December 9, 1980), pp. 291–92.

25. *Ibid.*, pp. 293–94.

26. *Ibid.*, p. 324. Translations from the Hindi are my own.

27. *Lok Sabha Debates* (December 17, 1980), pp. 322, 405.

28. *Ibid.*, p. 375.

29. *Ibid.*, p. 380.

30. *Ibid.*, p. 347.

31. *Ibid.*, p. 348. "The irregularities in our Government's conduct are a million-fold those of Auroville. Yet the Government rules the country unchallenged."

32. *Rajya Sabha Debates* (December 9, 1980), pp. 277–78.

33. *Ibid.*, p. 339.

34. *Ibid.*, pp. 344–45.

35. *Ibid.*, p. 342.

36. *Ibid.*, p. 341.

37. *Lok Sabha Debates* (December 17, 1980), pp. 362–64.

38. *Ibid.*, p. 395.

39. *Rajya Sabha Debates* (December 9, 1980), p. 350.

40. *Ibid.*, p. 306.

41. *Ibid.*, p. 299.

42. *Ibid.*, p. 301. Note that though he uses the term *society*, his reference is to Auroville itself, not just to the Sri Aurobindo Society.

43. *Ibid.*, pp. 326, 327.

44. *Lok Sabha Debates* (December 17, 1980), pp. 392–94.

45. *Ibid*, p. 367.

46. *Ibid.*, p. 372.

47. *Ibid.*, p. 373.

48. *Ibid.*

49. *Ibid.*, p. 388.

50. *Ibid.*, p. 399.

51. *Ibid.*, p. 338.

52. *Ibid.*, p. 336.

53. *Rajya Sabha Debates* (December 9, 1980), p. 286. See also p. 283.

54. *Ibid.*, p. 340.

55. *Ibid.*, pp. 297–98.

56. *Ibid.*, p. 309.

57. *Ibid.*, p. 344.

58. *Lok Sabha Debates* (December 17, 1980), p. 357.

59. *Ibid.*, p. 350.

60. *Rajya Sabha Debates* (December 9, 1980), p. 336.

61. *Ibid.*, p. 354.

62. *Ibid.*, p. 304.

Chapter 6

1. In *Auroville References in Mother's Agenda*, p.64, the Mother is quoted as saying that she used the phrase "nobody" in the Charter because it was a vague term. To say "no country," she believed, would make India "furious."

2. *Ibid*, p. 34.

3. *Ibid.*

4. *Ibid.*, p. 36. See also her brief comment in The Mother, *Collected Works* III, p. 373.

5. *Ibid*, p. 36.

6. *Ibid*, p. 37.

7. Mahendra Kumar, *India and Unesco* (New Delhi: Sterling Publishers, 1974), pp. 11–52.

8. UNESCO, *Conference for the Establishment of the United Nations Educational, Scientific, and Cultural Organization Held at the Institute of Civil Engineers, London, from the 1st to the 16th November, 1954* (London: UNESCO, 1954), p. 33.

9. James P. Sewell, *UNESCO and World Politics: Engaging in International Relations* (Princeton: Princeton University Press, 1975), p. 71.

10. S. Nihal Singh, *The Rise and Fall of UNESCO* (Riverdale, Md.: The Riverdale Company, Inc., Publishers, 1987), p. 30.

11. M. Kumar, *India and UNESCO*, p. 57.

12. UNESCO, *General Conference: First Session Held at UNESCO House, Paris, from 20 November to 10 December 1946* (Paris: UNESCO, 1947), p. 27.

13. *Ibid.,* p. 28. For Radhakrishnan, this was a part of the promotion of the essence of religion as he defined it. See Minor, *Radhakrishnan: A Religious Biography,* pp. 83–87.

14. James P. Swell, p. 316.

15. UNESCO, *Records of the General Conference: Fourteenth Session* (Paris: UNESCO, 1966), p. 222.

16. *Ibid.,* p. 71.

17. *Ibid.*

18. UNESCO, *Records of the General Conference: Fifteenth Session* (Paris: UNESCO, 1968), p. 56.

19. *Auroville References in Mother's Agenda,* p. 45.

20. The Mother, *Collected Works* XIII, p. 210. The words in brackets were not in the original message but added by the Mother in 1972 when she reread the text.

21. *Auroville References in Mother's Agenda,* p. 127.

22. The Mother, *Collected Works* XIII, p. 221.

23. UNESCO, *Records of the General Conference: Fifteenth Session,* p. 56.

24. "Text of the Policy Statement made on behalf of India by Leader of the Indian Delegation to the 16th UNESCO General Conference at the Plenary Session of the General Conference on 17–10–1970," in Indian National Commission for Cooperation with UNESCO, *Report of the Secretary–General for 1970–72* (New Delhi: Ministry of Education and Social Welfare, Government of India, 1972), p. 86.

25. UNESCO, *Records of the General Conference, Sixteenth Session: Resolutions* (Paris: UNESCO, 1970), p. 52.

26. *Ibid, Reports,* p. 96.

27. Indian National Commission for Cooperation with UNESCO, *Report of the Secretary–General for 1970–72,* pp. 29–30.

28. UNESCO, *Records of the General Conference: Eighteenth Session* (Paris: UNESCO, 1974), II, p. 140.

29. UNESCO, *Records of the General Conference: Twenty-second Session* (Paris: UNESCO, 1984), I, pp. 64–65.

Chapter 7

1. Robert D. Baird, "Religion and the Secular: Categories for Religious Change in Independent India," pp. 47–63.

2. Besides its existence in the Court records, a slightly abridged version can be found in *Auroville Review*, no. 5 (summer–fall 1981), pp. 68–80.

3. See, for example, the following cases: "Commissioner, Hindu Religious Endowments, Madras v. Sirur Mutt," *The Supreme Court Journal*, XXVI, 1954, pp. 335–61; "Panachand Gandhi v. State of Bombay," *The Supreme Court Journal*, XVII, 1954, pp. 480–93; "Shri Govindlaiji v. State of Rajasthan," *All India Reporter*, Supreme Court, 1963, pp. 876–1,667; "Yagnapurushdasji v. Muldas," *All India Reporter*, Supreme Court, 1966, pp. 1,119–35; "Seshammal and Others v. State of Tamil Nadu," *Supreme Court Cases*, II, Part I (1972), pp. 11–25. Most of these and others are carefully analyzed in Robert D. Baird, "Religion and the Secular. . . . ," pp. 47–63.

4. "S.P. Mittal, v. Union of India," *All India Reporter*, Supreme Court, 1983, pp. 25–26.

5. *Ibid.*, p. 26. See "Hiralal Mallick v. State of Bihar," *All India Reporter*, Supreme Court, 1977, p. 2,243.

6. *Ibid.*, p. 27. From "M. Giasuddin v. State of A.P.," *All India Reporter*, Supreme Court, 1977, p. 1,935.

7. *Ibid.*

8. The aforementioned quotations are from the Court's version in *ibid.*, p. 28. Compare it with the full Charter of Auroville as set down by the Mother and quoted with some apparently unconscious minor changes by the Court.

9. *Ibid.*, p. 19. The Court is actually quoting from its 1954 judgment in "Commissioner, Hindu Religious Endowments, Madras v. Shirur Mutt," p. 348.

10. *Ibid,*. p. 20.

11. *Ibid.*, p. 21. The aforementioned discussion of the position by the majority opinion is on *ibid.*, pp. 21–22.

12. *Ibid,*. p. 9.

13. *Ibid.*, p. 3.

14. *Ibid.*, p. 4.

15. *Ibid.*, p. 8.

16. *Ibid.*

17. *Ibid.*, pp. 8–9.

18. "Commissioner, Hindu Religious Endowments, Madras v. Sirur Mutt," pp. 347–48.

19. "S.P. Mittal v. Union of India, p. 10.

20. *Ibid.*, p. 11.

21. *Ibid.*, p. 30.

22. *Ibid.*, p. 12.

23. "S.P. Mittal v. Union of India," p. 21.

24. "M. Giasuddin v. A.P. State," p. 1,935.

25. Yagnapurushdasji v. Muldas, p. 1,135.

26. *Supreme Court Journal*, XVII, 1954, p. 486. See also Baird, "Religion and the Secular. . . . ," pp. 52–53, for an analysis.

27. From Counter Affidavit INCA in W.P. No. 5879 submitted by K. Tewari on behalf of the residents of Auroville, filed in the Supreme Court, January 1981.

28. For examples Wilfred Cantwell Smith has used to argue for the end of the use of the term *religion* altogether since he believes no truly religious person calls his beliefs a religion, see his *The Meaning and End of Religion* (New York: Mentor, 1963), pp. 114–15.

29. *Supreme Court Journal*, XXI, 1958, pp. 984–85.

30. S.P. Mittal v. Union of India," p. 29.

31. *Ibid.*, p. 30.

32. See "Saifuddin Saheb v. State of Bombay," *All India Reporter*, Supreme Court, 1962, pp. 853–76, where the Court upholds the right of the Dai-ul-Mutlaq to excommunicate a member of the Dawoodi Bohra community, against the Bombay Prevention of Excommunication Act of 1949; and "Bijore Emmanuel v. State of Kerala," *Supreme Court Journal*, II, 1986, pp. 395–412, where the Court upholds the right of Jehovah's Witness children to refrain from singing the National Anthem in school ceremonies, though they "do stand up respectfully" during the singing.

Chapter 8

1. It included, for example, former Indian Foreign Minister and then Defense Minister P.V. Narasimha Rao, the Director General of UNESCO, Indian industrialist J.R.D. Tata, and the education minister of Bulgaria.

2. *Lok Sabha Debates, 8th Lok Sabha* IX, no. 25 (August 28, 1985), p. 81; *Parliamentary Debates: Rajya Sabha: Official Reports* CXXXV, no. 181 (August 19, 1985), p. 347.

3. *Rajya Sabha Debates* CXLIV, no. 18 (December 1, 1987), p. 244.

4. *Rajya Sabha Debates* (August 19, 1985), p. 367.

5. *Rajya Sabha Debates* (December 1, 1987), pp. 219–20.

6. *Lok Sabha Debates* (August 28, 1985), p. 88.

7. *Rajya Sabha Debates* (December 1, 1987), p. 222.

8. *Ibid.*, p. 214; *Lok Sabha Debates* (November 12, 1987), p. 260.

9. *Lok Sabha Debates* (August 28, 1985), p. 105.

10. *Rajya Sabha Debates* (December 1, 1987), p. 251.

11. *Ibid.*, pp. 251–52.

12. *Lok Sabha Debates* (August 28, 1985), p. 87. There is a play here on the concept of India as the Mother, which Aurobindo used in his Nationalist days, but Munsi is referring to the Mother Mirra Alfassa, for in the next paragraph he speaks of "the death of the Great Mother" as the event that began Auroville's problems.

13. *Ibid.*, p. 90.

14. *Lok Sabha Debates* (November 12, 1987), p. 268.

15. *Lok Sabha Debates* (August 28, 1985), p. 85. Krishna Kaul (Rajya Sabha, Uttar Pradesh), called it "a living embodiment of the ideals of Shri Aurobindo." (*Rajya Sabha Debates* [December 1, 1987], p. 241).

16. *Rajya Sabha Debates* (December 1, 1987), p. 237.

17. *Lok Sabha Debates* (August 28, 1985), p. 90.

18. *Rajya Sabha Debates*, (December 1, 1987), p. 252.

19. *Lok Sabha Debates* (August 28, 1985), pp. 86–87.

20. *Rajya Sabha Debates* (August 19, 1985), p. 365.

21. *Lok Sabha Debates* (August 28, 1985), p. 83.

22. *Ibid.*, pp. 84, 97.

23. *Lok Sabha Debates* (November 12, 1987), p. 267.

24. *Ibid.*, p. 278.

25. *Rajya Sabha Debates* (August 19, 1985), p. 378.

26. *Lok Sabha Debates* (August 28, 1985), p. 104.

27. *Ibid.*, p. 97.

28. *Ibid.*, p. 87.

29. *Rajya Sabha Debates* (August 19, 1985), p. 357.

30. *Lok Sabha Debates* (August 28, 1985), p. 104.

31. *Rajya Sabha Debates* (December 1, 1987), p. 240.

32. *Lok Sabha Debates* (November 12, 1987), p. 274.

33. *Lok Sabha Debates* (August 28, 1985), pp. 98, 99.

34. *Lok Sabha Debates* (November 12, 1987), pp. 264–66.

35. *Rajya Sabha Debates* (December 1, 1987), p. 234.

36. *Ibid.*, pp. 244–47.

37. *Ibid.*, p. 239.

38. *Ibid.*, p. 214; *Lok Sabha Debates* (November 12, 1987), p. 260.

39. *Ibid.*, p. 238.

40. *Rajya Sabha Debates* (November 12, 1987), p. 268.

41. *Rajya Sabha Debates* (August 19, 1985), p. 352.

42. *Ibid.*, p. 369.

43. *Ibid.*, p. 374.

44. *Rajya Sabha Debates* (November 12, 1987), p. 277.

45. *Rajya Sabha Debates* (December 1, 1987), p. 253.

46. *Rajya Sabha Debates* (September 1, 1988), pp. 327–31; *Lok Sabha Debates* (September 9, 1988), pp. 477–79.

47. *Ibid.*, p. 331.

48. *Lok Sabha Debates* (September 5, 1988), pp. 480–81.

49. *Rajya Sabha Debates* (September 1, 1988), pp. 340–41.

50. *Ibid.*, pp. 332–34.

51. *Ibid.*, p. 336.

52. *Lok Sabha Debates* (September 5, 1988), pp. 491–92.

53. *Ibid.*, pp. 484–85.

54. *Ibid.*, p. 488.

55. *Rajya Sabha Debates* (September 1, 1988), pp. 337–39.

56. *Lok Sabha Debates* (September 5, 1988), pp. 492–93.

57. *Rajya Sabha Debates* (September 1, 1988), p. 345.

Chapter 9

1. Melford Spiro is referring, at least, to this observation when he argues that what he calls a "nominal" definition for a word should therefore have "intra-cultural intuitivity" or should, at least, not be "counter-intuitive." See Melford E. Spiro, "Religion: Problems of Definition and Explanation," in Michael Banton, ed. *Anthropological Approaches to the Study of Religion* (London: Tavistock Publications, 1966), p. 91.

2. Richard Robinson, *Definition* (Oxford: Oxford University Press, 1950), p. 191.

3. Wilfred Cantwell Smith, *The Meaning and End of Religion*, pp. 114–15.

4. See Robert N. Minor, *Radhakrishnan: A Religious Biography*, p. 77.

5. In my 1978 book, *Sri Aurobindo: the Perfect and the Good*, I offered the stipulative definition of "religion" used later to analyze the development of Aurobindo's thought. Treating it as though it were a real definition, it was used in the arguments before the Supreme Court of India in the Auroville case to argue that an "authoritative source" had declared that Aurobindo's thought was truly a religion. See "S.P. Mittal v. Union of India," p. 25.

6. Robert D. Baird, *Category Formation and the History of Religions* (The Hague: Mouton, 1971), p. 21.

7. The Mother, *Collected Works* IX, p. 354.

8. *BCL* XV, p. 100.

9. The Mother, *Collected Works* XIII, pp. 202, 221, 223, 224.

10. Savitra, "When Intensity Overtakes Integrality: A Personal Look at the Man and Myth called Satprem," *NexUS: Newsletter for the USA Centers of Sri Aurobindo and the Mother* (winter 1994–1995), p. 28.

11. Robert D. Baird, "Religion and the Secular: Categories for Religious Conflict and Religious Change in Independent India," pp. 95–99.

12. P.B. Gajendragadkar, *Law, Liberty and Social Justice* (New York: Asia Publishing House, 1965), p. 132.

13. *Ibid.*, p. 141.

14. P.N. Bhagwati, "Religion and Secularism Under the Indian Constitution," in Robert D. Baird, *Religion and Law in Independent India*, p. 15.

15. Rajeev Dhavan, "Introduction," p. lxiii.

16. Member state's difficulties and disagreements with UNESCO and its programs often are opportunities for nations to exert their competing sovereignties and thereby can be seen as clashes of "national interests," or national "religions," either between one "sovereign" state and another or between a "sovereign" state and UNESCO's stated ultimate concern. Though not analyses that use these categories, note how this often is a part of the "politics" of UNESCO. See James P. Sewell, *UNESCO and World Politics* and S. Nihal Singh, *The Rise and Fall of UNESCO*.

17. Gerald James Larson, *India's Agony over Religion*, p. 202.

18. Robert D. Baird, "On Defining 'Hinduism' as a Religious and Legal Category," pp. 41–42.

19. *Ibid.*, pp. 47–58.

20. *Ibid.*, p. 51.

21. J.D.M. Derrett, "The Definition of a Hindu," *The Supreme Court Journal* (1966), pp. 67–74.

22. J. Duncan M. Derrett, "'Hindu': a Definition Wanted for the Purpose of Applying a Personal Law," *Zeitschrift fur vergleichende Rechtswissenschaft, einschliesslich der ethnologischen Rechtsforschung* LXX (1968), p. 121.

23. Marc Galanter, "Hinduism, Secularism and the Indian Judiciary," p. 247.

24. *Ibid.*, p. 249.

25. For a further analysis, see Brian K. Smith, "How Not to be a Hindu: The Case of the Ramakrishna Mission," in Baird, *Religion and Law in Independent India*, pp. 333–50.

26. Robert D. Baird, "On Defining 'Hinduism,'" pp. 56–58.

27. Ashis Nandy, "An Anti-Secularist Manifesto," *Seminar* 314 (October 1985), p. 24.

28. For a fuller discussion and references to other scholarly analyses, see Robert N. Minor, *Radhakrishnan: A Religious Biography*, pp. 39–40, 132.

29. For complete references and a fuller discussion, see Robert N. Minor, "The Response of Sri Aurobindo and the Mother," pp. 92–97.

Bibliography

Adilakshmi, *Mother Meera*. Thalheim, Germany: Mother Meera Publications, 1987.

All India Conference on the Relevance of Sri Aurobindo Today, 1975: Souvenir Volume. Calcutta: Sri Aurobindo Samiti, 1975.

Aurobindo, Sri. *Birth Centenary Library*. Pondicherry: Sri Aurobindo Ashram Trust, 1971.

Auroville References in Mother's Agenda. Auroville: Auroville Press, n.d.

Baird, Robert D. *Category Formation and the History of Religions*. The Hague: Mouton, 1971.

Baird, Robert D. *Essays in the History of Religions*. New York: Peter Lang, 1991.

Baird, Robert D., ed. *Religion and Law in Independent India*. Delhi: Manohar, 1993.

Baird, Robert D., ed. *Religion in Modern India*. 3rd rev. ed. Delhi: Manohar, 1995.

Baxi, Upendra. *The Indian Supreme Court and Politics*. Lucknow: Eastern Book Co., 1980.

Coward, Harold, ed. *Modern Indian Responses to Religious Pluralism*. Albany: State University of New York Press, 1987.

Derrett, J.D.M. "The Definition of a Hindu." *The Supreme Court Journal* (1966): 67–74.

Derrett, J.D.M. "'Hindu': a Definition Wanted for the Purpose of Applying a Personal Law." *Zeitschrift fur vergleichende Rechtswissenschaft, einschliesslich der ethnologischen Rechtsforschung* LXX (1968): 110–128.

Dhavcn, Rajeev. *The Amendment: Conspiracy or Revolution*. Allahabad: Wheeler, 1978.

Gajendragadkar, P.B. *Law, Liberty and Social Justice*. New York: Asia Publishing House, 1965.

Gajendragadkar, P.B. *Secularism and the Constitution of India*. Bombay: Bombay University Press, 1971.

Galanter, Marc. *Law and Society in Modern India*. Delhi: Oxford University Press, 1989.

Heehs, Peter. *Sri Aurobindo: A Brief Biography*. Delhi: Oxford University Press, 1989.

Indian Constituent Assembly Debates. Official Report. Delhi: Manager of Publications, 1946–1950.

Indian National Commission for Cooperation with UNESCO. *Report of the Secretary General for 1970–72*. New Delhi: Ministry of Education and Social Welfare, Government of India, 1972.

Iyengar. K.R. Srinivasa. *Sri Aurobindo: A Biography and a History*. 4th rev. ed. Pondicherry: Sri Aurobindo Ashram Trust, 1985.

Iyer, V.R. Krishna. *Indian Secularism: Proclamation Versus Performance and a Viable Philosophy*. Delhi, 1975.

Iyer, V.R. Krishna. *Law and the People: A Collection of Essays*. New Delhi: People's Publishing House, 1972.

Johnson, David L. *The Religious Roots of Indian Nationalism: Aurobindo's Early Political Thought*. Calcutta: Firma K.L. Mukhopadhyay, 1974.

Kaylor, R. David. "Radhakrishnan as Proponent and Critic of Religion." *Indian Philosophical Annual* XII (1977–1978): 52–66.

Kumar, Mahendra. *India and UNESCO*. New Delhi: Sterling Publishers, 1974.

Larson, Gerald James. *India's Agony over Religion*. Albany: State University of New York Press, 1995.

Lohman, Ruud. *A House for the Third Millennium: Essays on Matrimandir*. Pondicherry: Ruud Lohman, 1986.

Luthera, V.P. *The Concept of the Secular State and India.* Calcutta: Oxford University Press, 1964.

Minor, Robert N. *Radhakrishnan: A Religious Biography.* Albany: State University of New York Press, 1987.

Minor, Robert N. "Radhakrishnan as Advocate of the Class/Caste System as a Universal Religio-Social System," *International Journal of Hindu Studies* I, no. 2 (August 1997): 386–400.

Minor, Robert N. "Sarvepalli Radhakrishnan and Religious Pluralism." *Studia Missionalia* XLII (1993): 307–27.

Minor, Robert N. "Sarvepalli Radhakrishnan on the Nature of 'Hindu' Tolerance." *The Journal of the American Academy of Religion* L, no. 2 (June 1982): 275–90.

Minor, Robert N. *Sri Aurobindo: the Perfect and the Good.* Columbia, Mo.: South Asia Books, 1978.

Minor, Robert N. "Sri Aurobindo's Integral View of Other Religions." *Religious Studies* XV: 365–77.

Mother, The. *Collected Works.* Pondicherry: Sri Aurobindo Ashram, 1978.

Nandy, Ashis. "An Anti-Secularist Manifesto." *Seminar* 314 (October 1985): 22–25.

Nehru, Jawaharlal. *The Discovery of India.* New York: The John Day Company, 1946.

Nehru, Jawaharlal. *Independence and After: A Collection of Speeches, 1946–1949.* New York: The John Day Company, 1950.

Nehru, Jawaharlal. *Toward Freedom: The Autobiography of Jawaharlal Nehru.* Boston: Beacon Press, 1958.

Phadnid, Umashanker. "Clean Up the Mess in Auroville." *The Overseas Hindustan Times* (July 12, 1986): 7.

Phillips, Stephen, H. *Aurobindo's Philosophy of Brahman.* Leiden: E.J. Brill, 1986.

Radhakrishnan, S. *Occasional Speeches and Writings. Second Series, February 1956–February 1957.* New Delhi: Ministry of Information and Broadcasting, Government of India, 1957.

Radhakrishnan, S. *President Radhakrishnan's Speeches and Writings. May 1962–May 1964.* (New Delhi: Ministry of Information and Broadcasting, Government of India, 1965.

Radhakrishnan, S. *President Radhakrishnan's Speeches and Writings. Second Series, May 1964–May 1967.* New Delhi: Ministry of Information and Broadcasting, Government of India, 1967.

Radhakrishnan, S. *Recovery of Faith.* Delhi: Hind Pocket Books, 1967.

Robinson, Richard. *Definition.* Oxford: Oxford University Press, 1950.

"S.P. Mittal v. Union of India." *The All India Reporter*, Supreme Court (1983): 1–43.

Sankhdher, M.M., ed. *Secularism in India: Dilemmas and Challenges.* New Delhi: Deep & Deep Pub., 1992.

Savitra. *Auroville: The First Six Years, 1968–74.* Auroville: Auropublications, 1974.

Savitra. *Auroville: Sun-Word Rising.* Auroville: The Community of Auroville, 1980.

Savitra, "When Intensity Overtakes Integrality: A Personal Look at the Man and Myth called Satprem." *NexUS: Newsletter for the USA Centers of Sri Aurobindo and the Mother* (winter 1994–95): 27–30.

Sewell, James P. *UNESCO and World Politics: Engaging in International Relations.* Princeton: Princeton University Press, 1975.

Singh, S. Nihal. *The Rise and Fall of UNESCO.* Riverdale, Md.: The Riverdale Press, Inc., Publishers, 1987.

Smith, Donald Eugene. *India as a Secular State.* Princeton: Princeton University Press, 1963.

Smith, Wilfred Cantwell. *The Meaning and End of Religion.* New York: Mentor, 1963.

Sullivan, Bill, "On Matrimandir: What About this Watertank?" *Auroville Review*, no. 6 (summer/fall 1982): 3.

UNESCO. *Conference for the Establishment of the United Nations Educational, Scientific, and Cultural Organization Held at the Institute of Civil Engineers, London, from the 1st to the 16th November, 1954.* London: UNESCO, 1954.

UNESCO. *General Conference: First Session Held at UNESCO House, Paris, from 20 November to 10 December 1946.* Paris: UNESCO, 1947.

UNESCO. *Records of the General Conference: Eighteenth Session.* Paris: UNESCO, 1974.

UNESCO. *Records of the General Conference: Fifteenth Session.* Paris: UNESCO, 1968.

UNESCO. *Records of the General Conference: Fourteenth Session.* Paris: UNESCO, 1966.

UNESCO. *Records of the General Conference: Sixteenth Session.* Paris: UNESCO, 1970.

UNESCO. *Records of the General Conference: Twenty-second Session.* Paris: UNESCO, 1984.

Wilfred, *The Mother: A Short Biography.* Pondicherry: Sri Aurobindo Society, 1986.

Index

A

Adiseshiah, Malcom, 82
Advaita Vedanta, 8, 21, 23, 26,
173n. *See also* Shankara
Ahmed, President Fakhruddin Ali,
80–81
"All India Conference on the
Relevance of Sri Aurobindo
Today, " 68, 80–82
Anbarasu, Era, 88, 93
Anger, Roger, 61, 69
Arunachalam, V., 132
Aspiration (the Auroville commu-
nity), 56, 61, 71
Aurobindo, Sri: on the Absolute as
Becoming, 20, 25–26, 28–29, 31,
41, 46, 50, 52, 155, 158; on the
Absolute as Being, 25–26, 29,
31, 50, 155; commemorative
stamp, 79–80; on community,
28, 34–35; as a cultural hero, 18,
78–82, 133–135; Day of Siddhi,
36, 39; on Mind, 27, 31, 37, 43,
51; on Overmind, 26, 37, 40; on
perfection, 24–25, 52, 155; on

"religion," 20, 28–35; "religion
of humanity, " 33, 35; on reli-
gious/spiritual experience, 24,
29, 32–33; on denying the "secular, " 20, 23–24, 28, 36; on saccidananda, 26; on Supermind, 25,
26, 37, 40–41, 55, 64–65, 94–95,
108, 109, 155, 158; on the
Mother, 39–41; on the world,
29; on true religion 29; his
Weltanschauung 20, 94
"Aurobindoism, " 122 , 126–128, 163
Auromitra, 75
Aurotrust, 70–72
Auroville, Charter of, 49–52, 69,
70, 72, 73, 84, 86, 88, 92, 97,
105, 108–110, 117, 125, 133,
140, 144–145, 147, 159, 190n
Auroville (Emergency Provisions)
Act, 1980, 75, 77–95, 112, 130
Auroville (Emergency Provisions)
Amendment Act, 1985 , 76,
130–143
Auroville (Emergency Provisions)
Amendment Act, 1987, 76,
130–143

Auroville (Emergency Provisions) Ordinance, 75, 82–83, 113
Auroville Foundation Act , 1988, 76, 143–149
Auroville Governing Board, 76, 143–144
Auroville International Advisory Council, 84, 110, 144,
Auroville Residents' Assembly, 144
Auroville Society, 70–71

B

Bahadur, Harikesh, 84–85
Baird, Robert D., x, 2, 4, 6, 7, 10, 14, 16, 25, 113, 114, 126, 154, 155, 158, 160, 163–165, 174n, 190n
Bande Mataram, 19–22
Bhagwati, Justice P.N., 159–160
Baxi, Upendra, 5, 159, 170n
Bhagavad-gita, 38, 145, 164
Bharat Nivas, 69, 73, 74, 75, 110
Bruteau, Beatrice, 175n
Buddhism, 29, 86, 120, 166

C

Calcutta High Court, 75
Central Bureau of Investigation, 75, 130
Chattopadhyaya, Debiprasad, 80, 81
Chaudhuri, Haridas, 175n
Chavan, S. B., 87–88, 91, 92, 93
Christianity, 11, 29, 88, 120, 127, 152
"Civil Religion, " 8, 13, 163, 165, 166–168
Comite Administratif d'Auroville, 69–70
Commissioner, Hindu Religious Endowments, Madras v. Sirur Mutt, 114, 117, 122, 125, 190n
Congress-I Party, 9, 15, 73, 84, 94

Constituent Assembly, 3, 4, 8–10, 77, 95, 139
Constitution of India, 2, 6, 112, 114, 121, 123, 156–159, 162, 169n, 170–171n

D

Daga, Mool Chand, 86, 88
definitions, 151; legal definitions, 162–166; real definitions, 151, 154; stipulative definitions, 151, 154
Derrett, J. D. M., 164–165
Desai, Morarji, 74
Dharma Rajya, 5, 11
Dhavan, Rajeev, 169n
Dias, A.L., 81–82
disciple, 24, 27, 29, 37, 39–40, 53, 56, 97, 106, 107, 122

E

East-West Major Project ("Major Project on Mutual Appreciation of Eastern and Western Cultural Values), 101, 102, 109

F

Faleiro, Eduardo, 138
Fidelity (the Auroville settlement), 74
42nd Constitution Amendment, 1976, 2, 12, 156–158, 169n
Fundamental Duties, 157–158

G

Gajendragadkar, Justice P. B., 15–16, 159, 164, 173n, 174n
Galanter, Marc, 15, 31, 164, 165, 173n

Gandhi, Indira, 73, 75, 79, 82, 91, 100
Gandhi, Mohandas K., 8, 13, 14, 15, 24, 29, 31, 101, 108, 147, 163, 166
General Fund, the, 67, 70
Gopeshwar, 137, 141
Gurupadaswamy, M.S., 139–140

Jena, Chintamani, 134–135
Jha, Bhogendra, 88
Jha, Siv Chandra, 93
Johnson, David L., 175n
Judaism, 29
Jhunjhunwala, Shyamsundar, 67, 69–70

H

Heehs, Peter, 174n
Hegde, Ramakrishna, 93
Heptulla, Najima, 145–146
Hinduism, 3, 8–11, 15, 16, 29, 88, 116, 118, 120, 122, 124, 127, 152, 153, 163–166
Hiralal Mallick v. State of Bihar, 116, 190n

I

inclusivism, 9–13, 79, 107, 118–119, 124, 125, 128, 136, 138, 146, 153, 165–166, 173n
Income Tax Act, 1961, 59, 117
India, as guru to the nations, 20, 75, 96, 136
Indian Civil Service, 18–19
Indian National Commission for UNESCO, 100–103, 108, 109–110
Indian National Congress, 19, 23
Integral Yoga, 1, 25, 27–28, 30, 33–35, 36, 42, 43, 51, 104, 116, 122, 128, 136, 142, 154–156, 166, 181n
Islam, 4, 29, 86, 88, 120, 127, 152
Iyengar, K.R. Srinivasa, 174n
Iyer, Justice V.R. Krishna, 16

J

Jagadish, 74
Janata (People's) Party, 12, 73

K

Kalyanasundaram, M., 89
karma-yoga, 36
Karmayogin, 20–22
Kaul, Krishna, 132, 192n
Kaur, Rajkumari Amrit, 99
Kaushik, M.P., 132
Kaylor, R. David, 13
Kirpal, Prem N., 100, 102, 105, 108
Kulkarni Committee, 73
Kumar, Mahendra, 99–100

L

Larson, Gerald, 4, 7–8, 13, 163, 165
Lohman, Ruud, 65
Luthera, V.P., 3, 8

M

M.H. Quareshi v. State of Bihar, 127
Madhva, 114, 173n
Mahab Chandra Bandopadhya and others v. State of West Bengal, 164–165
Mahavir, Bhair, 85
Manusamy, V.P., 93
Matrimandir, the, 61–65, 73, 74, 113, 147,
Minor, Robert N., 171n, 172n, 174n, 175n, 176n, 183n, 196n
Mirra Alfassa, 37–42. *See also* Mother, the

Mishra, Kailashpathi, 139–140
Misra, Justice R.B., 116
Mitra, Sankar Prasad, 80, 136
Mother, the: on Auroville, 46–54,
    55–58; divine anarchy, 56; on
    drugs, 57; on money, 58; on
    "religion, " 42–54, 152–154,
    155–156; on rules in Auroville,
    55–56, 58, 181n; on UNESCO,
    59, 97–99, 106–107
Mother Meera, 66, 183n
Mudaliar, Arcot L., 100
Munsi, Priya Rajan Das, 132, 134,
    138

N

Nahar, Bijoy Singh, 75
Nanda, Narasingha Prasad, 85, 90,
    92
Nandy, Ashis, 165
Narayanasamy, V., 132, 147
National Committee for Sri
    Aurobindo Centenary, 79
Nationalists, 4, 19–23, 40, 78, 79,
    81, 134, 135, 167
Navajata, Sri (Keshavdev Poddar),
    58, 68–70, 72, 80, 82, 97, 108,
    182n
Nehru, Jawaharlal, 5, 8, 9, 13–15,
    16, 78–79, 96, 101, 147, 163, 165
Neo-Advaita, 8–15, 18, 21, 29, 81,
    96, 118, 128, 138, 153,
    163–168
Neo-Hindu. See Neo-Advaita
Nigam, Justice L.P., 113, 130

P

Pal, Bipin Chandra, 12
Panachand Gandhi v. State of
    Bombay, 125–126, 190n
Panigrahi, Sriballav, 147
Pant, K.C., 131, 133, 138–139

Parashar, Narain Chand, 135–136,
    139
Paswan, Ram Vilas, 86, 88
Peace (the Auroville settlement),
    61
Phillips, Steven H., 175n
Pondicherry, 22, 24
Pour Tous Fund, 71, 184n
Prasad, Rajendra, 9, 171n
Prashant, Dharam Chander,
    133–134, 135
Purohit, Lal, 134, 140–141

Q

Qureshi, Aziz, 145

R

Radhakrishnan, Sarvepalli, 8–15,
    21, 29, 78–79, 100, 101, 118,
    124–125, 138, 153, 163–167,
    173n, 189n
Rajda, Ratansinh, 91
Rajneesh, 137
Ramakrishna Mission, 8, 101,
    164–165
Ramamurti, P., 77, 89, 184n
Ranga, N.G., 146
Rao, B. Ramachandra, 135, 140
Rao, Jagannath, 88, 108
Rao, P.V. Narasimha, 131, 133,
    140–142, 192n
Rao, V.K.R.V., 108
Rashtriya Swayam Sevak Sangh
    ("National Assembly of
    Volunteers"), 5, 11
Ray, Siddharha Shankar, 82
Reddy, B. Satyanarayan, 138–139
Reddy, B.V., 66
Reddy, Justice Chinappa, 116,
    119–123, 125–128, 162
Reddy, Kamala, 66
reification, 127–128

Richard, Paul, 38
Roy, Sudhir, 136–138

S

S.P. Mittal, the Sri Aurobindo
    Society and others versus the
    Union of India, 112–129
sadhak. See disciple
sakti, 20, 40–41, 64
sanatana dharma (the "eternal
    religion"), 20, 21–22, 23, 24
Sastri Yagnapurushadji v. Muldas
    Bhudaras Vaishya, 124–125
Satprem, 50, 75, 177n, 178n, 179n,
    180n, 182n
Savitra, 69, 156, 177–178n, 185n
Seshadri, H.V., 5, 11–12
Sewell, James P., 99
Shahabuddin, Syed, 139
Shankara, 8, 166. See also Advaita
    Vedanta
Shanker, P. Shiv, 143, 144–145
Shanmugam, P., 139
Shejwalkar, N. K., 86
Shinn, Larry, 66–67
Sikhism, 86, 88, 163, 171n
Singh, Jaswant, 141
Singh, Karan, 80, 90–91
Singh, Lakhan, 87, 92
Singh, Pratibha, 88–89, 93,
    138–139, 141, 145, 148
Singh, S. Nihal, 99
Singh, Sunder, 89
Smith, Brian K., 196n
Smith, Donald Eugene, 3
Smith, Wilfred Cantwell, 151–152,
    191n
Spiro, Melford, 194n
Sri Aurobindo Ashram, 18, 19, 28,
    36–42, 46, 48, 53, 56, 58,
    65–67, 70, 72, 79, 96, 106, 115,
    117, 134, 137, 141, 145, 156,
    177n
Sri Aurobindo Bhavan, 80

Sri Aurobindo Samiti, 68, 80, 90
Sri Aurobindo Society, 58–59,
    67–76, 77, 86, 102–104, 112,
    115, 117, 131, 156, 162,
    181–182n
Sudarshan, K.S., 5, 11–12
Sullivan, Bill, 64
Supreme Court of India: on "reli-
    gion, " 6–7, 15–16, 94–95,
    112–129, 148, 159–160, 162–163,
    167
Swaminarayan religion, 114

T

Tagore, Rabindranath, 15
Tamil Nadu government, 59, 73
Tata, J.R.D., 75, 192n
Theosophy, 31, 38
Tilak, (B.G.) Lokmanya, 12, 19,
    24
Tillich, Paul, 154
tolerance. See inclusivism

U

Unikrishnan, K.P., 93
United Nations Educational,
    Scientific, and Cultural
    Organization (UNESCO), 2, 17,
    59, 72, 78, 83, 91–94, 96–111,
    123, 131–132, 148, 156, 158,
    159, 160–161, 167, 192n, 195n;
    London Conference, 1945, 99;
    First General Conference,
    1946, 99; Ninth General
    Conference, 1956, 100;
    Fourteenth General
    Conference, 1966, 102–104;
    Fifteenth General Conference,
    1968, 104–106; Sixteenth
    General Conference, 1970,
    108–109, 110; Eighteenth
    General Conference, 1974, 69,

United Nations Educational,
Scientific, and Cultural
Organization *(continued)*
110; Twenty-second General
Conference, 1984, 110–111
United States Central Intelligence
Agency, 71, 131
Universality. *See* inclusivism
Upanisads 18–20, 25–26, 38, 145

V

Vivekananda, Swami, 8, 10, 12, 21,
29, 31, 118, 164–166, 176n

W

Weber, Max, 36, 183n
West Bengal Societies
Registration Act, 1961, 58, 113,
116

Y

Yadav, Ram Singh, 146–147
Yagnapurushdasji v. Muldas, 124,
125, 190n
Yoga Sutras, 38, 116